Nine Thousand Straws

Teaching Thinking Through Open-Inquiry Learning

Jean Sausele Knodt

Teacher Ideas Press

An imprint of Libraries Unlimited
Westport, Connecticut • London

Library of Congress Cataloging-in-Publication Data

Knodt, Jean Sausele, 1956–
 Nine thousand straws : teaching thinking through open-inquiry learning / Jean Sausele Knodt ;
 with digital photography technical support from Nicholas S. Knodt.
  p. cm.
 Includes bibliographical references and index.
 ISBN 978-1-59158-640-1 (alk. paper)
 1. Inquiry-based learning. 2. Active learning. I. Title.
 LB1027.23.K56   2008
 371.39—dc22   2008010436

British Library Cataloguing in Publication Data is available.

Library of Congress Catalog Card Number: 2008010436
ISBN: 978-1-59158-640-1

First published in 2008

Libraries Unlimited/Teacher Ideas Press, 88 Post Road West, Westport, CT 06881
A Member of the Greenwood Publishing Group, Inc.
www.lu.com

Printed in the United States of America

(∞)™

The paper used in this book complies with the
Permanent Paper Standard issued by the National
Information Standards Organization (Z39.48–1984).

10 9 8 7 6 5 4 3 2 1

To Richard and Nicholas

Contents

Contents

Chapter Six: Inquiry Project Sampler (*Cont.*)

INTRODUCTION, HISTORY, AND ACKNOWLEDGEMENTS

Nine Thousand Straws

During its first year in action, our open-inquiry lab, the Think Tank, went through nine thousand straws. If not used to build geodesic domes, as inspired by Buckminster Fuller and presented as a project in *Messing Around with Drinking Straw Construction* by Bernie Zubrowski, they were used for other structures based on the geometry of a triangle and seen going home in droves with the children. Inventions made from straws were even worn as hats as students hopped onto school buses.

Together with experience gained from my current consulting work, this book reflects the nine years I spent designing and directing a central inquiry learning lab for Kent Gardens Elementary, a public school in northern Virginia. During my time developing and teaching that program, the inquiry lab grew to serve more than six hundred regularly attending students. *Nine Thousand Straws* displays my particular take on what makes open-inquiry instruction purposeful and dynamic and emphasizes cultivating children's innovative and industrious thinking skills and dispositions through hands-on projects.

> *We had to use team work to get the marble to ring the bell.*
> —Lab student

It took the effort of many people, including those providing a major volunteer commitment, to set the Think Tank lab on its feet. I therefore honor and acknowledge the many parents, grade-level teachers, specialists, administrators, support staff, and community members who gave me and the program the resources, guidance, teaching help, assistance, and trust that made its growth possible.

I especially thank Robyn Hooker, the principal of Kent Gardens, who first conceived the idea of having a centralized critical and creative thinking lab for all children of the school and of establishing an open time specifically designed for student-led exploration. Acknowledged here are the early idea hatchers and developers who worked to meet her vision, such as Jane Renshaw, who led faculty input surveys; Gifted and Talented Itinerant Wendy Cohen who, along with other contributions, pegged the concept of Multiple Intelligences into the mix and who, together with parent Kathleen Hand-Bourgin, named the lab the Think Tank, called in the first volunteers (including myself), visited area discovery centers, and began developing the lab's projects. I also thank Wendy for her continued consultation and guidance when I stepped in to direct early program development and open the lab doors to the children. Warm thanks go to Reading Specialist Jean Strobel, who started the ball rolling for obtaining grants, and creating in-service links with Linda Stevens of the Smithsonian Institution.

> *About the most challenging thing was making the bridge with Kapla Blocks. It was really hard because we kept needing to add more and more weight and the first three bridges kept falling down. [Were you successful?] Yep. Very, very, very successful. [What helped your success?] Working together, and just thinking about it, and for a while.*
> —Lab student

The program would not have achieved success without the outstanding parent volunteers who stepped in and offered so many hours to teaching in the lab, provided PTA funding, scouted for materials, built projects, maintained the lab, supported program initiatives, and attended orientations. I am so thankful for their help (during one period of time, the lab had more than fifty regularly attending Room Guides), but also for the companionship and joy we experienced together in the lab.

> *I thought the hardest [inquiry challenge] was the fifteen-second marble race. You had to put certain objects together to make the marble go down in fifteen seconds. And if you got less or more then you had to keep on doing it. It took us about ten or more tries to do it. I thought that was really hard. I think we did a really good job on it, working together.*
>
> —Lab student

I am also thankful for the support of Assistant Principals Marilyn Wilson and Beatrice Whaley, and others in the administrative front office, such as Linda Baker, Deidre TeStrake, and Menda Ahart, who answered my many questions, proofed newsletter copy, and ordered countless supplies for the lab. I thank the Kent Gardens faculty, who gave their time to teach, confer with me, collaborate, and participate in the many Think Tank program orientations and in-services; in particular, I thank specialist Karen Schneider and the members of the English as a Second Language program for their enthusiasm and participation.

I thank Melanie McClure and Stephanie Hillebrand for their devotion to the lab; they became part of the permanent Think Tank lab staff and made it possible for me to teach part time while first starting this book. I also thank Gifted and Talented Itinerants Keri Putonen (who coined the phrase "Thinking Gears" for the ALPS [Active Learning Practices for Schools] Web site) and Barbara Ross for our thinking-centered coffee chats.

> *My favorite center was the toothpick spread. I liked it because we worked as a team and it took us three tries to do it. We were attempting to make a bridge with toothpicks [and clay] and tie a bucket and see how many marbles we could put in the bucket without the bridge falling off. We got one hundred and above [marbles in the bucket]. [Why do you think were you successful?] We worked together.*
>
> —Lab student

I am thankful for my professional connections with Diane Johnson, former "Think Tank South" director of Hilton Head Elementary, Hilton Head, South Carolina, and with David Perkins and Al Andrade of Project Zero, Graduate School of Education, Harvard University, who provided their guidance and led the Think Tank toward becoming a "Picture of Practice" on the ALPS Web site. Thanks to editors Tracy Casteuble, Rob King, Mary Claire Mahaney, and Cay Wiant for their work on various chapters of this book. And also, to Caroline Keens and Lynne Sausele for their design consultations.

I thank those at Libraries Unlimited/Teacher Ideas Press for believing in the direction of this instructional format and who now present the ideas of *Nine Thousand Straws* to a larger audience. I especially am thankful to my acquisitions editor, Sharon Coatney, and her steady, calm, and positive guidance.

> *My most memorable moment in the Think Tank this year was when we had these tubes and we had to make a marble go down through the tubes into this bucket. First the tubes could touch, and we were successful. And then the tubes couldn't touch. No one had ever done it before, and we accomplished it! [How did you meet the challenge?] Well, we put the tubes against the outer wall so that it wouldn't be as hard, that way they were all at the same level. That made it a lot easier, we just made a few adjustments and it worked!*
>
> —Lab student

Thanks also go to my parents, Lee and George Sausele, who gave me the freedom to explore my interests and who showed me throughout the years innovation and industrious doing in action.

> *Everything is possible.*
>
> —Lab student

Certainly the development of the lab and this book has been a family affair. I am endlessly thankful to my dear husband Richard Knodt, who supports me, clears my mind, and lovingly edits *so many* pages of my writing. And to our dear son, Nicholas Sausele Knodt, who originally motivated me to jump in and direct the Think Tank and develop open-inquiry learning experiences for young people, and who continues to inspire and delight Richard and I as his own explorations grow so dynamically.

> *You really have questions in your mind.*
>
> —Lab student

Finally, I thank the many children who make my walking into a lab and becoming part of the inquiry scene a true delight—a time and place where I will always feel at home, and find to be full of vital possibilities.

I always think of when I was using the Magnet Mural in the lab.
I think of the people I made dancing.
Lab student

Chapter One
Cultivating Innovative and Industrious Thinking

A PICTURE OF LAB TIME IN ACTION

Welcome

When you walk into an open-inquiry learning lab for the first time, it might take a few moments to absorb the scene. Before you is a group of twenty or more children exploring a wide variety of hands-on projects in "discovery-room" style. This lab time might be taking place in a grade-level classroom, a central inquiry lab in a school or children's hospital, or perhaps in a school or public library.

Children in one group whirl a bit loudly as they attempt to build a large arching structure with strawberry baskets, while two students work in whispers as they move large, colorful shapes to design an image at a magnetic mural board. A child sits in a cozy nook to construct a geodesic dome with straws and paperclips, as others nearby create a wall-mounted rebus story. Across the room a small team appears finally able to make a bell ring at the end of their newly constructed chain-reaction machine made up of angles and inclined planes. All in the room look up and turn with you to see the four children declare in triumph, *Look everyone! It's working!*

As you step closer to observe the unfolding action in the lab, you may find yourself as intrigued as the children are with the possibilities of the place. You see students finding challenges and solving problems by employing the same thinking skills and attitudes that you might use when faced with a new project or challenge. Brainstorming, classifying information, perceiving patterns, predicting outcomes, and employing strategy are a few of the skills seen on display as children work with their inquiries.

Yet you may also observe a focus placed on general thinking orientations and behaviors, identified to the group as *thinking dispositions,* or *habits of mind.* Widely applicable and positive dispositions are seen cultivating the inquiry action of the lab; examples include the habits of mind to *Wonder, Explore, and Ask Questions; Be Accurate and Precise;* or to *Contribute Positively to the Group and Inspire Teamwork* (see Chapter Two: "Project as Medium, Teacher as Coach"). Absorbing the beat of the place, you recognize that this is a unique time to share with children and *think about thinking together.* You may also take a moment to wonder, where was this inquiry lab program when I was in elementary school?

> *Then there is the instinct of making—the constructive impulse. The*
> *child's impulse to find expression first in play, in movement, and*
> *make believe, becomes more definite, and seeks outlet in shaping*
> *materials into tangible forms and permanent embodiment . . . .*
> *Children simply like to do things and watch to see what will happen.*
>
> (Dewey 1907, 59)

Children are naturals when it comes to jumping in with hands-on projects. They are driven to explore and tinker with things, examine possibilities, and produce results. You see one group at a favorite activity center called *Think It! Do It!,* eagerly seeking pieces of wood, corks, spools, or paperclips—tangible components to grab on to while pursuing a new quest, simple objects for children to use in designing and producing their own technologies. Today's goal might be to build a wind-generated machine, a chain-reaction device, or a paddleboat that moves on its own steam (and actually floats).

As students work, they delight in showing everyone (themselves included) what they can accomplish and what it takes to think through ideas. Even the very youngest students are eager to tell their story about what they figured out, not only with the project at hand but also about applying ideas and meeting challenges in general.

> *When you are doing a project you have to think how it's going to look*
> *and what you are going to do first. Or, if you are writing an*
> *assignment you don't just write something and say you're done with*
> *it—you have to decide how you are going to write it and how you are*
> *going to plan it out.*
>
> —Second grader

Children seem to be just waiting to be part of the conversation about what it takes to think well. Certainly this is the perception one gets while teaching cognitive skills and dispositions in an open-inquiry learning environment. Young people appear instinctively geared to develop and put into practice what many adults also try to cultivate for themselves: *finding and meeting challenges with competent, prepared, and inspired minds.*

Mission for Inquiry Instruction

Teacher: *What does it mean to inquire?*
Preschool student: *To ask about and explore!*

Open-inquiry instruction establishes a time and place in which children are led to engage their natural impulse to ask about and explore their world. The application of open inquiry, as developed in the instructional program presented in this book, is focused on building children's critical and creative thinking skills and dispositions. The mission is for *all* children to:

- discover that productive exploration is rewarding and enjoyable

- know there are unending positive and exciting inquiries to uncover

- develop thinking skills and dispositions that can be applied to the success of *any* endeavor

- transfer their learning from other instructional or activity arenas in order to personalize and strengthen their understandings

- build team skills

- actively contribute their abilities and insights

- experience the adventure and promise of innovative and industrious thinking

Whether established in a grade-level classroom during "Center Time" or as a separate "Inquiry Lab" within a school, museum, hospital, community center, library, or homeschooling network, the first program objective of inquiry instruction is for children to see innovative thinking on display, be inspired by it, and become active with it. At that point, an industrious thinking community is ready to grow.

The Essential Project

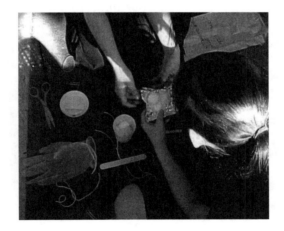

Challenges wake your brain up!
—Lab student

Well-designed inquiry projects set the instructional stage for this program. Often referred to in lab time as "challenges," they establish the sustainable energy from which children learn and through which educators teach. Ready to use when lab time begins, these specially designed hands-on projects together present a full spectrum of intelligences and interests and range from weaving patterns at the loom to identifying animal tracks, or from leading and documenting a group survey to analyzing and distinguishing complex rhythm beats. Altogether, the projects present a group of *inquiry possibilities*— some more open, and others with more finite goals—all from which students are able to choose for their day's inquiry (see Chapter Five: "Inquiry Project Design," and Chapter Six: "Inquiry Project Sampler").

Sharing and Guiding Children's Inquiries

On the floor with the children and their many sprawled items, you will see an adult or two, perhaps a parent volunteer or "Room Guide," a grade-level teacher, or a curious visiting educator. As inquiries unfold, you'll hear educators adding lines of questions and comments throughout the children's plans, concerns, negotiations, resolutions, and expressions of frustration. Instructors grab on to the interest that children have generated through the projects and, as opportunities present themselves, layer in lab-time teaching objectives. The "teacher as coach" *opens, employs,* and *guides* children's inquisitive energy (see Chapter Two: "Project as Medium, Teacher as Coach").

With a group of thirty students, there are perhaps fifteen individual project challenges underway. Certainly "the game is afoot" when you hear the familiar lab question: *So, where are you going to work? What is your challenge today?* Perhaps while viewing the scene, you become intrigued with a particular project to try out yourself. With the "Nail Challenge," you hear the problem: *Can you balance all six (filed blunt-end) nails on the head of the one hammered-in standing nail? No nails other than the standing nail can touch the mounting board!* (see Chapter Six: "Inquiry Project Sampler"). You begin to think through a few ideas. Likely you feel the irresistible call of a great challenge, believe you can make something happen, and really want to get your hands on those nails and give it a try. Once you get started, however, the initial thrill quickly turns into the realization that hard thinking is involved. Struggle declares itself throughout the room as the heavy six-inch nails sound their fall, time after time. As you urge your mind to stretch and ponder possibilities, you become more aware of the personal commitment it will take to brainstorm and strategize a solution. You want to quit. *Perhaps I should really be moving on now anyway.*

I learned not to walk away.
— Lab student

But from across the room, you have been watched. Although the lab teacher would often be the one to step in at this point, today she sends over two students who had previously discovered the solution to help you. To establish a skill development lesson with the art of questioning, the two students are given clear instructions: they cannot tell you how to solve the problem but instead provide *guiding* questions to frame your thinking. Perhaps they think back to questions asked of them when in your shoes—questions that were designed to teach spatial reasoning, flexibility, and fluency, such as, *What do you think the head a of nail could be used for other than what it was designed to do? Or What different patterns can you design using five nails that will establish a structure to hold the sixth?* These children are thrilled to be on the other side of the instructional table, perhaps even giggling as they lead your thinking toward meeting the challenge. When you find yourself raising your hands above your head declaring *I did it!,* you truly are the one who did the tough thinking. The students might then be asked to follow up their instruction by helping you identify the key skills and dispositions you employed with the Nail Challenge. *Yes, you used the habit of mind to be Open-Minded and Adventurous, as well as to Imagine Possibilities and Outcomes! Certainly to Persevere! Your fine motor and brainstorming skills were great!*

This is the familiar experience that unfolds when children head off to their inquiries (except for giggles from the two children as they watched you sweat it out). Lab time is a mix of excitement, frustration, wanting to pull out, regaining personal commitment, failing, and then usually finding a way, often with creative questioning provided to help out.

Real-World Thinking

The flexible and unfolding nature of open-inquiry and the focus on universal lifelong thinking skills and thinking dispositions lend this program perfectly to establishing a learning community for adults and children to share. The gist of each lab class is one to which adults can easily relate with a quick prompt from the lead instructor. *Come on in, Mr. Keens! We're talking about the habit of mind to Set Goals and Make Plans! Can you give us an example of how you engage that habit of mind to meet your own goals and challenges?*

Adults add to conversations and illustrate to students how a particular thinking disposition or skill is active in their own lives, either at home or their workplace. Not only are their comments revealing, but it also is *relieving* for each child to see that they are not the only ones who struggle with challenges and that developing effective habits of mind is a real-life quest. The child may even see an adult (like yourself) experience the same ups and downs while working through a tough age and skill-dimensional lab inquiry.

Building Connections to Home

She's making a Discovery Room in our basement!
—Parent

Children love the community experience of the lab, and especially so when folks from their home join in. Parents, grandparents, and even younger siblings participate and get on the same page with students to become fellow discoverers, as well as teachers. Interested parents are offered day and evening informational sessions to help them become aware of various lab goals, theoretical frameworks, and questioning techniques. All families receive information and ideas about working at home with inquiry concepts through lab newsletters. Habits of mind, Multiple Intelligences, and critical and creative questions can be seen on refrigerators or on special lab program bookmarks. Conversations inspired by lab time or by program materials take place during car rides, at the grocery store, or at the dinner table. Project ideas are seen developing in homes, with parents often asking lab instructors about where to find required ingredients. *By the way, how did you acquire all those strawberry baskets?* (see Chapter Seven: "Finding Parents as Partners and Sending Inquiry Home").

Focus, Reflection, and Celebration

Jake and I actually invented electricity!
—Lab student

Along with your own success with the Nail Challenge, you certainly can't miss the other celebrations of *I did it!* or *We did it!* bellowing out into the air. Toward the end of the class, after all students reluctantly put away their projects and move to a group "Reflection Circle," you hear more about what was experienced at lab time, how challenges were specifically met, and what new general insights were gained.

To meet our challenge, we had to take a chance.
—First-grade lab student

If you are doing teamwork, you have to learn how to deal with someone not using teamwork.
—Lab student

Group reflection will highlight the current lab "Focus Theme" with the lead teacher asking something such as,

Teacher: *So let's hear examples of how you were Adventurous and Open-Minded today. Any breakthroughs with your inquiries?*

Lab student: *Yes, I felt a lightbulb moment when I found out that there's lots of things we could do with those magnets. It just turned out I [we] can make anything!*

After reflections are wrapped up, the lead teacher provides the class with lab-time writing prompts for journal entries or short essays, follow-up research tasks, project ideas for home, or ways to extend various inquiries into whole-class investigations.

Often, as in the case of a centralized school lab, while the Reflection Circle is wrapping up, a new group of students is already waiting at the door to enter. With the age-dimensional inquiries easily returned to the shelves, the lab space is remarkably ready for the next class (see Chapter Eight: "Setting the Open-Inquiry Stage").

As the one class leaves the room, a new group comes in, sits in a circle, and begins discussing the opening Focus Theme, perhaps this time addressing the nature of Frustration (see Chapter Four: "Focus Theme Sampler"). *It's usually part of the process of working through any challenging problem. Everybody feels it at one time or another. Who can tell me about a time they felt FRUSTRATED?! What are things you can do to deal with frustration, to persevere and make it through? How do you feel when you are able to persevere? Anything else you would like to say about frustration?* You glance over to the other adults in the lab to share your surprise about what a child has offered to the conversation, something you had not thought of before, and that spurs further comment and exploration by the group.

You learn that frustration can be good for thinking.
—Lab student

Learning Through Inquiry

I learned that life is not just handed to you—you have to figure it out.
—Lab student

The experience and energy of an open-inquiry instructional format may take time for some adults to get used to, be able to keep up with, or even to appreciate. And as paper clips fly, blocks fall in crescendo, or a rubber-band car rolls by, one might really wonder what is going on. *This is instructional?* Look closer. If engaged effectively and with clear purpose, this program becomes a time and space that works hard for children. It is fully orchestrated and engineered, right down to the teaching opportunity presented when a child, struggling to self-structure and organize his or her own effort or to overcome the fear of performance, declares defiantly with the scapegoat phrase, *I'm bored.*

While loving a time and place to openly *ask about and explore,* students inevitably rub up against limiting skill levels or working attitudes and encounter various obstacles to meeting and sustaining their inquiries—*obstacles from which they can learn.* While pursuing the adventure of discovery, children are guided to identify productive and positive skills and thinking behaviors and put into practice what it takes to be great thinkers, innovators, positive team contributors, and, certainly, to be "challenge savvy."

What Children Have to Say

Folks who visit a lab to see open-inquiry instruction in action are often most inspired by what the children themselves have to say about the program. It is revealing to ask children collectively, *What are you learning in the lab?* Laced throughout this book are documented quotes (shown in italics) from children, Grades 1 through 6, that present their statements regarding the open-inquiry lab experience. Students' statements, as seen in the following, exhibit a variety of program objectives in action. *I learned . . .*

. . . to stop and think.
. . . to look at things from different angles. [Literally!]
. . . how to work with others and alone.
. . . to communicate with other people.
. . . if you don't take a chance, you can't really do anything.
. . . it's OK to fail.
. . . how to deal with frustration.
. . . to persevere with tough challenges.
. . . how to work with strategy.
. . . going step by step.
. . . to build and get new ideas.
. . . math skills, definitely.
. . . to make up a story.
. . . a lot of thinking words.
. . . about different ways we think.
. . . [that] you make goals for yourself.
. . . to pace yourself.
. . . to concentrate.
. . . you want to finish a project so you can feel good.
. . . to find the questions.
. . . everything is possible.

FINDING A HOME FOR INQUIRY

As mentioned earlier, open-inquiry instruction, focused on developing thinking skills and dispositions for children, can take place in a wide variety of learning environments. The following summarizes possible formats, with the final chapter of this book, "Setting the Stage and Starting Up Shop," offering more specific guidance.

A Central Lab

In this format, a school, children's hospital, community center, or museum establishes an open-inquiry *lab center* where one space in the building houses the entire inventory of projects. All children attend this specialized inquiry lab setting on a regularly scheduled basis. The director, or directing group, does all instructional preparation for each lab period, including developing Focus Themes and Reflection Circle questioning. Faculty and Room Guides (volunteer parents) who accompany the class are prepared, through specialized orientations, to be co-teachers at lab time and during group discussions. Later, grade-level teachers, specialists, and parents of the school or organization connect the themes and objectives that the lab has focused on to their own unique instructional settings. At monthly meetings, the current lab theme, introduction of new projects, and other lab objectives are presented to the entire group of faculty, staff, and volunteer parents.

Grade-Level Classroom

For some schools, establishing a separate lab space is not feasible or desirable, in which case bringing the program into the grade-level classroom is an option. Inquiry lab time can be developed to be an extension of Center Time, in which various hands-on projects are displayed in an area of the classroom. Besides the inquiry projects, the classroom teacher also establishes the specific inquiry learning goals for the year and which skills or habits of mind to focus on. Just as in a central lab setting, children start off with a circle Focus Theme discussion, work for a period of thirty to forty-five minutes on their inquiries, and then meet in a Reflection Circle. Parents also become part of the program in this setting.

As in the centralized program, thinking skills and dispositions and other objectives highlighted during the lab session are then applied to strengthen other classroom learning experiences and curriculum understandings. *Who can remind us about the Focus Theme we discussed today at lab time? Yes, the habit of Supporting Ideas With Reasons Why. Who can show where that disposition is located on our class habit-of-mind poster? How are we using that thinking disposition as we work together on this science section and experiment on metamorphosis?* Or, while instructing a social studies unit, *Do you remember how it felt to use the habit of mind to Persevere as you worked with your inquiry project? How did the early Iroquois employ the same disposition to help them survive and develop their culture? What challenges did they face?*

Inquiry Program for a Library

Integrating inquiry centers to become part of a library, either school or public, presents exciting new directions for research opportunities and for cultivating children's interests in reading. Children's hands-on investigations create personalized and pivotal experiential bases to engage other resources in the library or media center. As children identify and classify rocks and minerals, for instance, books on that subject are readily available for use during lab time, but also to bring home and show their family examples of the specimens they had their hands on that day. After a student builds a geodesic dome, the media specialist or librarian helps the child find a biography on its inventor, Buckminster Fuller. Or as a Focus Theme conversation with students explores the habit of mind to Persevere, the instructor might ask, *What book have you recently read that shows someone displaying the habit of mind to Persevere? Oh, the biography of Helen Keller, of course. Could you give some examples to the group? By the way, we have two copies. Is anyone interested in taking that book home today?* (An extensive listing of various thinking dispositions and their links to literature is presented in the Development Resources area of Arthur Costa and Bena Kallick's Web site, associated with their series of books, *Discovering and Exploring Habits of Mind:* http://www. habits-of-mind.net/booklists.htm).

Unified Classroom Approach

In this format, individual teachers throughout the school lead inquiry lab time in their own classrooms while following *schoolwide* Focus Themes. Everyone—grade level teachers, specialists, students, parents—follows the same themes that are established on a monthly or bimonthly basis. Again, as in the centralized lab, the children explore the habit of mind to *Listen Actively* in their classroom lab. They discuss ideas about that same disposition while in class with the music or art specialist, during physical education, or at a special presentation in the auditorium. Themes and objectives are reviewed at faculty meetings and sent throughout the school with writing prompts and questioning ideas, as well as accompanying graphics.

Inquiry project resources are shared by classrooms, perhaps housed and circulating through the school's media center or by exchanging them at faculty meetings.

Again, volunteer parents become part of the program and help out during classroom inquiry sessions. This approach requires at least one individual to direct the unified effort, develop and maintain projects, and to provide in-services for staff members and parent volunteers on program methodologies and theories.

Homeschooling Network

Open-inquiry program ideas can also be developed for homeschooling. The format can be for a single homeschooling family, or for a group of homeschool families who gather and develop project resources, select a list of target Focus Themes and create a shared, centralized lab time for their children to experience group open-inquiry learning.

INSPIRATION, GUIDES, AND GOALS

A Synthesis of Theories and Methods

Defining intelligence and how we as humans can become more effective with our thinking and learning remains an emerging science. How the mind works as it learns is an ongoing inquiry in itself. The open exploratory nature of this program makes it an ideal place to investigate and engage concepts and possibilities.

Once the lab is active with students and their inquiries, it almost appears to speak for itself as it reveals kinship with various theories and teaching methodologies. Theories interrelate and support each other, such as John Dewey's *Experiential Learning*, Piaget's *Constructed Learning,* or neurobiologist Marian Diamond's *Enriched Environments* (Fogarty 2001). As the program develops, new ideas and concepts continue to roll in to inspire, add support, or confirm directions, such as the insights gained from practices of Reggio Emilia, the Constructivists, or as new insights unfold in the field of cognitive science. Yet regardless of what becomes part of the mix of guides and influences, the focus remains on the developing inquiry program. The goal is to establish an instructional practice that develops its own clear voice. The teacher as instructional designer asks, *What part of this theory works for us? What does it add to the program? Why engage the idea? What should be emphasized? What concepts work well together?*

Chapter Two of this book, "Project as Medium, Teacher as Coach," highlights how theory and practice build sound inquiry instructional approaches. It includes a focus on thinking dispositions and habits of mind, with links to David Perkins, Eileen Jay, Shari Tishman, and Al Andrade and their work at Project Zero of Harvard University; Arthur Costa and his work with thinking centered instruction, as well as his and Bena Kallicks's series, *Discovering and Exploring Habits of Mind*; Mihaly Csikszentmihalyi's Flow Theory, and the Flow Room of the Key School of Indianapolis; David Perkins's work with Teaching for Transfer; Howard Gardner's theory of Multiple Intelligences (MI), and MI practitioners as represented by Tom Hoerr and the New City School of St. Louis.

Not only do these methods, practices, and theories provide guidance and structure to the program and its instructional objectives, but they are also on display for all participating educators (including parents) to see in action. The program therefore acts as an *ongoing* in-service center of sorts in which involved adults explore and put into practice a variety of instructional methods and directions and also gain help in applying them to other learning environments. The program director coordinates ways to connect the lab-time pedagogy to the entire grade-level classroom experience, the school as a whole, the hospital, or the children's museum, as well as the student's home. For example, as MI becomes part of the lab-time fabric, participating and visiting adults are offered supportive MI graphics, reading lists, writing and discussion prompts, questioning concepts, lesson plans, and new project ideas for use in other learning environments.

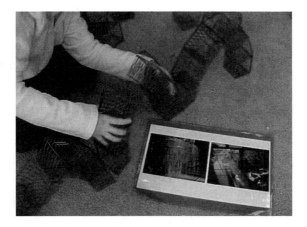

Opening Learning Possibilities and Meeting Needs

Nothing delivers more value to a business than innovation. Nothing.
Smooth the path to innovation and your whole company wins.
(International Business Machines 2004)

"Smooth the path to innovation," and children win as well. Group open-inquiry lab time often has the atmosphere of a collaborative artists studio, an engineering lab, or science research center, where new ideas and creations pop up for all to see. Some students become industrious right away with the many projects and challenges, while others engage more hesitantly. Yet all students gain insight and inspiration from seeing the exploration and discovery unfold in the lab. Inquiry becomes the thing to do, an energy that supports and builds on itself. Students feel safer and gain support for pursuing individual and group quests.

I've been learning to do things I thought might have
been impossible to do.
—Lab student

New levels of confidence develop, as do stamina and zest for finding and pursuing new challenges.

Whatever unfolds in a child's life—from mastering grade-level curriculum standards or coping with difficult health or life issues to taking advantage of academic, athletic, artistic, social or cultural opportunities—children are better positioned to meet new challenges with the buoyancy of an innovative spirit. Group inquiry places an identifiable thinking community by their sides and helps students develop and keep positive skills, dispositions, and vital industrious energy clearly *in mind*.

Teacher: *Why do people love challenges?*

Lab students:
It wouldn't be exciting (without them).
You want to be able to do it.
It makes them feel good.
If there were no challenges in the world, it would all be too easy ...
You have to actually think!
They make your brain stronger.

Teacher: *Why do people like to think?*

Lab student: *Because they like to use their brain.*

To meet the program's goals and objectives, students need to experience focused inquiry learning on an ongoing scheduled basis. It needs to become a time they can depend on.

During the summer [vacation], at 11:50 on Wednesday, I think about the Think Tank and my time going there.
—Lab student

While in the groove of working at regular lab times, children reflect and anticipate what they will do next.

When I see houses being built, I think about making a Dream House at the Think Tank.
—Lab student

Students also learn to recognize effective dispositions, either in action or perhaps as ones that are missing in action.

Hey guys, remember, we need to use the habit of mind to Brainstorm here!
—Lab student

They show clear signs of transferring emphasized skills to meet other grade-level curriculum expectations.

I had to plan a strategy [at lab time] with something. When I had to study at home I remembered back, and planned a strategy for the study.
—Lab student

Students display evidence of continuing to pursue inquiry interests outside of lab time, sometimes even with a parent's photo documenting their work. *Look at this arch system my son developed with strawberry baskets!* With consistent instructional focus, it is the *What can I do next? What are the possibilities? How will we think this new challenge through?* seen lacing through children's inquiries that sets the stage for prepared and inspired minds to grow, both in and outside the lab program.

Our fast-paced culture demands a growing number of individuals who are prepared to navigate through and find solutions to complicated problems in critical, creative, and cooperative ways and who are able to apply and transfer a great variety of skills and understandings to different situations. From the professional skill sets required by our corporations to those required by nations as they compete in the global economy, higher-level critical and creative thinking top the list of sought-after attributes.

It is obviously just a matter of time before the bulk of our workforce will require a much higher level of problem-solving skills than is currently evident. (Greenspan 2000)

In his many testimonies to Congress that focused on educational reform for economic health and growth, former Chairman of the Federal Reserve Board Alan Greenspan pointed to the role of developing higher-level thinking skills as key. His plea to the nation is direct: start early to help children develop momentum in building these essential skills.

Early success in problem solving clearly enhances the self-esteem of young people and encourages them to engage in ever more complex reasoning. We all tend to gravitate toward those activities that we do best. This is the self-reinforcing process [for problem solving] in which early success promotes further effort in a self-perpetuating direction. (Greenspan 2000)

Beyond supporting the economy, society also needs individuals to contribute vitally to the arts and to help resolve humanitarian, health, national safety, agricultural, and environmental issues. Our changing world demands of everyone—from the core workforce to those who lead our local and national governments—innovative, cooperative, and industrious individuals skilled to synthesize and apply complex understandings (Cox, Alm, & Holmes 2004) who have the dispositions to ask, *What are the possibilities? In what other ways can this be done? How will we think this new challenge through?* The raw material needed by our society for addressing these challenges is sitting in our classrooms now. Open-inquiry learning provides one vital instructional format that supports and encourages the growth of these young minds. Children's natural inquisitive energy is the resource to *tap into and guide* during their early years of development.

> *Education reform must, at its core, make schools into*
> *places that cultivate creativity.* (Florida, 2004)

Certainly children are poised and delighted to put into action what is needed: to explore, try various approaches, tinker with ideas, plan strategies, ask questions, and transfer skills and understandings to make new and productive things happen. Many educators, parents, corporations, theorists, and government officials continue to ask: *What educational commitments and standards are being set for building and developing our children's critical and creative thinking skills and dispositions? How are we providing children with the flexible cognitive tools necessary to confront and explore the unknown questions, realities, and opportunities of the future?*

This book specifically asks the following questions: *How are educational programs tapping into and engaging the natural inquisitive energy that children bring to the learning table? What instructional time is given to open up, employ, and guide their inquiries while developing positive thinking skills and dispositions.*

Finding Joy

Not only do we not know the answers to questions that will face us in the future—in many cases we don't even know what the questions will be. The graduates who will deal with such a future most effectively, and who will contribute the most to society, are those who are open-minded and have a spirit of discovery, who will not just confront challenges but will welcome them actively.

—David Porter, President Emeritus, Skidmore College (1996, 28)

Those who have caught the exploratory spark for discovery rub their hands together in excitement, knowing that new challenge opportunities will likely lead them to a feeling of being vitally engaged. They like their minds and abilities to be tested and stretched and to know that they will encounter situations in which they can employ and further develop their skills and understandings. Through their own inquiries, they have gained confidence for navigating through challenges in general and are therefore better able to take on new challenges that are presented to them by others. They become cherished students, productive employees, and inventive contributors—individuals who help cultivate healthy homes and communities. Zest for such industriousness is best developed by experiencing it firsthand, by seeing individuals of all ages and abilities actively pursue positive inquiries (Porter 1996), and by finding out together—as a thinking community—which skills and attitudes make a difference.

> *What I have learned from my own experience is that the most important ingredients in a child's education are curiosity, interest, imagination, and a sense of adventure in life.*
> —Eleanor Roosevelt (Purcell & Purcell 2002, 20)

The gift of open-inquiry learning is that it develops a sense of adventure and joy for finding new and positive individual quests.

> *Your mind opens up and you want to do all these different things.*
> —Lab student

And for adults guiding the children, this instructional format presents adventures as well. Indeed, the spirit of discovery is in the air for everyone. This remarkable time with children is exciting and satisfying because of the community learning experiences it stimulates and the creative teaching possibilities that unfold. Moreover, satisfaction comes when one sees children's potential and promise so openly presented. These moments reveal a sense of readiness as young individuals take the lead with their own thinking and learning.

Goals for This Resource

> *I wish I lived here.*
> —Lab student

Whether located in a grade-level classroom or a centralized lab, open-inquiry is a time and place that young minds intuitively seek out and welcome with delight. The purpose of this book is to provide a "picture of practice" resource focused on answering the following fundamental questions for its readers:

- *What does an open-inquiry learning format—focused on developing thinking skills and dispositions—look like in action?*

- *What do children, teachers, and parents gain from such an instructional direction?*

- *What are the format's basic instructional methods and teaching approaches?*

- *How do various theories and concepts support the program?*

- *What constitute effective Focus Theme and Reflection Circle conversations with children? What are specific Focus Theme possibilities?*

- *What constitutes effective inquiry project design? What are some specific inquiry project possibilities?*

- *What are concrete examples of lab-time dialogue and questioning with children?*

- *And finally, how does one go about setting up a practical and effective lab program?*

References

Cox, W. M., Alm, R., & Holmes, N. (2004, May). Op-Chart. *New York Times*, A27.

Dewey, J. (1907). *The School and Society*. Chicago: University of Chicago Press.

Florida, R. (2004, October). America's Looming Creativity Crisis. *Harvard Business Review,* 1–9.

Fogarty, R. (2001). Our changing perspective of intelligence: Master architects of the intellect. In A. Costa (Ed.), *Developing Minds,* (3rd ed., pp. 144–149). Alexandria, VA: Association for Supervision and Curriculum Development.

Greenspan, A. (2000, September). Statement of Alan Greenspan before the Committee on Education and the Workforce, U.S. House of Representatives. Retrieved January 27, 2005, from http://edworkforce.house.gov/hearings/106th/fc/mathsci92100/greenspan.htm.

Greenspan, A. (2004, March). Testimony of Chairman Alan Greenspan before the Committee on Education and the Workforce, U.S. House of Representatives. Retrieved January 27, 2005, from http://www.federalreserve.gov/boarddocs/testimony/2004/20040311/default.htm.

Kao, J. (2007). *Innovation Nation: How America Is Losing Its Innovation Edge, Why It Matters, and What We Can Do to Get It Back.* New York: Free Press.

Lobugilo, K., & Shein, D. (n.d.). *Habits of Mind Student Book Lists.* Retrieved May 7, 2007, from Habits of Mind Online: http://www.habits-of-mind.net/booklists.htm.

On Demand Business Division, International Business Machines (2004.) IBM Advertisement. *Time Magazine,* 164 (6), 11.

National Commission on Terrorist Attacks Upon the United States (2004, September 20). *The 9/11 Commission Report,* Information Page. Retrieved January 27, 2005, from http://www.9-11 commission.gov.

Perkins, D. (2003). *King Arthur's Round Table, How Collaborative Conversations Create Smart Organizations.* Hoboken, NJ: Wiley.

Porter, D. (1996, March). From Plato to Piano Strings: An Outward Bound for the Mind. *The Chronicle of Higher Education,* 32, 28; a52.

Purcell, S. J., & Purcell, L. E. (2002). *Eleanor Roosevelt.* Indianapolis: Alpha Books.

Chapter Two
Project as Medium, Teacher as Coach

PUTTING THEORIES, METHODS, AND INQUIRIES TO WORK

The Project as a Powerful Place to Start

Children sit ready at the Opening Circle Focus Theme discussion and think to themselves, *OK, if we don't get to that center, where else will we try? What are the possibilities? What can I explore and do today?* Many students even arrive on the scene with plans about how to continue their previous work with a particular inquiry. Indeed, the focused pursuit of children openly finding and self-structuring their own inquiries is a hallmark of the lab program and extraordinary to see in action.

The project is the primary tool or medium that sets the stage for inquiry teaching and allows the program to put various methods and theories into practice. The first step of this instructional format is therefore to establish a strong project inventory that inspires a wide variety of individual interests and sensibilities. Once the children make their choices from among the available centers, they take the lead in creating a lab time filled with positive explorative energy. From there, success requires mindful instruction to maintain and develop that energy. The lab staff, grade-level teachers, or parents working at lab time follow the action and establish conversations with students to develop the inquiries further and achieve program objectives. The open-inquiry learning dance has begun with the *project as medium and the teacher as coach.*

A Preliminary List of Inquiry Learning Objectives

As the inquiry projects unfold, a broad range of teaching opportunities present themselves. The perceptive lab instructor waits for the right moment, then cultivates the project experience by guiding students to:

- develop new individual interests

- develop the ability to sustain choices and self-structure their work

- build focus and experience "flow"

- identify and enrich the *process* of finding and meeting challenges

- build positive and productive habits of mind

- put critical and creative thinking skills into concrete practice

- develop a full "spectrum" of intelligences

- *transfer* their learning—to and from—other instructional and life arenas

- rethink, fine-tune, and personalize their grade-level curriculum learning

- experience alternative language-learning opportunities (English Speakers of Other Languages "ESOL" students)

- discover and build giftedness

- develop collaborative thinking and positive team contributions

- engage inquiry experiences for writing

- build new connections and working relationships with their teachers and parents

Offering Choices and Finding Challenges

With an emphasis on both problem finding and problem solving, and within a discovery-room-like setup, students are given choices for their inquiries. Offering choices generates children's inquisitive energy and helps to establish high levels of lab-time engagement. A well-developed inventory of projects will offer a number of choices based on common interests—various building and construction options, for instance. Choices lead to affirmation, with the teacher as coach essentially saying, *I believe in your choice, I will follow you there.* This is the message that lifts the children and helps build their confidence for pursuing and managing self-directed inquiries both in and outside the lab.

> *One of us wanted to do space and the other wanted to do the jungle* [story theme at the felt board]. *But then we decided on camping in the jungle.*
> —Second-grade lab student

Naturally, it is not always possible to offer complete freedom of choice. Not all students will end up where they first wanted to go because of the number of children present. However, children do accept the process of taking turns with favorite projects. And certainly in the meantime, cultivating and building other challenges always remains an option for inquiry, with valuable lab lessons unfolding: *You ended up at a project that wasn't your first choice; how can you build that inquiry to make it your own? How will you make that challenge an exciting or purposeful place for you to be?*

Or as things might go, children can literally be squirming to get their hands on a particular center, find themselves finally there, and run into a difficulty that makes them want to abandon it. Telltale signs unfold—bothering others, freezing up with anxiety, or proclaiming the classic stalling stance and comment, *I'm bored.* As inquiry learning goes, this becomes a prime instructional moment for teaching children different ways to cope, to adjust and personalize their challenges, and to self-structure their tasks and goals. These skills can later be transferred right into other learning and life situations.

With the lab standard understood—that the inquiry choice is for the entire period, without hopping around—if a child loses focus, the coach steps in to help as needed. They explore the project together, and the coach presents questions to spark new possibilities, find out what frustrations may be lurking, and guide the student to plan steps to meet his or her goals.

What drew you to this project, the one you now want to leave?

Are there specific parts of the project you find frustrating? What if you . . .

I know you have a big interest in building bridges. What are ways this project could somehow include that interest? Let's explore some possibilities.

So what are your goals now?

What steps will you take with this inquiry to meet your new goals?

What other steps could you take?

Finding "Flow"

In terms of offering choices, you might hear a visiting parent or teacher say, *But you go to that center every time! Try something new today!* This statement, meant to help children develop a diversity of experiences, can unfortunately be counterproductive and get in the way of a core lab-time purpose related to intrinsic motivation and promoting self-structure—for children to maintain vital focus with their work while finding joy in developing their interests. In other words, for them to be in *flow.*

> *The best moments [in our lives] usually occur when a person's body or mind is stretched to its limits in a voluntary effort to accomplish*

---

*something difficult and worthwhile. Optimal experience is thus
something that we <u>make</u> happen. For a child, it could be placing with
trembling fingers the last block on a tower she has built, higher than
any she has built so far; for the swimmer, it could be trying to beat his
own record; for a violinist, mastering an intricate musical passage.
For each person there are thousands of opportunities, challenges to
expand ourselves.* (Csikszentmihalyi 1990, 3)

The psychological theory of "optimal experience," as developed by Mihaly Csikszentmihalyi, is focused on what he defines as flow: a state of "total involvement" with some task, project, or thinking. Through his studies of individuals actively pursuing their vocation, such as artists, surgeons, and athletes, Csikszentmihalyi observes that they generally become so absorbed in their work, or in flow, that they tend to lose track of time (Csikszentmihalyi 1990). Flow is something all individuals experience and can cultivate further and represents an ultimately satisfying and happy time. Inquiry learning is an approach that is naturally geared toward generating sustained absorption and experiencing the positive feeling of a great challenge.

The Key School of Indianapolis (Key Learning Community) has adopted Csikszentmihalyi's flow theory, especially for its Flow Center (Key Learning Community 2007). Along with its focus on developing an atmosphere of sustained absorption, the Flow Room is geared toward learning more about children's intelligences through the project choices they make. "The Flow Room serves two main educational purposes. First, it allows students to explore various aspects of their intelligences, to experiment with different skills, and thus develop potentialities that otherwise may never be tapped. Second, the free, enjoyable, but orderly activity in the Flow Room is expected to infuse the rest of the more structured classes with a halo of intrinsic motivation" (Csikszentmihalyi & Whalen 1991, 3).

The key element of an optimal experience is that it is an end in itself.
(Csikszentmihalyi 1990, 67)

Inquiry educators will know if a lab time has the spirit of discovery and purposeful focus simply by scanning across the lab. They will see small groups of children with their heads and shoulders pointed toward their work and their hands moving to make things happen. The room may be loud in pockets, but the sounds are purposeful for the job at hand. This is the picture to look for—children vitally engaged with their projects. Such a high level of involvement is usually accompanied by children's receptiveness to going further with the challenge and reaching higher levels of thinking and understanding. Consequently, establishing a good healthy dose of flow meets two primary goals for an inquiry learning lab: to set positive patterns for finding and sustaining interests and to generate a productive learning energy. Thus, while working with students, instructors nurture the following key elements of flow (presented by Csikszentmihalyi):

1. A challenge is present, with clear goals "every step of the way."

2. Feedback about performance, in terms of skills or understandings needed for the task, is immediate and ongoing.

3. There is a balance between the individual's abilities and the skills needed to meet the challenge—the challenge is neither too easy nor too difficult.

4. An individual exhibits full concentration and focus. "Action and awareness are merged."

5. The high level of absorption with the challenge tends to wash away other life issues, troubles, or realities, the individual "aware only of what is relevant here and now."

6. "There is no worry of failure." The absorbed experience of flow washes away concern of potential failure.

7. Individuals' concerns about themselves are removed during this time, "yet paradoxically the sense of self emerges stronger after the flow experience is over."

8. One's sense of time is altered.

9. The experience is "an end within itself," or "autotelic." (Csikszentmihalyi 1990, 1996)

If children are able to catch the spark for deep involvement with positive activities, such as with the inquiry projects, they will more likely find ways to search out and build such experiences for themselves, again and again.

No, really, it's time to move to Reflection Circle! You have been so focused that you lost track of time! That's flow in action!

How has being able to focus helped your work and your thinking? What skills did you develop? Look, you were able to . . .

What other ideas do you have for this project? How will you explore it further the next time?

What other times do you lose track of time?

What was going on in those activities? Are there any common links or elements?

How can you build those elements into other projects in the lab?

Cultivating and Enriching the Process

For my part, I travel not to go anywhere, but to go. I travel for travel's sake. The great affair is to move.
—Robert Louis Stevenson

When focusing on and cultivating the *process* of working through a challenge, the end product or goal is not ignored; rather, the process needed to accomplish the goal at hand is simply given more serious consideration and is thus *enriched*. Cultivating the process involves adding (or taking away) activities and steps in order to strengthen the effort, resulting in overall stronger understandings, statements, or products.

As an example, imagine how an artist might develop a new series of still-life paintings. Often artists begin by exploring various objects. To open up and consider possibilities, they first make countless "thumbnail" drawings of potential angles and forms and experiment with various light sources. They then make larger drawings to investigate further their emerging interests and compositional ideas. The artist may also play around with color, making various small sketches to uncover combinations and concepts that work and feel right. This activity all takes place before starting to paint the first canvas of the new series. Each individual painting thus becomes a "statement" of the overall process that was built and nurtured. Altogether, each of the paintings in the group supports and establishes the series as a whole. Every artist develops his or her own unique process, adding and taking away parts and continually searching for new possibilities. Yet remove an essential step, and the series as a whole becomes limited and weaker in comparison—with the artist sensing that something is missing.

Enriching the process applies to cultivating industrious thinking and productivity for any type of endeavor: an attorney working on a case, a chef planning a menu, an educator designing a social studies unit, a student writing a paper.

Thinking about thinking through open inquiry brings awareness of the unfolding process at hand and helps individuals see that they themselves can enrich that process. With a "traveling" orientation of moving through an inquiry, children are set on an adventure to find new steps in the process toward working through a challenge that will strengthen their thinking and doing. Just as for the artist, the goal is to help children become sensitive to when critical elements, needed to support the overall effort, are missing.

What Does It Take to Meet a Challenge?

There are behavioral attributes that help make the process of meeting *any* challenge more successful. Examples are making a commitment to a challenge or evaluating the work accomplished. What is intriguing and inspiring to an inquiry program is discovering that many critical elements for thinking through and meeting challenges can be broadly applied and that individuals of all ages and interests can talk about, share, and *together* identify and develop these elements. When students are collectively asked, *What does it take to meet a challenge?*, many are often eager to present their insights, as the following actual quotes reveal:

You need to <u>want</u> to do it.

Patience.

On some things, you need teamwork.

Strategy.

Morale—if you don't have faith, nothing will happen.

Use what you know.

Don't just stop. Keep doing it.

You need to have the ability. In other words, I shouldn't try to do something I'm not ready for, like driving a race car.

Confidence. Believe you can do it.

Don't let your mind wander. Focus.

Be ambitious.

Be brave. Be strong.

Brainstorm. Get ideas. Think big. Use your imagination.

Let someone help.

Don't be hard on yourself.

You need to care.

Have fun!

Think ahead. Plan.

Take it one step at a time.

Have a backup plan.

[Use a] piece of paper to write out ideas.

Enthusiasm.

Start again if you mess up.

Look at what are the possibilities and what are the consequences.

Take your time.

Have the ability [and be willing] to switch ideas.

Time.

Control your temper.

Don't be upset if someone gets it [solves the challenge] before you.

Have a good attitude—don't get grumpy.

Don't be tired. Don't be hungry.

Relax.

Imagine it done.

Don't be afraid to wonder.

Identifying and Building Habits of Mind

Are the students missing anything? Not much! What the children listed above can be seen as general behavioral guideposts of productive and industrious thinking. Essentially, they were in the process of identifying positive and productive *thinking dispositions* or *habits of mind*.

> *Dispositions shape our lives. They are the proclivities that lead us in one direction rather than another within the freedom of action that we have. A thinking disposition is simply a disposition about thinking.* (Perkins 1995, 275)

Thinking dispositions are defined as "on-going tendencies that guide intellectual behavior" (Tishman, Jay, & Perkins 1992). And certainly, individuals can develop both positive and negative behavioral inclinations with their thinking. For example, individuals can move toward generally being more open-minded and adventurous with their thinking or generally more closed-minded and cautious. Just like other patterns of human behavior, thinking dispositions can be encouraged and guided, can be employed by individuals more consciously, and can also become nearly automatic. They can be taught.

> *I have no special talents, I am only passionately curious.*
> —Albert Einstein

Any individual or group can establish a target list of thinking dispositions or habits of mind on which to focus throughout the year. Indeed, there are many examples of such listings. The following is based on watching children, teachers, and parents at work in the lab and on two primary resources: *Teaching Thinking Dispositions: From Transmission to Enculturation* (Tishman, Jay, & Perkins 1992) and *Discovering and Exploring Habits of Mind* (Costa & Kallick 2000).

1. **Be Adventurous and Open-Minded**

   Brainstorm many ideas. Be flexible with thinking and doing. Think outside of the box!

2. **Wonder, Explore, Ask Questions**

   Investigate and be curious. Seek new challenges or projects. Inquire.

3. **Contribute Positively to the Group and Inspire Teamwork**

   Offer your skills, understanding, and abilities to the team. Help the group to work well together.

4. **Imagine Possibilities and Outcomes**

   What could be? What will likely happen? Put a picture in your mind. Visualize.

5. **Set Goals and Make Plans**

   Establish workable goals. Design a strategy and steps to meet goals and objectives.

   Organize the effort.

6. **Think Independently**

   Think for yourself. Be bold in asking questions. Step out to offer a new idea.

   Build confidence for managing your own work. Review and think about your own thinking. Be metacognitive!

7. **Use What You Know, Transfer Learning**

   Use the skills and understandings you already have in new thinking situations.

8. **Step Back and Look at the Whole Picture**

   Get a full view of the project, event, or situation. Seek relationships.

   Understand how parts—things, ideas, beings, or purposes—connect and link to one another.

9. **Strive to Be Accurate and Precise**

   Be focused and organized when checking work for accuracy. Be tough in uncovering possible errors.

10. **Look Carefully**

    Observe critically and carefully to understand what you see. Gather visual information.

11. **Listen Actively**

    Listen for understanding as you hear music or sounds in nature, or as others speak.

12. **Support Ideas With Reasons Why**

    Find evidence that proves your point. Weigh the importance of the facts and reasons found. Compare the importance of facts.

13. **Persevere**

    Find ways to deal with frustration and stick with difficult challenges. Ask for help if things get too tough!

14. **Communicate Clearly**

    Present ideas clearly and effectively as you write, draw, speak, or perform music.

15. **Understand Others**

    Be aware of others' thinking, abilities, interests, and feelings. Be perceptive and empathetic.

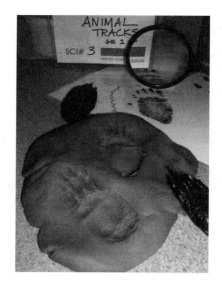

Knowing is not enough; we must apply.
Willing is not enough; we must do.
—Goethe

Certainly children love to be in the spotlight and share what they know about meeting challenges and which habits of mind make a difference for thinking things through. However, along with the rest of us, they can put a finger on what it takes but, once in the midst of a challenge, do not always put that knowledge into practice when it is needed the most.

I need to work on Think First—because usually I'm thinking so fast I
just put something there and the whole thing messes up.
—First-grade lab student

Much like the healthy habit of brushing teeth, which develops through prompting to become nearly automatic, building positive and productive thinking behaviors needs guidance to become something one *usually does.* As with other habits, establishing these dispositions takes time, practice, and constant reminders to become reliable tools for thinking and doing.

Abilities alone are dry and dormant. Passions, motivation, sensitivities,
and values all play a role in bringing intelligent behavior to life. Defining
intelligence as a matter of ability, without honoring all the other elements
that enliven it, fails to capture its human spark. (Tishman 2000, 43)

The habits of mind provide a clear foundation for teaching thinking to children. Through circle discussions and while students are at work, the aim is to identify and set positive thinking dispositions into a rhythm of continual practice. Students are led to see these dispositions in action while thinking and doing, or to see that they are missing. The goal is for children to integrate thinking dispositions consciously into the process of pursuing and meeting any challenge—from a lab inquiry to the taking of a standardized test. Habits of mind lead an individual to put related skills to work. As they sense a lack of Being Adventurous and Open-Minded students may say, *Hey guys, we forgot to brainstorm ideas here!* just as automatically as when they may sense a lack of caring for their health and say, *Wait! I need to run upstairs—I forgot to brush my teeth!*

Collecting Thinking

> Alice laughed. "There's no use trying," she said:
> "one *ca'n't* believe impossible things."
>
> "I daresay you haven't had much practice," said the Queen. "When I was your age, I always did it for half-an-hour a day. Why, sometimes I've believed as many as six impossible things before breakfast!"
> —Lewis Carroll, *Through the Looking Glass*

A list of habits of mind can become a unifying tool for a school, children's hospital, or homeschooling network. In a school setting, for example, thinking dispositions become identified and applied in various learning arenas, from the classroom to schoolwide assemblies. In the grade-level classroom, habits of mind are linked to unfolding curriculum, such as exploring what thinking dispositions were displayed by historical personalities or identifying those that aid an individual to work through a math problem. Various specialists also engage the dispositions; the music instructor might highlight *Active Listening* and *Striving to Be Accurate and Precise,* or the school librarian might guide children to identify the habits of mind seen in action while they read a novel or short story. (A supportive list of books for this purpose is available on Arthur Costa and Bena Kalick's Habits of Mind Web site http://www.habits-of-mind.net/booklists.htm.) Finally, the circle of pedagogy can expand further by sending home with students the list of habits of mind. When placed on the refrigerator for children and their families to review and engage in together, a school-to-home "culture of thinking" begins to develop.

Developing these lifelong thinking dispositions *together* with children, both at home and in the school or hospital, expands the program's capabilities into multigenerational learning experiences. Because they are of concern to all and can always be improved, all ages can share together in the cultivation of the thinking dispositions, including teachers, administrators, parents, grandparents, and younger siblings. At the same time, an intergenerational focus tends to engage the dispositions outside the lab and helps to create an expanding community spirit for the program.

As first introduced and then practiced during inquiry lab time, productive *lifelong* habits of mind are integrated into all corners of a child's thinking, learning, and doing:

What habits of mind are you building as you work on your inquiry with Animal Footprints? Which could you be using? How will those habits help your inquiry progress?

As we read Anne of Green Gables, *which characters in the story do you feel are showing the habit of mind to Persevere? How? What other habits of mind do you see in action?*

What habits of mind did Thomas Jefferson have in action as he wrote the Declaration of Independence? Which habits of mind did he engage as he designed Monticello?

I remember seeing you at work on your bridge construction during our inquiry lab period—you really showed the habit of mind to Strive to Be Accurate and Precise. Do you remember how it felt? How can you increase accuracy and precision with your math problem now? In what ways could it make a difference for your work?

Which habits of mind does our soccer team have working for it? Which do we need to work on? I agree, we could really use a little more accuracy and precision with our goal kicking! We also need to stay tough and persevere! What are some ideas that would get both of those habits of mind into better action?

What habits of mind does our family have in action? Wait a minute, are we <u>really</u> actively listening to each other?

Framing Up Thinking Skills

Habits of mind naturally engage supportive thinking skills into action. For example, if an individual senses the need to Be Accurate and Precise, putting that habit of mind into action will require calling into gear specific skills such as to analyze, evaluate, or compare and contrast. A group working successfully on the Rubber Band Car Derby project (see Chapter Six, "Inquiry Project Sampler"), while both rigging up a tension-and-release mechanism for the rubber band and organizing time and distance trials, will certainly need to apply these specific thinking skills in order to be accurate and precise. In addition, as the demands of the challenge unfold, students continue to need to be accurate and precise with other skills demanded by the project, such as communication, visual observation, data collection, graphing, and time measurement.

Good creative thinking always involves a measure of critical thinking, else it would simply be foolish. Good critical thinking always involves a measure of creative thinking, else it would be narrow. The two need one another. (Perkins 1995, 285)

Skills are seen in action at lab time in unique ways, shifting from one to the other as the challenge develops. At various points along the way, all skills—higher or lower, more or less complex, general or more specific—are essential to the job of thinking well (Costa 2001). As with any industrious thinking and doing, from working out a math problem to producing a painting, both critical and creative skills intermix and work together. From fine motor to computation skills, and from synthesizing ideas to analyzing and evaluating information, the inquiry lab's job is to clearly display the skills in action and to lead children to see how the skills can add significantly to meeting their challenges.

A program that spotlights developing cognitive skills serves to support the curriculum of a school, a homeschool network, or the learning goals of a children's hospital. In fact, an inquiry program that focuses on identifying and putting various skills into practice sets itself up to develop more easily a shared teaching mission with a broad range of participating educators. In addition, if the connection of shared skill objectives is made clearly and successfully, educators will see that time spent in the lab teaching, or otherwise supporting the program's objectives, will help them meet their own instructional objectives. Taking a look at state or county curriculum standards presents a possible source of skill strands that a lab program can help develop. For example, *Observation, Classification, Communication, Formulation of Models, Construction of Hypotheses,* and *Drawing Conclusions* are a few skills identified by the State of Georgia in its *Process Skills K–12.* These skills are certainly inquiry friendly, are part of many core curriculum objectives, and are ones that students will likely develop further throughout their lives.

Each lab program determines its own list of skills on which to focus. Target lists can be based on the skill goals of a children's physical therapy unit, a school's program of studies, faculty responses to questions about which particular skills students need, or on various published lists of critical and creative thinking skills. Another way to target skills is simply to observe what children are doing, or not doing, to meet their lab challenges. *What skills surface? Which should be surfacing?* The following list of skills is derived from all the above-mentioned sources:

- *Fine Motor*
- *Number Sense*
- *Computation*
- *Perceiving Symmetry*
- *Estimation*
- *Measurement*
- *Data Analysis*
- *Graphing*
- *Organizing*
- *Applying Concepts*
- *Problem Finding*
- *Problem Solving*
- *Abstract Reasoning*
- *Spatial Reasoning*
- *Construction*

- *Phonetic Pronunciation*
- *Writing*
- *Recalling Information*
- *Transferring Understandings*
- *Visualizing Outcomes*
- *Predicting, Hypothesizing*
- *Brainstorming*
- *Planning Strategy*
- *Perceiving Patterns*
- *Comparing and Contrasting*
- *Classifying Information*
- *Determining Cause and Effect*
- *Sequencing Ideas and Information*
- *Forming Relevant Questions*
- *Researching*

- *Mapping*
- *Using Vocabulary*
- *Interviewing*
- *Oral Communication*
- *Discussion*
- *Listening*
- *Observing and Recording a System*
- *Synthesizing Information*
- *Designing*
- *Analyzing*
- *Evaluating*

Throughout the inquiry lab time, intriguing instructional opportunities unfold as each project calls specific skills into action.

Yes, I agree, this project does require the habit of mind to Step Back and Look at the Whole Picture! What skills or tools will you engage to do that? Certainly, use your interviewing skills and survey the group for their observations about this project.

Have you used a Venn diagram before? Great, let's set one up.

What are other skills or tools that would help you Step Back and Look at the Whole Picture with this inquiry? Oh, a Mind Map!

Who Is Smart?

When people think of their intelligence as something that grows incrementally, they are more likely to invest the energy to learn something new or increase their understanding and mastery of tasks. (Costa & Kallick 2000, 3)

Intelligence is a high-profile commodity, and children know it. *They feel it.* Related comments often ring in their ears, drifting in from various sources. *Oh, that child is so bright. He is so smart.* Or one might hear children say, *That's stupid.* Worse yet, *You're dumb.* Grades, test scores, and IQ numbers are often passed around. Children spend time questioning themselves, even those who receive clear messages of being "bright." Such doubts can spiral into lack of confidence, perfectionist tendencies, an inability to engage in activities, and other behaviors that limit individuals. How children understand the concept of intelligence, and how they perceive themselves as being "smart" within a group, makes a big difference in terms of their taking chances, self-structuring their own learning, addressing their areas of weakness, and displaying giftedness.

Most educators and psychologists have moved beyond focusing on IQ or other standardized tests to define intelligence. Forgotten are the ideas that intelligence is a single entity, or one that it is set solid at birth. (This is what you get, thank you very much.) Instead, most have adopted more dimensional and flexible concepts of what it means to be smart. Although genetically influenced, intelligence will grow through opportunity and *can be taught*. Robert Sternberg's *Analytical, Creative, and Practical Intelligence*, Howard Gardner's *Theory of Multiple Intelligences,* and David Perkins's *Neural, Experiential, and Reflective Intelligence* all support the idea that intelligence is not static and set, and that individuals are able to develop their intelligence (Costa & Kallick 2000). Thankfully, we are in the midst of an "affirmative revolution" (Perkins 1995) when it comes to teaching thinking.

Multiple Intelligences

I found I could say things with color and shapes that I couldn't say any other way—things I had no words for.
—Georgia O'Keeffe

To set the empowerment stage and to nurture a *full spectrum* of intelligences, many educational communities have engaged Howard Gardner's Multiple Intelligences (MI) theory. Through human cognitive studies, Gardner has isolated the following eight distinct areas of intelligence that each individual possesses (Gardner, quoted in Checkly 1997). Each intelligence develops on its own timetable through relevant experiences and opportunities, yet all work together to help an individual think productively, gain skills and understandings, and meet any challenges he or she may take on.

Math-Logic Intelligence: our capacity to understand and work with numbers. To perceive and understand underlying principles, systems, and structures (for example, exercised as we play chess, make computations, estimate, perform scientific experiments, engineer, design).

Visual-Spatial Intelligence: our capacity to perceive and work with two- and three-dimensional spatial relationships (for example, exercised as we navigate; work with mapping; observe and record visual phenomena, draw, design, build; to judge distances and space in sports).

Verbal-Linguistic Intelligence: our capacity to understand and communicate through language (for example, exercised as we write, speak, read, research).

Body-Kinesthetic Intelligence: our capacity to engage and refine our movement, both gross and fine motor, to produce specific results or products (for example, exercised as we dance, make sculpture, handwrite, play soccer, draw).

***Musical-Rhythmic:** our capacity to perceive, understand, and work with sounds and rhythm. "To be able to hear patterns, recognize them, remember them, and perhaps manipulate them"(Gardner, quoted in Checkly 1997) (for example, exercised as we play music; memorize musical sequences; recall sounds, music, rhythm).*

***Interpersonal:** our capacity to understand others—their motivations and needs (for example, exercised as we cultivate team skills, help someone work through an issue, teach).*

***Intrapersonal:** our capacity to understand ourselves—our needs, interests, strengths and weakness (for example, exercised as we reflect, weigh out our strengths and weaknesses, consider our interests, think metacognitively).*

***Naturalist:** our capacity to understand the world around us and to discern differences in flora and fauna. "The human ability to discriminate among living things (plants, animals) as well as sensitivity to other features of the natural world (clouds, rock configurations)" (Gardner, quoted in Checkly 1997) (for example, exercised as we observe and identify nature, discern qualities, similarities, and differences in our life surroundings).*

We each have our own developing "MI profile," our own set of highlighted intelligences, gained both through genetics and experience. MI profiles tend to lead individuals toward the ways in which they understand and learn best and toward what they will pursue in life. For instance, an engineer, mechanic, or architect's more dominant intelligences are likely to be Visual-Spatial and Math-Logic; a surgeon, hygienist, or dentist's are likely Body-Kinesthetic, Naturalist, Math-Logic, Visual-Spatial; and an attorney, journalist, real estate agent, or politician's are likely Verbal-Linguistic, Math-Logic, and Interpersonal.

> *Certainly Gardner's pluralization of intelligence ranks as his major contribution to the way in which schools view kids. Not far behind, though, in our opinion, is his identification of the personal intelligences and his distinguishing between Interpersonal intelligence (understanding others) and Intrapersonal intelligence (understanding oneself). While these concepts and terms appear logical, and almost simple, they revolutionize the way in which one looks at child development and the role of the teacher.* (Hoerr 1996, xix)

A more dimensional and flexible conception of intelligence changes a school's working, learning, and thinking climate. Such a change moves right into the instructional arena by saying, *OK, each of us has all the different ways of being smart; let's respect, use, and build them all.*

Layering Intelligences

Specifically designing a project that requires a child to employ a variety of intelligences within the inquiry challenge, or layering intelligences, becomes an effective instructional tool. For instance, children with highlighted Visual-Spatial and Math-Logic profiles will likely pursue challenges in the area of building and construction. Perhaps they become deeply engaged in building a bridge. As they work, the coach asks the students to explain what they are doing and to provide advice to others pursuing a similar challenge. After the inquiry, the children give a short oral presentation about how they designed their bridge. Finally, the students write about the experience for a class journal or homework assignment. Along with the Visual-Spatial and Math-Logic experience, the children are also led to develop Verbal-Linguistic, Intrapersonal, and Interpersonal intelligences. As the building of the bridge becomes more complex and intricate, Body-Kinesthetic intelligence (fine motor) also gets stretched. Because the children are so committed to and excited about the inquiry, they are able to move more easily beyond their usual comfort zones and become more involved in developing their other intelligences.

Identifying MI Profiles

Because the goal is to keep the door open for all intelligences to grow, it just doesn't feel right to hear a seven year old label himself or herself: *It's pretty clear, I am a Math-Logic and Visual-Spatial kid.* Even though instructors are aware of the students' emerging MI profiles, instead of emphasizing those perceived profiles to the children, they highlight the *project's use* of intelligences: *Which intelligences are you using to meet the challenges of this lab inquiry? When you work on this book report, and new cover design, what intelligences will you be getting into action?* Children thereby still receive a strong empowerment message—something they can or love to do is being identified to themselves and the group as intelligent. All will celebrate as they display their strengths, yet the growth picture for all intelligences is left open. The child is led to know and feel, *I have all the different ways of being smart. They are all supported and respected here in my school. Even the ones I love most are grown here! I'm part of the thinking scene. You know, it could be I'm even getting somewhere with my Word Smart. Hmm, I do love music, but haven't worked on that one too much. I wonder if I could . . .*

USING WHAT WE KNOW: TRANSFER OF LEARNING

While in the pantomime of picking up an item and moving it to another place, an instructor might explain to a young group of children that *transfer of learning* is when we pick up and "take our learning along" to help out in a new thinking or challenge situation. An individual's learning becomes stronger and more personal as it sets out to serve in another context. Even a standardized test is a transfer of learning experience.

Without transfer—without this connecting of one thing to another—human learning would not have anywhere near the capacity to shape and empower our lives that it does. (Tishman, Perkins, & Jay 1995, 156)

Establishing transfer of learning has long been a concern for educators. After all, the point is to employ what is taught. The reality, however, is that transfer is not as automatic as many would hope: "transfer does not take care of itself" (Perkins & Salomon 2001). "For example science instructors commonly complain of having to reteach mathematics to their students, even though the students seem to be doing well enough in their math classes. Why has their mathematical knowledge not traversed the corridor between the math room and the physics room?" (Perkins 1992, 122). Although many educators apply methods to engage transfer, the message here is that in order for a broader base of students to consciously apply what they are learning, teaching for transfer needs to be engaged as a specific curriculum tool and as a more deliberate instructional focus.

A transfer experience can be more direct and akin to what was originally learned, such as a student applying the same multiplication skills to a new math problem. Or the transfer experience can represent a more synthesized understanding and application of the initial learning, such as applying math skills to a study of economics (Perkins & Salomon 2001). Ideas drawn from *How to Teach for Transfer* by Robin Fogarty, David Perkins, and John Barell (http://learnweb.harvard.edu/ALPS/thinking/docs/10tips.htm) and the Harvard Graduate Department of Education's Web site ALPS (Active Learning Practices for Schools; Harvard Project Zero, Cognitive Skills Group 1999) present a series of tools for teaching for transfer using the concepts of "Hugging" and "Bridging." Hugging is generally employed for the more direct, or "near" transfer, and Bridging supports the more complex and synthesized "far transfer." Some of these methods, as presented in the following, apply well to inquiry lab instruction.

Examples of Hugging

Match the Learning. Create a series of lab projects through which similar concepts, skills, or understandings are presented and laced—for example, a series of projects that require using simple machines in a variety of different ways.

Set Expectations. Highlight to students where else they might see an observed concept or skill in action. Dialogue example: *Certainly triangles are a big part of building a geodesic dome. Where else might you find yourself working with geometric forms as you pursue lab projects? How do triangles add strength to the dome? How might other geometric forms add strength and structure to other constructions?*

Model and Demonstrate the Learning. The educator displays his or her own thinking and doing while working alongside students and exploring a project with a group of children, providing insight as to how they might transfer various skills and understandings.

Examples of Bridging

Anticipate Applications. Children are led to visualize how a concept, understanding, or skill could be applied in a different situation. *What skills and habits of mind are you using here to get the job done? Where else could you employ these same skills, habits of mind, and understandings? Could you use the habit of mind to be Accurate and Precise while building here as well as with the Rocks and Minerals project? How?*

Use Analogies: Set up a Compare and Contrast experience between the content or skill at hand and its use in another possible application. *How is working and thinking things through with Bridge Building similar to working with the Mobile in Balance center? How are they different?*

Engage Metacognitive Thinking and Reflection. Give students time to review and reflect on how they are thinking through their particular project. Help students to be more mindful of the process of transfer, and see clearly what connections they are making with their learning. *Tell me what you already know about the properties of color. Ah, primary and secondary color, value and hue! How are you transferring those understandings now—how are you using what you know—as you work on the Magnetic Mural?*

A Transfer of Learning Station

With its hands-on explorative orientation that engages various skills and understandings, an inquiry learning lab is in an ideal position to display transfer of learning in action. Indeed, lab time could even be identified as a "Transfer of Learning Station"—a proving ground for making learning connections. As transfer experiences are actively pursued in this setting, children are more likely to make similar connections in other learning arenas. Instructors help children identify and employ grade-level content and other learning, and lead students to *interact* with the concepts at hand:

I see you have chosen to work with origami today.

Certainly you are building the habit of mind to Persevere!

This work requires dealing with frustration! It's tough! Good for you.

By the way, this project reminds me of something we studied in math this week.

Do you also see anything familiar?

What connections to our study of math can you make?

What understandings can you transfer?

Yes, I also see geometric shapes in your crane.

Can you name the shapes you see?

Great! You have identified many geometric shapes!

Do you also see a hexagon or parallelogram? Where?

How can your understanding of geometric shapes help your work with origami?

Ah, the square is equal on all sides. What you folded is a rectangle instead . . .

How will this observation change your crane?

Students are also led by instructors to transfer the understandings and skills gained during their inquiry time to other learning arenas outside the lab:

Do you remember yesterday when you were working with origami during our inquiry lab time? Now while we are here in our math period, I have a few questions for you . . .

Which habit of mind did you build while working with origami? I agree, you were able to deal with your frustration well, and persevere through that challenge.

What helped you to persevere with that work? Oh, take it one step at a time, review the plans, ask for help, step back and try again . . .

Which of those skills could help you persevere again, now, with this math problem? Are there any other ways that would help?

Certainly, you have already shown you can persevere when things get tough . . .

FURTHER TEACHING ON THE THINKING FLOOR

Differentiating Skills and Understandings

Teaching for transfer connects well with differentiating learning objectives for each student. As an instructor observes a child call into action a content, understanding, or thinking skill, he or she sees clearly how well that child grasps the given area of learning. Educators then work with each child individually to rethink and fine-tune their skills and understandings or to stretch them to higher levels. Indeed, lab time can be seen as a time and place when a school or other organization can meet some of its differentiation goals or requirements.

Surprises often happen as children transfer their understandings and skills within this open environment. For example, those who test well in a given curriculum content area may have difficulties applying that content to a lab challenge, whereas those who did not test as well may display a better grasp of the understandings and skills as they work with their inquiry. Lab time can thus become an interesting and valuable alternative evaluation opportunity for educators.

Supporting Special Programs

Inquiry lab time offers a unique social and working environment for various specialists to observe students applying their specialized instruction, as in special education, counselling, or gifted and talented programs. Various specialists—for example, those who work in the area of physical rehabilitation, speech, learning disabilities, or child psychology—are always welcome in the lab and also to contribute as coteachers. As they work alongside children, they are able to reinforce their own particular teaching objectives. The format can be enlightening for these specialists, especially to see how children "air out" their specialized instruction and how they integrate with other children while working in groups on inquiry projects. Overall, the inquiry program sets itself up for many instructional collaborations that will help an organization or school develop its learning and community building objectives. Making it clear that the lab space and program are open for active use to all educators in the school or organization can develop new professional relationships and understanding.

An example of such a collaboration is when the English for Speakers of Other Languages (ESOL) program makes more active use of a school's centralized inquiry lab program. As with other groups, ESOL can formally schedule additional lab times, with the door simply left open for these specialized instructors and their students. Then at the regularly scheduled lab with their entire class, seeing these ESOL students active in the inquiry format and breaking through their language barriers as they work alongside their native English–speaking classmates is a true joy. Lab time quickly becomes their place as well. Further, even though children can often move into complex thinking challenges through self-directed hands-on projects that require little up-front verbal instruction, all delight—teammates, educators, the new students themselves—as their vocabulary and communication skills clearly improve through the process of working together. Eyes twinkle as these children make valuable contributions to the group.

Affirming Thinking and Cultivating Belief in Oneself

I had no idea!
—Teacher

This does not surprise me.
—Teacher

When the full spectrum of intelligences, thinking skills, and dispositions are openly engaged, the door is flung wide open to support all areas of giftedness. Intriguing questions surface as students pursue self-directed projects in the open-inquiry lab: How might children display giftedness in this particular format? How can emerging gifts, including ones newly discovered, be encouraged and supported?

What individuals believe about themselves, how they reveal their gifts, and how an educator can help build those gifts certainly appear to be intertwined. How students work through their inquiries will often indicate children's underlying beliefs about themselves, both positive and negative. Each child works at an individual place on the spectrum of *being able* to show his or her gifts and build skills, with the extremes essentially saying either *I have nothing to do here. I'm frozen. I want to quit.* Or, *I just can't stop my ideas! What can I try next?* Which of these extreme attitudes is more likely to empower positive and purposeful gifted thinking and behavior? For the many dimensions of learning, thinking, and doing, who would be in a better position to move forward?

With each unfolding project, educators work alongside children and open positive new paths for their gifts to emerge and strengthen. In addition, they help students with issues that may hold them back in their development. Again, the instructional task begins by affirming the choices children make for their day's inquiry and then builds with continued affirmations as their work unfolds. Comments and questions, based on observation, are presented as the child works and tend to spiral upward in complexity as the child's thinking evolves and grows. Divergent questions are formulated to inspire critical and creative thinking and to help the child establish momentum with a positive energy. That energy, in turn, naturally helps to open up his or her many gifts and abilities:

You have decided to build and race a rubber-band car! What will be your first step? Ah, locate your parts and pieces. Good luck! I'll be back . . .

These pieces are assembled differently from what I have seen before. Interesting choice. What will you now do with them?

Stuck on the axle concept? Hmm. How do you see the axle working on this wooden model car?

Tell me what you discovered about how the axle works. Great insight! How does that thinking help you construct your own car? Nearly there! Be back . . .

This is a unique solution for getting the axle to function and creating a rubber-band car. I'm not sure I've seen it before.

Fantastic! We now we have another example of wheels in motion! Now, can you evaluate your axle design? What will be the criteria for your evaluation?

Would you be interested in designing a fleet of cars? Perhaps you could make three different designs and then compare how the cars function? Perhaps conduct time and distance trials?

Collaborative Thinking

In this open time and place designed to welcome everyone, seeing children build new working relationships with each other is perhaps the greatest benefit of an inquiry lab environment. Students who may not normally work or play together will often end up working with each other at a center, where a challenging project can overcome personality or learning differences that may arise. Students are in a great position to develop new levels of sensitivity for working with others and to find positive ways to contribute to a group.

Especially for the fifth- and sixth-grade age levels, who have grown to be more concerned about the group dynamic, establishing a set of challenges that *specifically depend* on team problem solving suits their emerging social sensitivities. Because these children's interests are growing into a higher consciousness of others, why not establish for them a specialty focus on social awareness and team-building skills? A good handful of such inquiry projects in the lab also makes a *significant* difference to maintaining the level of flow and work ethic for this age group.

Many published resources present such hands-on team-building projects that emphasize collaborative thinking and the group dynamic. One such project highlighted in this book, developed by industrial/organizational psychologist Sam Sikes (1995), is an ideal team-building experience that especially appeals to the upper grade levels. In People and Pipes, each participating student is given a PVC pipe of a different length. One golf ball needs to travel through all the pipes, from one pipe to the next, and then drop into a tin bucket (see Chapter Six, "Inquiry Project Sampler"). The hitch is that neither the pipes nor the students themselves may touch. This aspect makes the task extremely challenging, if not impossible, without the team members actively engaging their collaborative thinking skills and habits of mind. An intriguing solution to this challenge was once observed when a group (after much struggle, reflection, and team brainstorming) figured out that the pipes could be held up and steadied against a wall. After many adjustments, the ball was dropped into the top of the formation and, after consecutively cascading through each pipe (with neither hands nor pipes touching each other), it pinged into the bucket!

INQUIRY TEACHING ETIQUETTE

Lab-Time Instruction in a Nutshell

Watch.
Follow.
Let children's inquiry unfold and develop.
Keep inquiries open for surprises.
Observe how children process intelligences, skills, dispositions, and content understandings.
Wait.
Establish an "on the spot" teaching objective for each inquiry.
Brainstorm a line of questions to support the objective.
Find the best time to step into the inquiry.
Affirm the students' efforts.
Guide. Coach.
Pose questions.
Wait. Listen.
Affirm, reflect, celebrate, clarify.
Model the thinking skills and dispositions.
Be a fellow discoverer.
Try an age-dimensional project yourself and ask children to help guide your inquiry.

Inquiry learning practices are often identified as *open,* and at other times as *guided.* The short-term inquiries presented in this book tend to be a mix of the two. The design of the project itself may be more open and exploratory as when, for example, students set off on general investigations about magnetism. Or projects can be designed to present a more finite and guided challenge, as with the quest to build a geodesic dome. Yet each of these inquiries could move toward becoming either more finite or more open, depending on the particular inquiry path. Lab instruction can also be either more open or more guided. As the inquiries develop, teaching requires finding a balance between these two and becoming more sensitive to when it's time to wait and see what unfolds with a child's work, thus leaving things more open, and when it is time to step in and guide the effort.

Open to Surprises

When to step back during a child's inquiry becomes more clear with experience and as one gets to know the various teaching and learning possibilities of each project. As instructors see that children are engaged in flow, even if the inquiry appears limited, they may do well to wait and see what happens. Or when a group attempts a challenge and things do not work out well with the team dynamic, as with the People and Pipes project mentioned earlier, an instructor may choose to let things get even worse before stepping in with guiding questions. The teacher as coach may want the group to see for itself how a lack of team skills can negatively affect collaborative thinking, as well as the outcome of the project. They are looking to see the group uncover for themselves ways to amend the organizational crisis and then move forward more effectively.

Besides allowing the students to find their own solutions, instructors also need to be careful not to let their own ideas about a project's outcome overly influence the route the students might take toward finding possibilities. Even the most open-ended questioning can be focused toward a preconceived goal of the instructor, thereby controlling the outcome. With some inquiry teaching, such as helping students acquire a particular content understanding, targeted questioning is certainly appropriate and needed. However, in terms of the more open-ended challenges, why not leave the door open to see what the children come up with—perhaps possibilities that the instructor had not even thought of. The place becomes more exciting and engages higher levels of critical and creative thinking if it is kept open for surprises. As with the struggling members of the People and Pipes challenge, the instructor carefully opens the student's ability to organize their efforts and brainstorm ideas, yet at the same time the instructor, too, remains *open* to the uncovering of new possible solutions. Certainly the unexpected solutions often become the ones that are remembered longest.

Encouraging Student Reflection

From the Socratic approach to other guidelines for divergent questioning, there are many effective methods that can develop the "art of questioning." The goal of such questioning is to position the individual so that he or she can reflect on the question, generate new ideas, and evaluate possibilities. An instructor can often see when a child truly takes on a question. The blocks and hands might sit still for a moment, and the individual appears to look inward as his or her unfocused gaze is set off to the side.

A useful listing that helps frame effective questioning is presented by Arthur Costa (2001) and is represented by the following acronym, *SPACE:*

Silence *(wait time for students to answer)*

Provide Ideas *(provide feedback, give perspectives, offer resources and equipment)*

Accept Without Judgment *(establish a safe thinking and questioning "climate," affirm)*

Clarify *(position for more specific application, clarification or elaboration)*

Empathize *(communicate understanding of students' observed feelings)*

The Art of Questioning

When it comes to inquiry learning, everyone, educators and students alike, pursues the art of questioning. Building children's ability to cultivate questions as tools in the process of thinking through their inquiries, however, requires specific instructional focus. You may at first see blank faces if you ask students, *What questions do you hear yourself asking with this challenge?* It takes practice for children to be able to listen while their minds are at work and to hear their many questions unfold.

At Reflection Circle, asking children about the questions that drove their inquiries forward that day illustrates to the group as a whole how useful it is to be mindful of questions. To stimulate students' questioning further, some inquiry projects take the form of a "lab survey," in which students actually interview their working classmates and ask questions that focus on a particular theme, such as on the habits of mind being employed that day (see Chapter Six, "Inquiry Project Sampler"). Another way to get students into the practice of questioning is to use cards that list questions similar to those teachers ask. Questions such as the following rotate around the lab, asked by children: *What are the goals of your inquiry? What steps are you taking to meet your goals? Where else do you make use of strategy?* When equipped with a tape recorder, the question cards can themselves become an inquiry center, making for some great student-led interviews (see Appendix O, *Student Lab-Time Question Card*).

An Experience to Write About

Inquiry lab times create rich experiences about which children can write. After children have a solid work time with their inquiries, they can write about them in either a lab journal or for a class assignment. As in the case described earlier of the student who wrote about building a bridge, children have been seen to move well beyond their usual writing levels to document their vital lab-time experience (see Appendix A, *Student Writing Samples*). Critical for a successful writing experience is, of course, to ensure that the student's lab experience has been rich and full.

Writing often takes place naturally in the lab, from outlining the parts of a story being created at the Felt Story Board to making notes and diagramming how a puzzle is being solved. Writing quietly for a while following a rich lab experience also becomes a time for effective reflection. Once children have fully completed their inquiry, they can then settle down to document their experiences. Any notes or drawings made during lab time can also add a prewriting dimension to this writing experience. Setting this writing time in place can also act as a well-positioned transition from the more open lab experience to that of the more teacher-led group instructional arena.

(A) yes! #8

Nicholas

Yesterday I went to the
Think Tank and used Kapla
Bolcks to create a
Kapla bridge. I discovred
that to make the Kapla
bridge, you have to
have a lot of back
support and top support
The back support levels
out the weight and the
top support holds up
bouth sids Another thing i
discovered is that it takes a
groupe of two or three
people that will work toghter
and will not fiddle around

The Project Holds the Show

Have you ever noticed while working on a project with a child—playing a game of chess or cooking a meal together—that conversation with them flows more easily? In the child's mind, your focus is not so much on them but, rather, the project holds the show.

Consider children new to a school or hospital, perhaps a child from another country, a student acting shy and withdrawn, or someone who is otherwise going through a challenging time. A project can offer that individual a relieving and welcomed haven of activity. Other teaching objectives (such as developing specific thinking skills or transferring learning) are put aside for a while as the project establishes a comfortable zone in which educators can more easily connect with the child. Acting as a neutral spot, the project as medium carries things along, suggesting conversation possibilities and pointing the way for future questions and dialogue:

You have been so involved with your challenge today! Such great focus and flow!

Tell me about it. What do you like the most about this work?

Oh, you need me to hold this piece while you build the support? Sure.

By the way, I notice you have been quieter today than usual.

Is your new orthopedic brace somehow causing trouble? How? Perhaps you would be more comfortable if you . . .

Making New Connections

Both parents and grade-level teachers have noted that after spending time with children at their chosen inquiries, and working alongside them, their relationships have grown. Students especially seem to love when the tables turn, and they are able to guide their teachers to learn something new about a tough problem at hand. The time is like a field trip—a discovery excursion for thinking. This shared time can lead to new connections and understandings that linger with a quiet and pleasant satisfaction for both child and educator.

> *I remember my first visit to the lab. I didn't know what I would be able to offer. All those projects! Quickly I realized all I had to do was to sit with a child and ask them to teach me. I asked what the challenges were, how they got through the challenge, or what they liked best. By the end of one session, not only did I know at least eight new projects, I felt I had given something to the children and the lab. The kids love telling their stories and showing me things. Now when I see the children, I feel connected to them in a new way.*
>
> —Parent

For those who are just starting to work with students in the lab, it helps to know that making a positive and powerful contribution is simple—just work alongside the students and listen. Show interest, follow along, and learn from the children's innate ability to ask questions joyfully and to explore. The rest will unfold quite naturally.

REFERENCES

Carroll, Lewis. *The Annotated Alice: Alice's Adventures in Wonderland & Through the Looking-Glass by Lewis Carroll, 1832–1898.* New York: Modern Library, Random House.

Checkley, K. (1997). The first seven . . . and the eight: A Conversation with Howard Gardner. *Educational Leadership* 55 (1), 8–13.

Costa, A. (2001). Teacher Behaviors That Enable Student Thinking. In A. Costa (Ed.), *Developing Minds: A Resource Book for Teaching Thinking* (rev. ed., Vol. 1). Alexandria, VA: Association for Supervision and Curriculum Development.

Costa, A., & Kalick, B. (Eds.). (2000). *Discovering and Exploring Habits of Mind.* Alexandria, VA: Association for Supervision and Curriculum Development.

Csikszentmihalyi, M. (1990). *Flow: The Psychology of Optimal Experience.* New York: Harper Perennial.

Csikszentmihalyi, M. (1996). *Creativity: Flow and the Psychology of Discovery and Invention.* New York: HarperCollins.

Csikszentmihalyi, M., & Whalen, S. P. (1991, May). *Putting Flow Theory into Educational Practice: The Key School's Flow Activities Room.* Report to the Benton Center for Curriculum and Instruction, University of Chicago.

Fogarty, R., Perkins, D., & Barell, J. (1992). *How to Teach for Transfer.* Palatine, IL: Skylight.

Gardner, H. (1983). *Frames of Mind: The Theory of Multiple Intelligences.* New York: Basic Books.

Gardner, H. (1993). *Multiple Intelligences: The Theory in Practice.* New York: Basic Books.

Georgia Department of Education. *Basic Process Skills K–12.* Retrieved May 16, 2008, from http://www.glc.k12.ga.us/pandp/science/in-basic.htm.

Harvard Project Zero, Cognitive Skills Group. (1999). *Ten Tools for Teaching for Transfer.* Retrieved June 2007 from http://learnweb.harvard.edu/ALPS/thinking/docs/10tips.htm.

Hoerr, T. R. (1996). Why the Personals? In S. Boggeman, T. R. Hoerr, & C. Wallach (Eds.), *Succeeding with Multiple Intelligences: Teaching Through the Personal Intelligences.* St. Louis: New City School.

Perkins, D. (1992). *Smart Schools: From Training Memories to Educating Minds.* New York: Free Press.

Perkins, D. (1995). *Outsmarting IQ: The Emerging Science of Learnable Intelligence.* New York: Free Press.

Perkins, D. (2003). *King Arthur's Round Table, How Collaborative Conversations Create Smart Organizations.* Hoboken, NJ: Wiley.

Perkins, D., & Salomon, G. (2001). Teaching for Transfer. In A. Costa (Ed.), *Developing Minds: A Resource Book for Teaching Thinking* (rev. ed., Vol. 1). Alexandria, VA: Association for Supervision and Curriculum Development.

Sikes, S. 1995. *Feeding the Zircon Gorilla and Other Team Building Activities.* Tulsa, OK: Learning Unlimited.

Tishman, S. (2000). Why Teach Habits of Mind? In A. Costa & B. Kalick (Eds.), *Discovering and Exploring Habits of Mind.* Alexandria, VA: Association for Supervision and Curriculum Development.

Tishman, S., & Andrade, A. (n.d.). *Thinking Dispositions: A Review of Current Theories, Practices, and Issues.* Retrieved January 22, 2008, from http://learnweb.harvard.edu/alps/thinking/docs/Dispositions.pdf.

Tishman, S., Jay, E., & Perkins, D. (1992). *Teaching Thinking Dispositions: From Transmission to Enculturation.* Retrieved January 22, 2008, from http://learnweb.harvard.edu/ALPS/thinking/docs/article2.html.

Tishman, S., Jay, E., & Perkins, D. (1995). *The Thinking Classroom. Learning and Teaching in a Culture of Thinking.* Boston: Allyn & Bacon.

What Intelligences are you getting into action as you together design and build your structure? Where else do you find yourself using those intelligences? How? How do other people put these same intelligences into action as they pursue their work?

Chapter Three
Setting Up Inquiry for Mindful Practice

FOCUS THEMES

> *[For] some reason, whenever I climb my tree,*
> *I think about what smarts I'm using. Is it Visual?*
> —Lab student

As inquiry learning goes, thinking about thinking is an exploration in and of itself. Useful to such exploration are Focus Themes, which are instructional tools that spotlight the program's learning objectives. A Focus Theme frames a thinking-centered concept for children, so that they can set the idea into clear practice, at lab and other times—perhaps even as they climb a tree.

A Focus Theme conversation is a teacher-led discussion designed to establish an open yet clear-thinking agenda before students head off to work with their inquiry projects. In the initial discussion circle, the goal is to establish a common reference point for teachers, parents, and children to share while they work together with the projects, and later to employ in other learning arenas. The following chapter, "Focus Theme Sampler," presents thirty-three sample Focus Themes. Each highlights another program goal, such as the habits of mind, critical and creative thinking, Multiple Intelligences, or the concept of flow. The Opening Circle conversation generally begins by stating the focus of the session and then engages children's contributions through a series of unfolding questions.

Today our Focus Theme is all about the habit of mind to Listen Actively.

First off, what does it mean to be active?

What do you listen to (music, nature, what people say . . .)?

In what ways could you listen actively in these different arenas (restating ideas presented by another, asking for clarification, focus, replay a piece of music, etc.)?

How does listening actively help your thinking and doing?

How does it feel when someone is really listening to what you have to say?

How is it sometimes difficult to be a great listener?

What helps one to overcome the things that can get in the way of listening actively?

Focus Themes add structure to lab-time teaching. The initial circle dialogue especially helps visiting parents or faculty by providing ideas for the conversations they will have with students during lab time. With no previous review or preparation needed on their part, these various educators are ready to coach and work with the children. As a Focus Theme conversation wraps up and children set off to their inquiries, questioning possibilities have been well prompted and follow naturally.

I see you both have settled into working with a great inquiry project.

How have you been Listening Actively to each other today while working?

Where do you think Natalie is heading with her idea?

Could you try restating her idea? Let's see if you two are on the same page!

After the inquiry lab period, the Focus Theme is again visited at the group Reflection Circle. During this wrap-up, children share their experience of putting that day's theme into action.

> *After the third try to solve the marble challenge, we felt like giving up. Everyone had so many ideas, but no one was listening. But then, all of a sudden, we started brainstorming together, and really listened to each other. Pop! New ideas! And it worked!*
>
> —Lab student

Finally, as seen in the chapter that follows, "Focus Theme Sampler," the class is given a writing prompt that can be used for a journal entry or short essay, such as: *Describe your lab project for today. How were you an active listener? How did it help the project as a whole to listen actively? Where else will being an active listener help you* (in school, at home, with sports or music, or when out on a nature walk)*? How?*

Children Hearing Children

Students are the primary contributors to any Focus Theme discussion. Indeed, in between the lines of the next chapter's Focus Theme question possibilities, one can imagine the voices of children saying fantastic things. Once engaged in conversation, many will have a lot to say when given such prompts as, *What do you think people really mean when they say they are bored?* or *How does the habit of mind of Communicating Clearly make a difference for a group effort?* Educators lead the conversation along by affirming, illustrating various points, and guiding students to uncover and contribute their ideas. Yet children hearing other children is what sets the pace for exploring and taking chances with the thinking concept at hand and is critical to get in place while directing a Focus Theme conversation. The goal is that the children personalize and take ownership of the thinking-centered objective and be ready to use it.

Adults Sharing Thinking Goals

The open-inquiry format lends itself beautifully to students, parents, and teachers reflecting on and developing thinking skills and dispositions *together*. Therefore, another element to engage while leading an opening conversation is to display how the theme at hand is also of vital interest to adults. Visiting parents, teachers, and administrators are called on to contribute to the Focus Theme conversation. The principal might be asked, *Mrs. Shanon, what are some examples of you developing your own habit of mind to Listen Actively?* A unique cross-generational learning experience unfolds with children and adults sharing similar ups and downs, developing new ideas, and inspiring one another. Children get the message: we are here talking about lifelong thinking skills and dispositions.

Making Content Connections and Establishing Transfer

An essential objective of the Focus Theme conversation is to set up the given concept for transfer and make links with other life and learning experiences (see Chapter Two, "Project as Medium, Teacher as Coach"). The grade-level classroom teacher is in an ideal position to make these connections while leading an inquiry lab session in his or her own classroom because the related curriculum is right there. As in the case of a centralized lab, hospital, community center, or museum, the lead instructor collaborates with colleagues and parents to gain input for uncovering potential connections to the theme of the day. Examples might be a group of students who are studying metamorphosis in their grade-level classroom, children who have just reviewed new orthopedic equipment in their rehabilitation clinic, or a group that has just begun a new project in the art room, perhaps one on animation. If the theme of the day is *Looking Carefully to See Things Clearly,* one way to link their study and experiences to the lab conversation might be:

I hear you are studying the life cycle of the butterfly in your classroom.

How do you employ the skill of direct observation with that study?

What are some examples of things you have learned about metamorphosis by looking carefully and critically?

Or

I have seen the new equipment that has just arrived in the clinic! How are you finding it important to employ the skill of direct observation as you learn to work with these new pieces? How are you engaging the habit of mind of Looking Carefully to See Things Clearly?

And

Certainly, the art of creating an animation requires critical observation skills. By the way, what does the word "sequence" mean? Why is it important to look carefully and see the sequence of a developing animation clearly?

Likewise, those at the helm of designing and leading effective Focus Theme discussions seek purposeful ways to connect and transfer the inquiry thinking agenda to support the school or organization. For instance, a simple way to build a helpful link is simply to ask (speaking together or through a questionnaire) a teacher, parent, or hospital therapist: *What is on the children's plate right now that they seem to find challenging? Which habits of mind do you see as needing to be strengthened?* A grade-level teacher might respond, *The students are having a tough time with working and Thinking Independently. I need to help them with every step along the way! And also, interestingly, I don't know what happened, but my class that worked so well earlier this year as a team is sorely lacking cooperative skills this spring. They could use a focus on the habits of mind of Thinking Independently, Understanding Others, Listening Actively, and Contributing Positively to the Group and Inspiring Team Work!*

As another example, a conversation with the school's math specialist might reveal that students in all grade levels are not taking the time to be accurate with their computations, which would prompt a Focus Theme conversation about Striving to Be Careful and Precise.

In the case of a centralized lab, the participation of visiting grade-level teachers, staff, and parents during a Circle Conversation establishes direct links to experiences students are having in their grade-level classrooms, other special area classrooms, physical therapy, or home. A grade-level teacher might contribute by saying, *Class, this conversation relates to our discussion this morning about Benjamin Franklin. How do you think he employed the habit of mind to be Adventurous and Broad Minded?* The physical therapist might ask, *Did you see yourselves employing the habit of mind to Step Back and Look at the Whole Picture as we took on that new piece of exercising equipment in our therapy center? How?* Parents representing the homefront offer examples that illustrate how a family might develop skills and habits. *Our family is working together to build the habit of mind to Listen Actively. Just yesterday my youngest even said, can you say your idea once more?*

Illustrating the Focus Theme for the day from various perspectives also helps students better transfer and decompartmentalize the particular thinking-centered concept at hand. It aids the program in moving its pedagogy out to other learning environments. For example, if an educator or parent offers a comment during the Focus Theme conversation, he or she is more likely to later spotlight that theme when in a different environment. *Where have you seen evidence of other historic personalities of the American Revolution engaging the habit of mind to be Adventurous and Broad Minded?*

Keeping Themes About Thinking

However, as connections are made to children's other life and learning experiences, a Focus Theme conversation helps keep the exploration "on task" with its objective. A discussion can easily drift toward elaborating on, or even teaching, a highlighted component of a theme's conversation. As that may happen, the thinking skill or disposition focused on for that day can get lost in the sauce, with students missing the point of the theme's lesson. For example, as a Focus Theme conversation explores the habit of mind to *Set Goals and Make Plans,* it might highlight the use of mind maps and outlines. The caution is not to turn the conversation into an involved lesson on how to go about making these tools. (Making mind maps is an essential teacher-led lesson for another time.) For students to be ready to employ the Focus Theme idea at lab time and then transfer it to other learning environments, the Focus Theme discussions need to stay on task.

Keeping the theme clear and general again helps teachers, school specialists, and parents to better prompt students to employ the Focus Theme concepts when outside the lab in other learning or life situations. Adults will ask the children at home and in the grade-level classroom and throughout the community:

Do you remember when we talked about the skill of brainstorming at inquiry lab time?

I remember you brainstormed many ideas then for creating a wind-generated machine. What did it feel like to come up with so many ideas? How did it help your project?

How might brainstorming ideas now help with the story you are working on?

Ultimately, the goal is for the student to see the need for a particular habit of mind or skill, and then put it into action themselves:

Oh boy, I need more ideas. I need to brainstorm some more before writing my story.

In a Nutshell, What Makes a Great Focus Theme Conversation?

As mentioned earlier, a successful Focus Theme conversation has certain elements or characteristics. For starters, the discussion:

- has a clear purpose
- presents the thinking-centered objective for the session
- sets up a group-inquiry discussion with the concept at hand
- is teacher orchestrated, yet establishes students as the primary contributors and speakers
- lends itself to the teacher to affirm, restate, and acknowledge contributions from the group
- presents the lifelong aspect of the thinking skill or habit of mind
- invites visiting adults to share their insights to the theme at hand
- displays how the theme relates to real-world vocations and professions
- connects the objective to unfolding curriculum contents, skills, or other life experiences
- stays focused on the thinking-centered idea
- sets up the highlighted objective to be practiced during lab time
- sets up the idea to be visited again after students work with their inquiries at the Reflection Circle
- sets up the thinking objective for transfer to other learning environments
- presents writing prompts, thus engaging lab time as a prewriting experience
- is age dimensional—the same Focus Theme discussion can (with adaptation) be engaged for all age levels

A Focus Theme Lineup

A list displaying the Focus Themes selected for the year, with its unfolding timetable, is an effective program reference for students, families, specialists, visiting educators, and administration. Everyone gets a clear picture of the program's goals. If someone happens to step in at the middle of a lab time, the listing allows them to immediately become part of the scene. As they wander in and sit by a group of children working at the invention station, they might ask, *Do I have it right, is today's Focus Theme "Rubber-Band Thinking"? What is that?!*

With the goal to establish a culture of thinking for the entire community, the Focus Theme listing is distributed for display at home, in each classroom, and in the lobby of the school or children's hospital, and posted in newsletters, presented at Back-to-School Night, or even on the school's daily news report. As opportunities arise, specialists, staff, parents, and grade-level teachers then link the concepts to their individual learning arenas by asking children questions related to the current Focus Themes: *I see the Focus Theme right now is Strive to Be Accurate and Precise. How are we practicing that habit of mind as we play these notes on the recorder?* Or *What intelligences are engaged by our class investigation of simple machines?* A parent at home might ask his or her child, *How are you using your habit of mind to Persevere as you work on this tough project for social studies? I see the Focus Theme this month is Set Goals and Make Plans. What steps can you plan for meeting your goals with your book report?*

In the case of a centralized lab or inquiry cart program, the director might select the year's Focus Theme lineup or could collaborate with the Gifted and Talented itinerant; another alternative is that the entire school faculty and staff establish the lineup. In the latter case, a potential list of options, based on the inquiry program's thinking-centered learning objectives, is presented at a staff meeting and voted on. One might hear the faculty say, *Oh boy, I need my students to explore that one!* Or, *I don't see it here on your listing. Could we develop a new theme to help students understand the nature of frustration and how to manage it?*

Variations on Delivering the Theme

The Focus Theme sampler in Chapter Four is meant as a guide, and can be employed in a variety of ways. Some educators will be interested in moving through the entire "script" of a presented theme, while others may select just three questions to highlight in their conversations with the children. In addition, the dialog of a theme might perhaps span over two or more sessions.

Some educators will be interested in shortening the Opening Circle discussion to allow children more inquiry lab time with their projects. For those situations, a shorter opening announcement is given to identify the theme's thinking concept or skill. Then, while students are working on their projects, dialogue and question ideas relating to the Focus Theme are elaborated on and presented. The Reflection Circle, as usual, follows the inquiry period.

The theme today is Using What You Know. Transfer Learning!

What does it mean to transfer something?

Right! Pick it up and move it over to some other place.

While you are working today with your inquiries, think about how you are using something you have already learned or understand or a skill you have already gained. Together we will think about how you are transferring your learning.

Another more open variation on developing the focus for each lab session is to help guide students to establish their own theme for the day. With this direction, the themes evolve based on what the children are learning about while finding and meeting challenges with the lab inquiries. The listing essentially grows out of the Reflection Circle and sets the agenda for the next inquiry lab session. A listing of Focus Themes becomes established throughout the year, with the lead instructor mindfully aiding along its development. Visiting teachers or parents are asked to review the list with the group and make suggestions. *Mrs. Stern, this looks like a rather complete list that the students have created up to this point. Do you see any essential thinking skills or habits of mind missing?*

This direction for establishing a list of Focus Themes works especially well for grade-level classroom investigations, but it also works in interesting ways for a centralized lab. Each individual visiting class can establish its own "What Makes Our Thinking Great!" poster, which is displayed for other classes to watch as it develops (thus helping all to grow). An entire wall of highlighted thinking skills and dispositions inspires everyone to take a closer look. *Mr. Hinton's class has Thinking Independently on its list. We ought to think about that one for ours.* Lists are also duplicated and given to each classroom for reference. Bookmarks are made, and lists are put on the refrigerators at home. As the inquiry sessions unfold throughout the year, so do the students' lists of "lab-grown" choices of thinking dispositions and skills. For some, this individualized process for determining a Focus Theme listing will work great; for others, moving right into a predetermined listing for everyone might be of greater benefit.

Still other educators might prefer to keep lab time even less structured and not engage any initial Focus Theme conversations with the children. In this case, the lead instructor simply employs various Focus Theme ideas and questions while moving about the room and working with the students. The reflection circle then reviews the action of that day's inquiries, highlights the various thinking skills and dispositions that have unfolded, guides transfer possibilities, and prepares children to write about their inquiry experiences.

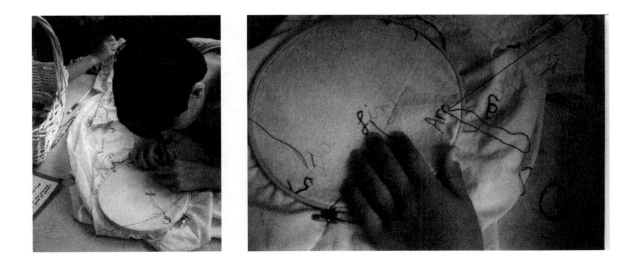

Open for Practice

Teacher: *Which habits of mind do you think you need to work on?*

First-grade lab students: *Sticking to it, don't give up.*

Being flexible. Because once when I was drawing a picture I messed up and I just crossed it out and got a new piece of paper instead of making it into something.

Discovery. I just think it's a great habit.

Regardless of how the Focus Themes are developed and presented, they are meant to guide children to put productive thinking skills and dispositions into concrete practice. As noted earlier, all ages are able to talk about and contribute ideas to a Focus Theme conversation. However, the reality is that developing the learning objectives requires children's active time with tangible work and interacting with the teacher as coach. Students also need to understand that as they work to establish thinking skills and habits of mind, their efforts will not be perfect. Their development will take practice, patience, and ongoing focus.

How are you employing the habit of mind to Strive to Be Accurate
and Precise as you work with Point Value Pick-Up Sticks?
Where else does it help to employ that thinking disposition? How?

Chapter Four

Focus Theme Sampler

This chapter lists thirty-three Focus Theme possibilities with conversation and questioning possibilities for Opening Circle, lab time, and Reflection Circle. Each theme also presents follow-up journal or short essay-writing ideas. Themes are written for mid to higher grade levels, with the understanding they can be customized for younger students as needed. Names of students are added to animate the text and are fictitious.

As a general rule of thumb for lab time and a follow-up writing session, allow twenty minutes for the Opening and Reflection Circles combined, thirty to forty-five minutes for the actual inquiry lab period, and another fifteen to twenty minutes for reflective writing.

1. THE ADVENTURE OF A NEW PROJECT

Objective

Students see that inquiry lab time is full of projects with unfolding possibilities and challenges. Children explore how curiosity builds inquiry and strengthens thinking. The group examines the nature and characteristics of challenges.

Opening Circle Time

A project is an adventure! A challenge can be an adventure.

Let's look at some of these inquiry projects. (Teacher displays and explains a few projects.)

Does anything about any of these projects make you curious?

What are some possibilities? What would you want to do if you worked with this project?

Does anyone have any suggestions for building on these ideas?

What is a challenge?

What are some challenge possibilities you can imagine with this project? (Teacher displays another project.)

Where might your curiosity and interest lead you with these projects? How could the challenges build? (Teacher shows a few more project ideas.)

Why do people love to find a great new project for themselves? Why do they often enjoy a great challenge?

How is a project like an adventure? How can a new challenge be an adventure?

What is your challenge going to be today? Where would you like to work? (Teacher displays a few more projects as needed, and students choose their inquiry for the period.)

Conversation and Question Possibilities for Lab Time

What are you most curious about? What brought you to this project?

How are you building on that interest? What are the different parts of your challenge?

When have you worked with a project like this before?

Reflection Circle Prompts

What was your challenge today? Did your curiosity and interest grow? How?

How did your challenge develop? What were the different parts to your challenge?

How do you think a project is like an adventure?

Writing Prompt

Describe the project you worked on today. What was your challenge? Did your curiosity and interest grow? How? How did the challenge grow?

From *Nine Thousand Straws: Teaching Thinking Through Open-Inquiry Learning* by Jean Sausele Knodt. Westport, CT: Teacher Ideas Press. Copyright © 2008.

2. ASK ABOUT AND EXPLORE. INQUIRE!

Objective

Students understand and explore the word *inquire*. Students discuss how curiosity and zest for problem finding and solving develops strong and industrious thinking.

Opening Circle Time

I have no special talents, I am only passionately curious.
—Albert Einstein

Curious people are big thinkers. What does it mean to be curious? What does it mean to be passionate? What are some things you are "passionately curious" about?

Someone might say, "Today I would like to inquire about the rain forest."

A teacher might say, "Today we are going to inquire about simple machines."

Let's take a look at a few projects here in the lab today. (Teacher displays some projects.)

With this project, someone might inquire about (give examples such as rocks and minerals, simple machines, color, building and construction, and so on).

So, what do you think the word "inquire" means? (Possible answers: ask about, explore, discover, investigate, think about, research.) *That's getting there! Some people call a lab time like you are in now an inquiry lab, inquiry time, or inquiry learning.*

Let's see what Merriam-Webster's Collegiate Dictionary *has to say: It defines* inquire *as "To ask about. To search into: investigate."*

How does an interest to inquire build strong thinking, doing, and learning (examples: uncover new information, gain experience, gain new understandings)*?*

What would you like to inquire about in the lab today? Where would you like to ask about and explore?

Conversation and Question Possibilities for Lab Time

What are you inquiring about today? Are you "passionately curious" about anything here? Can your curiosity develop? How?

Are there different parts to your inquiry? What are they?

Does everyone in your group with this center want to inquire about the same thing?

Can you think of new challenges for this project? What else could you inquire about?

What research could this inquiry lead to? What sort of books or resources might be of interest?

What other projects or challenges in the lab are similar to this inquiry center?

From *Nine Thousand Straws: Teaching Thinking Through Open-Inquiry Learning* by Jean Sausele Knodt
Westport, CT: Teacher Ideas Press. Copyright © 2008.

Reflection Circle Prompts

Describe your inquiry today. What steps did your inquiry take? What challenges were part of the inquiry? What advice would you give someone working on this inquiry project?

What would you want to inquire more about with the project you explored today?

How and where did your curiosity build?

Writing Prompt

Describe something in class or at home that you have been curious about. How did that interest lead to an inquiry? What were the challenges? How can you develop your inquiry further?

(or) Describe your lab inquiry today. What did you learn as you investigated and explored? What were the challenges? How do you think your inquiry made your thinking stronger? What else would you like to explore with this project?

From *Nine Thousand Straws: Teaching Thinking Through Open-Inquiry Learning* by Jean Sausele Knodt.
Westport, CT: Teacher Ideas Press. Copyright © 2008.

3. WHAT HABITS OF MIND DO YOU HAVE WORKING FOR YOU?

Objective

Students establish a working relationship with thinking dispositions or habits of mind. Children see that habits of mind can be employed in all learning and life arenas and are lifetime thinking tools. The group understands that habits of mind take practice and patience to develop. Students see that we adults (parents, teachers, principals, and others) also work to develop habits of mind.

Opening Circle Time

What are some good habits you have (brushing teeth, exercising, eating a salad, etc.)*? What do these good habits do for you?*

Do you have any "bad" habits? What might they be?

How do you develop these habits, good or bad (practice, someone guides you, etc.)*?*

Getting into some good habits can make your thinking more powerful and strong. What do you think a positive habit of mind might be (or use "thinking disposition")*?*

Habits of mind are productive habits—ways of being, thinking, and doing—that make your thinking overall stronger. You already have named a good number of positive habits of mind. Let's look at this list . . . (or) *Could you consider . . .* (or) *I might add a few more . . . .*

Do your parents and teachers use these same habits of mind? How?

I'm working myself on the habit of mind to be . . . (lead instructor gives own examples). *Mrs. Anderson, which one(s) are you working to develop* (lead instructor asks visiting parent or teacher to give examples)*?*

Who would like to get some habits of mind in action? What will be your inquiry today?

Conversation and Question Possibilities for Lab Time

Which of the habits of mind do you think you have in action right now? Let's look at our list. Which habits do you think could help you out now as you work on this project?

Reflection Circle Prompt

Let's look at our habits of mind poster again. Who sees a habit of mind that he or she had in action? How? How did it make a difference for your thinking and doing? Where else could that habit of mind be used?

Writing Prompt

What habits of mind do you have going for you on a regular basis? Which ones do you think you often use? How do they make a difference in your thinking and work? What habits of mind do you feel you would like to develop? How will they help you with your challenges and class lessons?

(or) *Describe your lab inquiry today. What habits of mind did you use? How?*

Materials and Other References

Habits of Mind Student Reference Sheet, which also could be made into classroom poster (see Appendix V).

Quick Link: Lab Time Conversations to Build Habits of Mind (see Appendix D).

Quick Link: Focus Theme Conversations to Build Habits of Mind (see Appendix C).

4. DEVELOPING HABITS OF MIND TAKES PATIENCE AND PRACTICE

Opening Circle Time

Developing a new skill or positive habit of mind takes practice and patience.

What are some examples of skills you have? Things you can do (examples: swim, play piano, read, write, play soccer)?

Did it happen right away? Poof! And you had these new skills like magic?

How did you develop these skills?

Ah, you perfect a skill or habit by doing it! By practicing it! By seeing others practice or do the skill. By asking questions!

Habits of mind, just like skills, develop over time. Just like the skills you mentioned, they take practice and patience to develop. Some habits will take us more time to develop, and some come more easily.

Think about where you would like to work today at lab time. Think about the inquiry's challenges and what you might experience as you work with the project.

Now let's look at our habit of mind poster. Which habits of mind would help your thinking and doing with that project and its challenges? Perhaps being Accurate and Precise? Looking Carefully? Understanding Others?

When you say where you would like to work today, tell us also which habit(s) of mind you will focus on and practice. Tell us how that habit(s) of mind will likely help your work today with the inquiry.

Conversation and Question Possibilities for Lab Time

What habit(s) of mind are you practicing today? How?

Where else in your life can you build and practice these habits of mind?

Reflection Circle Prompts

What habits of mind did you practice and develop today?

How did developing those habits of mind make your work go better?

Where else can you develop those same habits of mind?

Writing Prompt

Describe your lab inquiry today. Which habits of mind did you develop and work on? How did they make your work with the project stronger and help it go better?

Materials and Other References

Habits of Mind Student Reference Sheet, which could also be made into classroom poster (see Appendix V).

Quick Link: Lab Time Conversations to Build Habits of Mind (see Appendix D).

Quick Link: Focus Theme Conversations to Build Habits of Mind (see Appendix C).

---

5. TEAM THINKING AND DOING

Objective

Children explore how working in the lab is often shared with others. Students see that a large part of their success with a project depends on how well they understand others and develop team working skills. This Focus Theme highlights the following habits of mind: Understand Others, Contribute Positively to the Group and Inspire Team Work, and Listen Actively. The theme also lays the groundwork to develop Focus Theme 29, "What Skills Does It Take to Be Part of a Team?"

Opening Circle Time

Working with others is often part of the thinking and doing scene. How many people do you usually see working on one challenge during inquiry lab time? I also see usually two to three people at one inquiry center.

How can working well together make the project more successful?

In what ways can it sometimes be hard to work with others? What becomes difficult? How can things go wrong?

How many of you think that adults—teachers, parents—have the same team-related challenges you mentioned? You bet they do!

What habits of mind make a difference for successful teamwork?

What are ways that you use the habits of mind to Understand Others? Listen Actively? Communicate Clearly?

What are some specific skills you use to develop these habits of mind?

Working on these ideas to be a good team member and understand others is a lifelong quest. It is something we all work on.

Where are the inquiries today? Where will you practice team thinking and doing?

Conversation and Question Possibilities for Lab Time

How is the team effort going with your project?

What team skills are going great? What skill is your team struggling with? How can you solve that problem? How can you work together more effectively?

Have you taken time to brainstorm together?

Have all team members had the chance to present their ideas clearly?

Are you all open to each other's ideas and interests?

Are you using the habit of mind to Listen Actively as you work?

Is everyone committed to solving the problem? How can you become committed? How can you help others become committed?

How can you share the leadership and tasks needed?

Does the team have a plan? Have you all agreed on a strategy?

Does everyone have a part to do? Is everyone contributing?

Reflection Circle Prompts

How did your group's ideas work together today to make your inquiry project experience successful?

What team skills did you see in action?

Let's list those specific team skills you came up with. (Teacher Note: Hold on to list for future work together, or incorporate it into developing Focus Theme 29, "What Skills Does It Take to Be Part of a Team?")

Writing Prompt

Describe your last inquiry group challenge. How did your group work together well? What wasn't working? How did you try to fix the problem? How did your ideas work together to make the inquiry, or part of the inquiry, work successfully?

6. BRAINSTORMING UNLIMITED!

Objective

Students explore how the skill of brainstorming strengthens thinking through a challenge, quest, or project. Brainstorming is a skill that supports the habit of mind to Be Adventurous and Open-Minded.

Opening Circle Time

Imagination is more important than knowledge. —Albert Einstein

Do you agree or disagree with Einstein? Why?

What does it mean to be imaginative?

What does the word "creative" mean?

A big part of being creative involves brainstorming. Certainly, meeting a challenge takes brainstorming. What does it mean to brainstorm? How does brainstorming help you to be imaginative? Has your brainstorming time ever felt limited or weak? Brainstorming takes time and practice to get the creative juices going and use our imaginations.

Brainstorming can be like popping popcorn. Have you ever heard popcorn cooking? You hear one pop, then a couple more. Then, pop, pop, pop! And it starts getting faster, pop, pop, pop, pop, pop! Brainstorming can be like that. You get started, and then the ideas start coming faster. You could call it popcorn brainstorming!

What are some possibilities with this new inquiry project? (Teacher displays an inquiry project.) *Great brainstorming!*

Let's get some brainstorming popping with other inquiry projects in the lab as well. . . .

Where do you want to work? Where are the inquiries today?

Where will we see popcorn brainstorming in action?

Conversation and Question Possibilities for Lab Time

I see you managed to meet this challenge by . . . (Teacher observes the way child worked ideas through.) *What could be another way to work and think things through?*

OK, I see you're stuck here with your project. Let's brainstorm some ideas together.

Have you gotten to a popcorn level with your brainstorming yet?

How can you help yourself to get ideas going when you feel stuck (work with a partner, look for ideas in various places, approach the situation from another viewpoint)*?*

When are other times you need to generate a lot of ideas?

From *Nine Thousand Straws: Teaching Thinking Through Open-Inquiry Learning* by Jean Sausele Knodt.
Westport, CT: Teacher Ideas Press. Copyright © 2008.

Reflection Circle Prompts

How did the brainstorming go with the projects today? Let's hear some examples.

When did your ideas really get popping? Did you feel yourself shift into gear?

Where else does it make a difference to brainstorm?

How does using your imagination make thinking through any project or lesson stronger?

How do you feel when you are brainstorming?

With which lessons or projects you are working on in class could brainstorming help?

Writing Prompt

Think about time you actively brainstormed. How did brainstorming make a difference for what you were doing? How could you employ brainstorming with . . . (grade-level teacher selects an upcoming classroom project, journal writing, or other curriculum content like science or math).

(or) *Describe your lab inquiry today. How did your brainstorming go? What different ideas did people in your group have? How did the ideas make a difference in working with the project? How does brainstorming make your thinking and work stronger?*

7. PUT A PICTURE IN YOUR MIND—VISUALIZE

Objective

Students cultivate the ability to visualize possibilities and outcomes with their projects. Students discuss how thinking about what could happen and what could be strengthens their thinking. Students put "pictures in their minds."

Opening Circle Time

Put a picture in your mind of what you could do with this inquiry project. (Teacher displays a project.) *What do you think the phrase "putting a picture in my mind" might mean* (to see possibilities, what could happen, see outcomes . . .)*? So what do you see is possible with this inquiry? How do you think putting a picture in you mind could help you to think through challenges and do activities?*

When you put a picture in your mind, you are visualizing and imagining possibilities with a project. How can visualizing help your work? What sort of information do you gain? Right! Visualizing can help you think about and see new possibilities and also see when different actions should happen. It also can alert you to where you might need to be more cautious and careful with your thinking and doing.

For what kinds of projects or situations can you visualize, imagine possibilities, and put pictures in your mind (a book report, a science experiment, painting a picture, the route to a soccer net with ball, parts in the process of creating a perfect birthday party, a social studies group project, a dance or musical production . . .)*? Does it take some time to generate a picture in your mind? To see possibilities? Does it take a quiet moment? Do you need to "stop" the action for awhile? Do you only visualize or put a picture in your mind at the beginning of a project? Why?*

Where are the inquiries today? Before you start working (once you are settled at your lab projects), take three to five minutes to visualize possibilities and put a picture in your mind. If you are in a group, discuss together your ideas after quiet thinking time.

Conversation and Question Possibilities for Lab Time

Take a moment. Do you have a picture in your mind of what the possibilities are with this project? What could happen here? What possibilities and outcomes do you visualize?

What questions come up as you imagine possibilities and outcomes?

What will be the likely outcome if you try a different approach?

How are you using the information you gain as you visualize?

Reflection Circle Prompts

Who had a picture in their mind today? Let's hear about it!

How does imagining what could happen help you with your work?

How does visualizing outcomes and possibilities make your thinking stronger?

Writing Prompt

Describe the picture you had in your mind before you started working on your project today. What were the possibilities? What were areas of concern? If you worked with a group, describe how you explored possibilities together. How did things work out? How did visualizing help?

---

8. SETTING GOALS AND PUTTING STRATEGY TO WORK

Objective

Students explore what it means to make plans and be strategic. This Focus Theme highlights the habit of mind to Set Goals and Make Plans.

Opening Circle Time

What is a goal?

What could be some goals for this inquiry project? Let's visualize some possibilities. (Teacher displays a project.) OK, what might be some plans to meet these goals?

Why is it helpful or even essential to identify a goal before you make a lot of plans?

What does the word "strategy" mean? When do you use strategy (soccer game, chess, math problem, planning a trip, building a Kapla bridge . . .)?

How does putting strategy to work help our thinking and doing as we work to meet challenges and reach goals?

How can taking time to make plans and consider strategic ideas actually save you time?

What are some tell-tale signs that strategy or planning is needed?

Can your plans change? Can a new strategy be added while you work?

How do you plan strategy as a team?

How can it be difficult to plan a strategy together? How is it helpful or essential to plan together?

Let's set goals and put strategy to work with the lab projects! What inquiries do you have in mind?

Conversation and Question Possibilities for Lab Time

What is your goal(s)? What are your plans and strategy to meet your goal(s)?

Reflection Circle Prompts

What were some ways in which strategy was in action today with your inquiries?

How does building the habit of mind to Set Goals and Make Plans make your thinking stronger?

Writing Prompt

Describe your lab inquiry today. What was your goal? Was there a team goal? What was it? What was the plan to meet your goal? What strategy did you employ? How did making plans help your project?

---

9. THINKING INDEPENDENTLY

Objective

Children consider how they think and work independently. This Focus Theme explores building confidence to think individually and self-structure one's own efforts. It highlights the habit of mind to Think Independently.

Opening Circle Time

What does the word "independent" mean? What does it mean to think independently?

What are some examples of you thinking independently—times when you have taken chances, thought of a different way, tried a new approach, for example?

How does thinking independently make your work and your thinking stronger?

What does it feel like to come up with ideas and try them out, or to manage your own work effort well? Right! Great! Why does it feel great?

Does thinking independently mean you are working or doing things alone?

How does each of us thinking independently help a group or team (offering different ideas, build diversity, etc.)*?*

Do you agree or disagree with this statement: Thinking independently sometimes takes courage. Ah, everyone's hand is up. So the question is, then, why is it hard sometimes to think and do things independently? What are some of the thoughts or things that may get in our way?

How many of us, at some time in our lives, have felt unsure about offering an idea we have or answering a question? Yes, this is a human trait!

Who has ever felt unsure about asking a question? Sure, asking a question can be taking a chance as much as answering one!

What are we concerned about (group acceptance, others might laugh . . .)*?*

Presenting independent ideas and asking questions can feel like—or actually are—taking risks. Why is it often worth taking the chance? What helps you to take a chance (taking a deep breath, accepting that it's difficult, it's OK to make a mistake . . .)?

Do independent thinkers ask for help? Of course!

How is the asking of questions a sign of independent thinking?

So where are the inquiries today? Where will we practice some independent thinking?

From *Nine Thousand Straws: Teaching Thinking Through Open-Inquiry Learning* by Jean Sausele Knodt.
Westport, CT: Teacher Ideas Press. Copyright © 2008.

Conversation and Question Possibilities for Lab Time

Who has a new idea to try or suggest? Take a chance and offer your thoughts! Trust your brainstorming abilities!

What "stepping out" ideas do you have? It doesn't matter if it seems silly or weak at first; you/we can help your idea grow. Trust yourself . . .

Reflection Circle Prompts

Did anyone feel that they stepped out with an independent idea today? What was the idea?

Did you contribute to the team with your ideas? How did you see your idea used?

Is it OK when our ideas are sometimes not used or even not accepted by the group? How? Elaborate.

Writing Prompt

Describe your inquiry project for today. What ideas did you think of? Which ideas did you share with the group? Did you see your ideas at work? How did your ideas grow?

10. USING WHAT WE KNOW. TRANSFER IT!

Objective

Children consider ways to employ the skills and understanding they have already acquired to help out in the development of a new challenge. Students learn the term "Transfer of Learning." This Focus Theme highlights the habit of mind to Use What You Know—Transfer Learning.

Opening Circle Time

When you are able to transfer (teacher uses hand gesture—picking up, arching over, and placing down) *something from one learning arena to another, you really know your stuff!*

Who knows what the word "transfer" means (taking something and placing it in a new place, moving something . . .)?

What could the term "transfer of learning" mean?

Describe someone transferring something he or she understands, or can do, from one thinking situation to another.

When do you find yourself transferring your skills in reading? Math?

Do you transfer your skills when you take a test?

What are some other ideas of transfer in action (examples: buying popcorn at a baseball game, reading an article in the newspaper, reading road signs, contributing to a family conversation about recycling and helping developing a healthful environment, contributing what you know about Americans Indians as you work on the Spirit Stone inquiry center)?

What skills might you transfer as you work on the Tower of Patterns project (geometry, patterns, estimation . . .)?

Transferring something shows a high level of personal understanding. If you can transfer successfully what you have learned, you know that skill or understanding well!

Can you transfer what we talk about here with, say, the habits of mind, to other learning situations? How? Where? Let's take the habit of mind to Listen Actively as an example. Besides working on an inquiry lab project in a group, where else does active listening help your learning, thinking, and doing?

How does transferring, or using what you know, make your thinking and doing stronger?

So what are the inquiries today?

With your inquiry today, think how you are transferring what you know and putting your learning to work!

From *Nine Thousand Straws: Teaching Thinking Through Open-Inquiry Learning* by Jean Sausele Knodt. Westport, CT: Teacher Ideas Press. Copyright © 2008.

Conversation and Question Possibilities for Lab Time

What is your challenge with this project?

Where have you worked on a challenge like this before?

Where have you used some of these ideas, concepts, or understandings before?

What part of this challenge reminds you of work you/we have done with math, science, writing, or another subject?

Tell me what you understand and know about . . . .

Where else could you use these skills and understandings?

Who builds and uses these sorts of skills and understandings in the world, in their job or a special interest they have (name vocations and professions)?

Reflection Circle Prompts

Who found themselves transferring a skill or understanding today? What skills and understandings? How? Look around—where else in the lab might you be able to transfer those same skills?

What new skills or habits of mind did you develop today while working (team skills, fine motor, visual, perception, strategy, various habits of mind, etc.)? Where could those skills transfer to? Where could you use those skills again?

Writing Prompt

Describe your inquiry challenge. Think of all the skills you transferred while you were working at that center. In other words, where did you use some understanding, skill, or knowledge you already have for the new thinking situation? What new skills did you develop at your project today? Where could those new skills be used again—or transfer to—in our classroom or at home?

11. STEPPING BACK AND LOOKING AT THE WHOLE PICTURE

Objective

Students recognize that a challenge is not made of just one but of multiple parts. Students consider how the parts of a challenge relate to each other. The group explores how stepping back to take a look at the whole picture strengthens the thinking and doing with the challenge at hand (a habit of mind).

Opening Circle Time

It's time to step back and look at the whole picture, folks! Let's take a moment to look at this wooden rubber-band car. It is part of our Rubber Band Car Derby project (see Chapter Six). What are the parts of this car?

Let's step back and look at the whole picture with this car. How do the parts of the car relate?

What parts make the car whole?

Which parts do you <u>have to have</u> to make the car roll? What parts are essential?

Imagine you are now taking on the challenge to build your own rubber-band car with the Lego blocks. Let's step back and take a whole picture look at the process—or the steps—you might take to see the challenge through. What will be the parts of the process—<u>have to have</u> steps—of meeting this challenge (brainstorm ideas, gather pieces, make a plan, build the body of the car, work out the axle, attach the rubber band to the axle)*?*

What could be some unexpected parts of meeting this challenge (teamwork issues, ideas not working out, frustration, running out of supplies . . .)*?*

Let's imagine you have a tough math problem in front of you. What could be the parts of that challenge? How might those parts connect? Now imagine working on a class assignment to make a book report along with a new book cover design. What might be the different parts or steps you would take to do this project well?

What if you were trying to work out a personal problem that you and a friend were having—maybe a misunderstanding over something that happened one day. Are there parts of that problem to understand? What are they, and how do they connect? How could you step back to see the whole picture in this example? How would seeing the whole picture help?

Stepping back and looking at the whole picture is one of our target habits of mind. Work with our projects has several parts; different thinking situations have separate parts, too. It is often worth taking some time to step back and look at the whole picture! How come?

In what situations will we use the habit of mind to Step Back and Look at the Whole Picture in our inquiries today?

From *Nine Thousand Straws: Teaching Thinking Through Open-Inquiry Learning* by Jean Sausele Knodt. Westport, CT: Teacher Ideas Press. Copyright © 2008.

Conversation and Question Possibilities for Lab Time

What are the parts to your challenge today?

Let's make a drawing or diagram of all the parts.

Let's step back and take a look at the whole picture. How do the parts link to one another?

How are the parts dependent on each other to get the job done?

Which parts are essential? Are there any parts that surprised you?

Reflection Circle Prompts

How does stepping back and looking at the whole picture help make your thinking and doing stronger? Give some examples from your work today.

How did the different parts of your project connect?

Use the habit of mind to Step Back and Look at the Whole Picture, and review in your mind the work you did today. What were the most essential areas you needed to get right to meet your challenge?

Writing Prompt

Think of a challenge or project you have had here in school or at home. Step Back and Look at the Whole Picture. Make a drawing or diagram of that challenge. Show all its different parts. Now write about your challenge and all its parts. How did the parts work together? Which parts were essential to meet your challenge?

12. STRIVING TO BE ACCURATE AND PRECISE

Objective

Students consider how a project experience or a particular part of a challenge can require precise work and thinking to get things "just right." The group explores ways to cultivate the habit of mind to Strive to Be Accurate and Precise as they think through their inquiries and challenges.

Opening Circle Time

When do you need to be very careful?

What does the word "accurate" mean?

How about the word "precise"?

What does it mean to strive for something?

One of our habits of mind is to Strive to Be Accurate and Precise. Who has a feeling about how developing that habit could strengthen our thinking and doing?

What projects and activities need a high level of careful and precise actions and thinking (kicking the soccer ball into the goal, flip-turns with swimming, solving a math problem, performing a piece of music, spelling, making a chess move)?

Describe different ways you check your work for accuracy to make sure it's right. What skills support the habit of mind to Be Accurate and Precise (proofreading, observing critically, listening, fine motor skills)?

Let's look at a lab project and think together how we would engage the habit of mind to Be Accurate and Precise as we work with the inquiry . . .

Where are the inquiries today? As you work with your projects, take some time to think how you are striving to be accurate and precise.

Conversation and Question Possibilities for Lab Time

What is your challenge with this project?

Part of this project requires precision! There is little room for errors here.

How tough are you when it comes to being precise?!

Why is it important to be tough when precision is needed?

What adult jobs and activities require work to be done carefully and precisely (car mechanic, parent keeping family schedule, editor, balancing a checkbook, Shakespearian actor, pharmacist, engineer, surgeon, dentist, attorney checking detail on a contract, chemist, electrician)?

How does it pay off to take the time to be Accurate and Precise? How does it make your thinking and work stronger?

From *Nine Thousand Straws: Teaching Thinking Through Open-Inquiry Learning* by Jean Sausele Knodt. Westport, CT: Teacher Ideas Press. Copyright © 2008.

Reflection Circle Prompts

Where was there little room for error today with the projects? Give us advice on the challenge you worked on . . . Who can add advice for . . .

In what other situations do you need to be careful, accurate, and precise with your work?

Writing Prompt

Imagine you are giving someone advice about how to get through the inquiry challenge you just worked on. How does the person need to be careful and precise as he or she works through the different parts of the challenge? What parts require being tough and taking extra care?

13. LOOKING CAREFULLY TO SEE THINGS CLEARLY

Objective

The group identifies visual observation as a key lab-time and lifelong skill. Students consider how developing the habit of mind to Look Carefully enhances one's ability to explore, collect essential information, and think through possibilities.

Opening Circle Time

We are all too much inclined to walk through life with our eyes shut. There are things all around us, and right at our very feet, that we have never seen; because we have never really looked.

—Alexander Graham Bell

What does it mean to "really look"?

The habit of mind to Look Carefully is supported by the skill of "visual observation." What does the word "visual" mean? What does it mean to observe? In what ways have you developed the skill of visual observation?

To what sorts of challenges, class lessons, or projects does engaging the skill of visual observation make a big difference (geometry, science lab, being a detective, "Finding Waldo" puzzles, seeing how to make a new move in gymnastics or basketball, painting or drawing, seeing a move in chess, comparing and contrasting historical photographs, identifying a species of animal, finding differences in rocks and minerals, seeing how a simple machine functions, other science projects you have done)*?*

What adult careers and jobs in our society depend on the skill of visual observation (surgeon, artist, designer, mechanic, chef, chemist, filmmaker)*?*

How do you develop and practice your skill of visual observation (drawing from nature, puzzles, taking time to really look at your surroundings, nature walks)*?*

What inquiry projects require a high degree of visual observation? Let's look . . .

Let's see how the inquiries go today and how you use your visual observation skills and the habit of mind to Look Carefully.

Conversation and Question Possibilities for Lab Time

Why is it important to Look Carefully with the project you are working on? How does taking time to observe closely make a difference for this challenge?

When else do you use the skill of visual observation in school, at home, or in other things you do? When is it handy to have a well-developed habit to Look Carefully?

Reflection Circle Prompt

What was your inquiry challenge today? How did your project require you to develop and practice visual observation skills?

Writing Prompt

What was your challenge today? How did your project require you to develop and practice your visual observation skills? What are some activities at home, in the community, and in our classroom for which you find yourself developing and practicing your visual observation skills? Where are you building the habit of mind to Look Carefully?

(or) Draw three to five "sequence frames" (like a comic strip, but with larger frames) of different stages of your inquiry challenge that required you to look carefully. Write how each stage used visual observation skills. How does seeing clearly build stronger thinking and understandings?

From *Nine Thousand Straws: Teaching Thinking Through Open-Inquiry Learning* by Jean Sausele Knodt
Westport, CT: Teacher Ideas Press. Copyright © 2008.

14. LISTENING ACTIVELY TO HEAR CLEARLY

Objective

Students identify and develop the skill to be an active listener. The group discusses how building listening skills strengthens the ability to hear music, nature, or what others say more clearly and fully. This Focus Theme highlights the habit of mind to Listen Actively.

Opening Circle Time

Developing the habit of mind to Listen Actively helps you to hear things clearly.

What do you listen to (music, nature, what people say . . .)?

What does it take to be a great listener?

How does it feel when you sense someone is really listening to what you have to say?

How well do you think you listen to others?

How can it be difficult to be a great listener?

What are some things that can get in the way?

Does listening take time? Does it take patience? Focus? Discipline? Do you have to try?

Has anyone ever drifted away as someone was speaking? Has anyone ever gotten into trouble for not listening? Has anyone missed or felt confused as they were presented with important information (for example, when doing math, finishing an assignment, following instructions)?

What can you do if you don't understand when someone is speaking? Right! Active listeners ask questions! An active listener asks others to clarify and repeat what they have said.

Have you ever "restated" something someone has said to you?

What does it mean to restate something someone said? Let's hear an example. How does restating help?

Why is it worth being an active listener?

How many think that practicing the skill of listening and building the habit of mind to be an active listener can help you become stronger in your thinking and doing? Explain? I agree.

With which inquiry challenges will we develop active listening today?

Where are you interested in working today?

From *Nine Thousand Straws: Teaching Thinking Through Open-Inquiry Learning* by Jean Sausele Knodt. Westport, CT: Teacher Ideas Press. Copyright © 2008.

Conversation and Question Possibilities for Lab Time

How well do you think you have been listening to each other today with this project? Where do you think Lee and George are heading with their ideas? Try restating Lynne's idea. Let's see if you are on the same page.

Who can build on the idea that Anne just presented?

How is being an active listener helping your work today?

How is active listening making your team stronger?

Reflection Circle Prompts

Who took the time to really listen to their working partner(s) today? Describe how it went.

How did being active listeners help you work with this inquiry?

Writing Prompt

Describe your inquiry today. What did you learn about your partners' ideas? How were you an active listener? Where else will being an active listener help you in school, at home, with sports or music, or when out on a nature walk?

15. MANAGING FRUSTRATION

Objective

Children discuss how frustration is often part of the process when moving through a tough challenge. The group explores how frustration may indicate that new learning or skill acquisition is underway. Children discuss ways to handle frustration, ways that work for them in particular, and knowing when it's time to ask for help. This Focus Theme highlights the dispositions to Persevere and to Think Independently.

Opening Circle Time

Frustration is often part of meeting a challenge. Certainly frustration is often part of the inquiry scene here! Who here has ever felt frustrated? When? How? Why do things get frustrating (new skill level, distractions, "too hard")? Does hard mean bad? Explain.

What do you sometimes want to do when you feel frustrated? Yes, but does it feel good to quit? Can leaving a challenge or class project—for good—cause some trouble?

What else could you do when you feel frustrated? What are things that can help you (take a quick break, deep breath, review the problem, step back, ask for help)?

Does everyone cope with frustration in the same way?

Sometimes people seem afraid of feeling frustrated. They might leave the challenge, or say, "I'm bored." Others might start acting silly or disturb someone else who is working. Why would someone say, "Frustration can actually be a good sign for thinking" (new learning or skill developing, trying something new or more challenging, risk taking)?

How could it help to accept the frustration, and say something like, "OK, it's there, I accept it. The good news is that I'm likely to learn something new here. My skills are growing. My thinking is going to become stronger."

What if your frustration gets too heavy—too much to handle? For example, you can hold one dictionary, but can you hold ten? (The teacher can get dictionaries out and have children give it a try.) *That's what frustration is like. You can hold some, sometimes more, but there will be a limit as to how much frustration you can, or should, try to take on.*

A young girl once asked me, "What do you do if you are always frustrated? I am with my reading." What would you have said to her? Or imagine yourself, what do you do if the frustration level gets too much? If you have reached your limit? Right! Be brave and sensible, let someone you trust know you are frustrated. Ask for help.

Where are the lab inquiries today? Where should we air out some frustration?

What parts of this project do you find frustrating?

Have you accepted feeling frustrated?

How have you worked with your frustration? What has helped? What works for you?

What has dealing with the frustration taught you about yourself? How has dealing with the frustration built new skills and helped you to move ahead with your project?

Reflection Circle Prompts

What was your challenge today? Were some parts of the challenge frustrating? How did you work with the frustration?

How did you work as a team to deal with frustration?

Writing Prompt

Describe a time you had trouble dealing with frustration. What was the new skill or learning at hand? How would you try to work with that frustration differently? Describe a time you had success managing your frustration. What did you do? What worked for you?

(or) Describe your project today. What parts were frustrating? What were the new skills or understandings being developed? Give some advice to someone working on the project. How would you suggest that person deal with the frustration that may come up and then meet the challenge?

16. TO SAY, "I DID IT!" YOU HAVE TO DO IT! PERSEVERE

Objective

Students examine the habit of mind to Persevere. Children consider ways to nurture the patience and stamina needed to persevere. Students reflect on the conversation focused on Managing Frustration and how those ideas link to perseverance.

Opening Circle Time

You hear it said here all the time, often with a dance about the room with flying hands and arms! I did it! We did it! How many people love to say, "I did it!" What does it take to be able to say, "I did it!" Right, you have to do it!

What does the word "persevere" mean (to stick with it, make it through)?

Can it be harder to persevere with one type of activity or lesson than another?

What have been tough challenges you have had? Where have you needed to work hard to stick with a challenge, to persevere (play a new piece on the piano, solve a tough math problem, learn to read, learn to ride a bike, write a long English paper, swim the butterfly stroke)?

Do we all have different areas that are tough for us? Are we all the same?

What stops us from sticking with a problem until we solve it (frustration, being unsure of what to do, lack of information, being tired, being hungry, lack of guidance, missing supplies, teamwork issues, time management, lack of self confidence)?

What are ways you have learned to persevere when things get tough (ask for help, manage frustration, take a break, draw out ideas, find a partner, look for ideas somewhere else, try another approach, ask a question, take a deep breath, get a drink of water, laugh a bit, look for ideas from a book)?

Is everyone different? Do things that work for one person not work for others?

A student once said something like, "I shouldn't try to take on a challenge I am not ready for." What do you think about that statement?

If you are unsure of your problem or challenge in some way, or if a project gets too tough—too tough to persevere—what should you do? RIGHT! Talk to your teacher and parents! Ask for help! Discuss together what the challenge is and gain their perspective—their view of your challenge at hand. Ask them—Do you think this is a good challenge for me? If so, what are some ways I could keep going?

Let's practice perseverance with the projects here today.

From *Nine Thousand Straws: Teaching Thinking Through Open-Inquiry Learning* by Jean Sausele Knodt. Westport, CT: Teacher Ideas Press. Copyright © 2008.

Conversation and Question Possibilities for Lab Time

You want to quit? Why? Let's look closer at why you want to leave this challenge.

Do you find anything about this challenge frustrating today? How are you dealing with your frustration? How are you managing that part of the challenge?

What helps you persevere at other times when things get tough? What works for you?

How does a team help you persevere?

How can you make this project more interesting to you? What effort and energy can you put into working here? How can you make this challenge your own? How does building a challenge and making it more your own help you persevere?

Reflection Circle Prompts

Describe your project today. What was the toughest part of the challenge?

How did you persevere? How did the group work together to persevere?

What worked?

Writing Prompt

Remember how you worked with frustration and perseverance today with your inquiry challenge? What worked for you? Describe another challenge you have in our classroom (upcoming projects due, learning new math content). *Write down things you can do that will help you to persevere with that challenge.*

17. OK, WHY?!

Objective

The group members explore how finding ways to support their ideas with reasons why strengthens their overall thinking process and efforts with challenges. Students consider evaluating and weighing evidence. This Focus Theme highlights the habit of mind to Support Ideas with Reasons Why.

Opening Circle Time

When someone says "OK! Prove it!" What are they saying? What are they asking you to do?

How does it help to back up your ideas with facts, proof, or reasons?

How does finding evidence strengthen your thinking about something?

Have you ever said to yourself, "I want to prove this idea. I want to test out my idea."?

With your inquiry projects, I see you testing and proving ideas to yourself all the time! What are some examples you see?

What are different ways you can find proof, reasons, or evidence?

Imagine you have collected five facts or reasons to support an idea. Do they all have the same weight? Are they all equal? Could one be more important?

Let's take a look together at a lab project. What are some facts we know about this particular project? (Teacher selects project, polls for facts, writes ideas on board.) *Now, let's weigh our facts—evaluate the facts at hand. From one to ten, which fact on our board is most important?*

Where could you research to uncover more facts and reasons to support your ideas?

How can you gain ideas from other people's experiences?

How can you run experiments or test ideas?

How can you create questions that will uncover essential evidence for your ideas?

Where should we find evidence and support our ideas today?

Where are the inquiries today? Where are you interested in working?

From *Nine Thousand Straws: Teaching Thinking Through Open-Inquiry Learning* by Jean Sausele Knodt. Westport, CT: Teacher Ideas Press. Copyright © 2008.

Conversation and Question Possibilities for Lab Time

I see you feel strongly about your idea; tell me why are you so sure about it? What ideas and reasons help support your idea? What evidence have you collected?

Consider your group of facts and reasons. How are they similar? How are they different? Which facts do you think hold the most weight? Which are the strongest to support your idea or concept?

Reflection Circle Prompt

Describe your lab inquiry today. What ideas did you come up with? For which idea did you work on gaining evidence? How did you test your ideas? How did you find evidence that the ideas would work?

Writing Prompt

Describe your lab inquiry today. What ideas did you come up with? How did you test your ideas out? What idea or fact did you uncover that you think is the most important for meeting your challenge? Why? What evidence did you find?

18. COMMUNICATING CLEARLY

Objective

Children learn how communicating clearly helps in our work and experiences with others. The group explores ways to develop the habit of mind to Communicate Clearly as we write, speak, draw, or perform music.

Opening Circle Time

If someone is to understand your ideas and interests, it really helps to think about how you can communicate your ideas more clearly.

Who plays an instrument, or sings? What are ways you perform your music clearly? What are examples of your work with music when it is not clear?

How about those of you who draw or paint? When do your visual ideas communicate clearly? What are examples of when the work is not clear?

How about when you are writing—perhaps a book report, journal entry, or essay? What are some aspects or elements of a written piece that are communicated clearly?

How many of you have presented ideas in front of a group? Perhaps an oral book report? What are some of the elements of communicating well when you speak?

When you work in a group, or a team, and you have an idea, is that also an important time to communicate clearly? Why? How does Communicating Clearly make a difference for a team effort?

Where should we practice the habit of mind to Communicate Clearly today?

Where are the inquiries today?

Conversation and Question Possibilities for Lab Time

You have a great idea there! You are on to something! I especially like how you . . . .

What else could you add—or take away—to state your ideas? Explain again what you just said. Take it slow, and take care to state your idea clearly. Think about how you are communicating your idea so that we understand it clearly.

When are other times you need to take this kind of care in presenting your ideas effectively?

You have some nice (visual) ideas developing in your mural. I see how . . . (teacher comments on specific mural). What else would you like to add to make your ideas more clear? How can you go further with these ideas? What do you want to say with the colors you select? What areas do you want to develop further?

Reflection Circle Prompt

Who took some time to think about how they were communicating clearly to others? What worked? Explain. Are there any examples of when your communication broke down—when it didn't work? When are other times you need to take this kind of care to present your ideas effectively and communicate clearly? What are some examples of adults working toward communicating clearly in their work and lives?

Writing Prompt

Think about one of your favorite inquiry projects. Communicate clearly in writing what your ideas were and what you did with this project.

19. UNDERSTANDING OTHERS

Objective

Students consider how understanding the needs, thinking orientations, and ways of being of others help them to work more happily and successfully as a group. The group considers ways to build the skills, orientation, and habits of mind to Understand Others.

Opening Circle Time

When you are working, thinking, or doing things with other people, it helps to take some time and try to understand your coworkers—perhaps what they are thinking or feeling, or what their needs might be.

What does it mean to be perceptive? When does it help to be perceptive and see what someone else is thinking or feeling?

What does it mean to be sensitive? Is being sensitive a strength? How?

How can you use your habit of mind of Listening Actively as you try to better understand someone?

What are ways people express their feelings? If I sit here like this (teacher displays a despondent expression and slump), *do I appear happy and ready to work? How about if I sit here like this instead* (teacher displays a curious and happy expression and posture)*?*

Is there ever a point during a project when if you don't take the time to understand your team member, that the project might run into trouble? Let's hear some examples.

How is understanding and being sensitive to others' needs or feelings important? How does it make the team stronger?

How can it be difficult to take the time or effort to understand another person's needs or feelings? Why is it worth making the effort?

Where today should we practice the habit of mind to Understand Others?

Conversation and Question Possibilities for Lab Time

What are the different contributions from each person in your working group today?

I'm curious, in what various ways did you see each of your team partners thinking through ideas? Oh, Kyle likes to draw out concepts, which makes ideas clear for all to see. Nicholas is quiet but then adds an important idea just at the right moment.

Oh, your partner isn't speaking to you right now? How come? You don't know? Have you tried asking why? Be brave! Oh, she does want to work with you! You thought she said something else! Good work clearing that up! Great risk taking!

Ben, how is your thinking/idea similar to Caroline's? How is it different?

Reflection Circle Prompt

Who feels they took the time to better understand what someone else was thinking about or feeling today? Explain. How did you gain your understanding? How did your new understanding help your working together?

Writing Prompt

Describe a time you were working with someone else and it became important to stop and understand what that person was thinking or feeling. How did you gain your understanding? What did you notice? Hear? See? How did your new understanding help your project or time together?

20. RUBBER-BAND THINKING

Objective

Students explore how being flexible with thinking and doing opens possibilities for greater success finding and meeting challenges. Children see how being flexible allows a broader range of ideas and solutions. The group considers how flexible thinking is an aspect of employing the habit of mind to be Adventurous and Open-Minded.

Opening Circle Time

Sometimes my thinking feels hard as ice, frozen and stuck. Other times it feels like a rubber band. It feels flexible.

What does the word "flexible" mean? When you say someone is flexible, what are you saying? If you say you are a flexible thinker, what are you saying?

If you try one way to solve a problem or work through a challenge, and it doesn't work, are you able to change gears and find alternatives?

How does it help to be flexible? How does it make for stronger thinking?

What is it like to work with someone who is not flexible with his or her thinking and doing?

Is it easy to think if you are frozen? I agree, if you are flexible, new ideas come to you more easily.

Is it easy to work on a team project with people who are not flexible with their thinking?

How can you help a group loosen up?

Who wants to practice being flexible today with some tough, open-ended challenges? Let's get some rubber-band minds in action!

Conversation and Question Possibilities for Lab Time

How flexible is your thinking today with this challenge?

Are you able to move around with your ideas—change them if it makes sense to do so?

How flexible are you to see and work with others' ideas?

How flexible is your team's thinking today?

Reflection Circle Prompts

Who had some rubber-band thinking in action today? Describe the process of how your thinking and doing went with the project and how it was flexible. How does it feel to be flexible with your thinking and doing? How is being flexible helpful when finding, thinking through, and meeting challenges?

Writing Prompt

Write about a time you did not feel flexible with your thinking. Then write about a time you did feel like a flexible thinker. Compare the two. How did your work go in both cases?

From *Nine Thousand Straws: Teaching Thinking Through Open-Inquiry Learning* by Jean Sausele Knodt. Westport, CT: Teacher Ideas Press. Copyright © 2008.

21. WHAT IS YOUR GROUP STYLE?

Objective

Students recognize their own individual "way of being" while in a group. The group sees how a variety of skills, personalities, and interests makes a team stronger. Children reflect on ways to offer their ideas and talents to a group and to be positive contributors. This Focus Theme highlights the habits of mind to Understand Others, Contribute Positively to the Group and Inspire Team Work, and Think Independently.

Opening Circle Time

We all have different group styles, sensitivities, and personalities. Does everyone have different abilities, interests, and skills to offer a group? What are some examples (drawing, math, writing)*? What are some examples of various styles or group personalities* (talkative, quiet, bold)*?*

Is it OK that we are all different? I hope so!

Why is it great to have a variety of skills, interests, and personalities in a group?

How is variety needed?

Think alone for a moment. What is your group style? How do you tend to be in a group?

Can you be one way in one group and different in another? Do you expect to have exactly the same skills, interests, and group style in ten years?

What is a contribution? How is a contribution a gift?

What does it mean to be a positive contributor?

How does a group project depend on positive contributors?

What do you like to contribute to a team's effort?

Is it always easy to contribute to the group? How can it be difficult?

What can hold someone back from contributing an idea or effort? How can people overcome holding back their ideas and contributions?

How can a working group make it easier for all its members to contribute their skills and interests?

Where will you offer positive contributions today? What will be some group inquiries?

Conversation and Question Possibilities for Lab Time

What different individual interests are in action in this group?

What is everyone contributing to the effort of this project?

How are you being a positive contributor?

Reflection Circle Prompt

What were the different contributions today in the various inquiry groups?

If you have become part of a team, do you have the responsibility to be a positive contributor? How? Why?

Writing Prompt

Describe a group project you were part of. How did you see your group style in action? What positive contributions were you able to make?

22. LISTEN TO YOUR MIND AT WORK. BE METACOGNITIVE!

Objective

Students learn what the word "metacognitive" means: *"Thinking about your own thinking."* Children consider how reflecting and evaluating one's own thinking is effective and purposeful. Theme highlights the habit of mind to Think Independently.

Opening Circle Time

Let's be metacognitive today. Let's have fun with a really big word! Metacognitive. Now you don't hear that every day! How many syllables do you hear? Let's see how big a word we're talking about!

Met-a-cog-ni-tive. Who's got it? Five syllables, great!

Who wants to say the word? Anyone else? Slow it down, try again.

Who can say it five times fast?! Wait, let me time you with my stopwatch!

So after all that, I suppose we should all know what metacognitive means!

Hans was metacognitive as he reviewed how he solved the math problem.

Lee thought metacognitively as she thought through her main idea for her story.

George was metacognitive as he considered once again how to solve the Kapla Bridge challenge.

What do you think the word "metacognitive" means? Good tries! You almost have it!

Metacognitive means thinking about your own thinking. Not mine! Yours!

When you are metacognitive, you are reviewing and evaluating your own thinking process. You think about your thinking strengths, what you could develop, what kind of thinking you should use at different times, such as brainstorming or strategizing.

When have you thought about your own thinking? You all do it (Examples: reviewing a strategy while playing chess, how you thought through a math problem, reviewing an outline or mind map before writing)*!*

How do you think it helps you to be metacognitive?

How does being metacognitive help you be an independent thinker?

Who is going to say to their folks at home tonight, "I was metacognitive today. How about you?"

Let's get some metacognition going with some tough inquiry challenges!

Oh, but wait! We forgot to spell the word! Who is ready to give it a try?! You can do it if you take it one syllable at a time!

Conversation and Question Possibilities for Lab Time

Review out loud to me how you have been thinking through your challenge.

Be metacognitive out loud . . .

Now, where do you think your thinking was strong?

Where does your thinking need to bend, or consider some other route?

How might a new thinking plan make this project go better?

Reflection Circle Prompts

What does the word metacognitive mean again?

How did being metacognitive help your work today?

Where else could you be metacognitive as you work and do things?

Writing Prompt

Think about the inquiry project you took on today. Make a mind map of how your thinking developed to solve the problem, pursue your inquiry, or meet your quest. What does the word "metacognitive" mean? Look at your mind map and write about how you were metacognitive with your inquiry.

23. THINKING ABOUT THE PROCESS

Objective

Students become familiar with the word "process" as applied to finding, meeting, and thinking through their inquiries. Children see how enriching the process will mean stronger outcomes, statements, and products. The group explores ways to enrich the process of being engaged in an inquiry.

Opening Circle Time

An enriched process makes stronger products. When you work on a project, do you expect to have it done right away? Wouldn't that be great! Like a genie in the bottle. Bing! It's done! There wouldn't be any reason for these great challenges here, that's for sure! We would just be here nodding our heads, "bing this, bing that!"

Actually, who would miss the fun? Even working through some frustration? Who would miss the time spent thinking and doing? Would you miss your inquiries? Me too.

What does the word "process" mean? How is working with an inquiry project—a process?

Imagine making a great soup. That's a project, and a process. Can you add parts to the soup to make it great? Can you add parts to the soup that would not make it great? Would a rotten banana work? Can you take away parts to make the soup work out better? Right, that old shoe doesn't need to be in there!

How are all projects or challenges we take on like making a great pot of soup? Let's look at that last book report you all did. What was part of the process to make your report work out well? What could you have added to the process of making that book report that would have made it an even better, fuller, richer, more developed report? What does enriching the process of meeting a challenge or pursuing an inquiry take (time, thinking of ideas, patience, interest, research)? Let's take a look at the process you get in action with some inquiry challenges . . . Let's make some great soup!

Conversation and Question Possibilities for Lab Time

What are the different parts of the process of meeting your challenge today?

What are new things you can add to your process to make it stronger, richer, and more developed? What about brainstorming? Are you planning strategy?

Reflection Circle Prompt

What advice would you give someone working on this challenge? What would you tell that person to add to the process to make the end result richer or better? How did enriching the process make for stronger outcomes with your challenge?

Writing Prompt

Reflect on a project or challenge you have had recently. Make a map on a piece of paper showing the route or process you took with that project. What could you add to your travel to make the end result richer or better?

24. HOW MANY WAYS ARE THERE TO BE SMART?

Objective

Students understand that there are many ways of showing how they are smart. The group explores Howard Gardner's Multiple Intelligences and sees how "being smart" means developing *all* our intelligences, as well as respecting the intelligences of others.

Opening Circle Time

It's time to think about how many ways there are to be intelligent. So let's have a show of hands. How many ways do you think there are to be smart? (That many?! Just one?!)

In the last twenty-five years, so much has changed with what we understand about the brain and how it works. With MRIs (explain), *we can even see the brain in action!* (Show MRI examples.) *Most of those who study the brain and how we think say that intelligence is not just one single thing, but that there are many different intelligences or ways of showing how we are "smart."*

One way to show multiple ways of being smart is the theory of Multiple Intelligences, developed by a man named Howard Gardner. What does "multiple" mean?

Dr. Gardner would agree with those of you who said there are thousands of ways to be smart! Through his studies, Dr. Gardner was able to identify eight intelligences. Here's the line up: (Note: teacher observes to see all hands go up as they review each intelligence.)

- *Interpersonal, or People Smart: The intelligence used as we work with and understand others. How many of you sometimes try to understand what other people are thinking or feeling? How many of you have ever seen someone upset and tried to help that person? Who has ever been part of a team? In what ways do you see adults engage People Smart? How? How many of you are People Smart?*

- *Verbal-Linguistic, or Word Smart: The intelligence used to speak, read, or write. How many of you love to write or play Scrabble? How many of you are often reading or thinking of the book you are reading? How many of you have ever worked with words by learning to read, listen, speak, or write? How many of you are Word Smart? In what ways do you see adults use Word Smart?*

- *Body-Kinesthetic, or Body Smart: The intelligence used to position and move your body (fine and gross motor). How many of you can't wait to get out on the playing field, ride a horse, swim, or get to gymnastics class? How many of you have ever kicked a soccer ball, learned to ride a bike, bead a necklace, draw a picture, or danced? How many have their hands up for Body Smart? In what ways do you see adults use Body Smart?*

- *Naturalist, or Nature Smart: The intelligence used to identify and tell differences between animals and plant life, including their behavior and needs. How many of you love to observe nature in action? How many of you have ever seen the differences between two types of butterflies? Who here has ever tried to understand what one type of dog bark or another meant? Who has ever helped pick out a ripe banana? How many have their hands up for Nature Smart? In what ways do you see adults engage Nature Smart?*

- ***Musical-Rhythmic, or Music Smart:*** *The intelligence used to hear rhythmic beats and tones with music. How many of you hear music in your minds, perhaps something you're learning to play on the piano or violin? How many of you can clap this beat. . . . Now try this one, it's harder . . . . Here's another. Now which of you have just been using your Music Smart? In what ways do you see adults engage Music Smart?*

- ***Visual-Spatial, or Picture Smart:*** *The intelligence used to work with and understand two- and three-dimensional space. Which of you love to draw and look for opportunities to doodle or paint? How many of you have ever worked with a puzzle? Who plays chess? Who has ever worked with geometric shapes like these? Who has tied their shoe? How many hands up do we have for Visual-Spatial Intelligence? In what ways do you see adults engage in Picture Smart?*

- ***Intrapersonal, or Self Smart:*** *The intelligence used when we work to understand ourselves, our strengths and weaknesses, and our likes and dislikes. Who here loves to spend time reflecting quietly about things? How many of you have ever thought of your likes and dislikes? Who has ever tried to understand why they might feel unhappy or happy about something? Who has ever thought about how they thought something through? Has anyone reflected on what they might want to do? Let's see the hands up for Self Smart. In what ways do you see adults using Self Smart?*

- ***Math-Logic, or Math Smart:*** *The intelligence used to work with numeral systems and logic. Who here enjoys solving tough mind-bender problems like this Rubik's Cube? How many here work with numbers—adding them, subtracting, multiplying, dividing, fractions, positive, negatives? Who here has ever played chess or checkers, or some other strategy game? Well then, raise your hands for Math-Logic Intelligence! In what ways do you see adults engaging Math Smart?*

How many of you raised your hands for all the intelligences we talked about? It's clear we have all of these different intelligences in action!

Are they all equally important? Yes! They are all important for our lives and for doing necessary and exciting things.

Are there some intelligences that you feel somehow closer to, or better at? Ones that come easier for you? We all have different intelligences we feel stronger in at different times in our lives.

Can intelligences grow? Sure! How?

If you give an intelligence an opportunity, it will grow. The Smarts are like plants, not stones. What are some examples of building or growing our intelligences?

For instance, you could have great abilities with music, but if you never give music an opportunity to grow—by actually doing some music through learning an instrument or listening to music—that intelligence might not grow as quickly as it could.

Could I grow my intelligences today at the age of fifty? That old?! Yes I can!

How many have found that something you love to do, like painting, observing nature, reading, or dancing, is an intelligence? Great—we have them all, let's use them all! Let's put some of those intelligences to work! Where are the inquiries today? Let's build and grow some intelligences.

Conversation and Question Possibilities for Lab Time

Which of your intelligences are you using to meet this challenge? How?

Reflection Circle Prompt

Which intelligences did you have in action today? How?

Writing Prompt

Which intelligences did you have in action today? How? Which intelligences would you soon like to get into action? How?

Note: This Focus Theme needs a longer time frame than others.

25. WHICH INTELLIGENCES ARE YOU USING TO GET THE JOB DONE?

Objective

The group explores how the intelligences work together to get a job done. Students see that there is no hierarchy with the intelligences. They discuss how intelligences work together to perform tasks and create products.

Opening Circle Time

Intelligences work together to get a job done. OK, let's say I'm part of a team to build a bridge with the Kapla blocks. What intelligences would I likely be using (Math Smart, Picture Smart, People Smart)*?*

Let's take a look at a recent class assignment—say, your one-page work, "These Are Things That Are Important to Me," with a self-portrait picture. What intelligences were working together to get that job done (Word Smart, Picture Smart, Self Smart)*?*

Let's look at some jobs that adults might have. What intelligences do we see at work (chef, architect, lawyer, car mechanic, sales person, teacher, Mom or Dad, soccer coach, realtor, manager)*?*

Is any one intelligence more important than another?

So let's see which intelligences we can mix together today with our project inquiries!

Conversation and Question Possibilities for Lab Time

What intelligences are helping you get the job done today?

Where else have you developed these intelligences?

Reflection Circle Prompt

Which intelligences did you have in action today with your inquiries? How?

Writing Prompt

Describe your lab inquiry today. Which intelligences did you have in action as you worked? Where else do you use these intelligences?

26. BEING "IN FLOW"

Objective

Students learn the term "flow" to identify times when they are focused and absorbed in an activity. Children understand and appreciate how flow strengthens thinking and work. Children see how flow can be cultivated in other learning arenas.

Opening Circle Time

You can lose track of time when you are really focused on a project and in "flow." In what situations do you loose track of time?

Have you ever been doing something and were surprised when someone said, "Time to go!"? What were you doing at those moments?

Some people refer to that kind of time, when you are so absorbed with what you are doing, as being in flow.

When was a time you felt the happiest? What were you doing then?

Studies have shown that people are the happiest when they are in the middle of a great project or challenge (in sustained absorption with some activity, in flow). *Would you have thought it was more likely when they were with a bowl of popcorn, a remote control, a couch, and the TV? Even though that is nice to do, the happiest times listed were when people were doing things like you mentioned—designing a new garden, building a group sculpture, making a model of a bridge, fixing a car, working on a soccer skill. Times when they were in flow—when they were truly focused on doing something.*

Have you ever been in flow doing something you didn't choose to do yourself, like writing in your journal, cleaning your room, or raking the yard? Great examples! Did you feel a switch go on the moment you really took on and accepted the project?

Yes! I agree, if you can make the challenge yours, get the energy going, you can find flow with all sorts of activities! What are ways to make a challenge your own?

How do you think that being in flow can make your work and thinking stronger?

I'm curious, it seems you have all had experiences with flow. What do you think can break your focus on a project, or flow?

Have you ever heard a teacher say, "Let's get back on task, folks!"? When you are in flow with an activity, you're definitely on task!

Some people call an inquiry lab like ours a "Flow Room."

Where should we get some flow going with our inquiries?

From *Nine Thousand Straws: Teaching Thinking Through Open-Inquiry Learning* by Jean Sausele Knodt.
Westport, CT: Teacher Ideas Press. Copyright © 2008.

Conversation and Question Possibilities for Lab Time

Has there been a time today with this project you felt in flow?

What are other times in your life you feel in flow?

What are ways you can cultivate your focus or help flow into being?

Reflection Circle Prompts

Was anyone surprised the time went by quickly today? Who felt they were in flow?

Did anyone help the focus or flow happen? How?

Writing Prompts

Times when I feel in flow are when I am . . .

The part of the challenge I seem to get most involved with is . . .

A time I got flow into action with an activity I didn't choose on my own was . . .

The way I made the challenge my own and got flow into action was by . . .

27. WHAT ARE PEOPLE REALLY SAYING WHEN THEY SAY, "I'M BORED"?

Objective

Students identify reasons for the feeling, or saying, "I'm bored." Students see that they can cultivate challenges or projects to become *their own*—both challenges they receive from others, and those they choose. Children discuss ways to take responsibility, develop stamina, and personalize their challenges. The group discusses a quote from one child, "You can make your own challenges." The Focus Theme highlights the dispositions to Think Independently, Be Adventurous and Open-Minded, and Explore and Investigate.

Opening Circle Time

When someone says they are bored with a project or challenge, it makes me think other things could really be going on. What do you think could be some things that are happening when someone says, "I'm bored" (frustration, unsure of what to do next, out of ideas, tired, hungry, afraid they will do something wrong, might look "bad," might look like they don't know what they are doing)? *Something usually is going on—or not going on—when people say they are bored. When things are going right, people usually really love to be engaged in a challenge. It's a purposeful, active time.*

What do you think the student was saying in this quote: "You can make your challenges."? Can you personalize any challenge? Even one you were given? How? Can you add parts to a challenge? What is an example of doing that? Can you make your own decisions on what to inquire about further?

Seems to me, when you build a challenge, inquiry, or lesson, you <u>own</u> it more. You make it yours. It can continue to grow and build as you want it to. Is it harder to get bored if you have made a challenge your own? How?

Where should we build and make our inquiries our own today?

Conversation and Question Possibilities for Lab Time

At what point of "jumping in" are you with this challenge?

What about this challenge interests you most?

How can you build your interest in the project?

Is there an obstacle in your way to truly taking on this challenge (hungry, tired, frustrated, don't understand the project, not sure how to)? *What could it be?*

I know you have an interest in . . . how could you combine that interest with this project? I'll be back to see what you figured out.

Reflection Circle Prompts

Were any of you feeling bored with your challenge today? What did you do about it?

Did any of you work out some things that were in the way of working well and happily with your inquiry? What did you do?

How did you build your challenge or inquiry experience today? What were some ways you made the challenge your own?

Writing Prompt

Write about a time that you felt it was going to be impossible to accept a challenge, a time you felt bored. What were you doing instead of the challenge? What was in your way of taking on and building the challenge for yourself? Did you finally jump in? How or what did you do to make the challenge your own? What were you able to accomplish with your challenge? If you were not able to jump in, do you now see any ways in which you could have built the challenge to become your own?

28. IDEAS AND INTERESTS IN CONFLICT

Objective

Students explore how conflicts can often arise when working on projects and developing ideas together with another person or within a group. Children discuss ways to negotiate and compromise as conflicts of interest surface. This Focus Theme highlights the habits of mind to Think Independently, Understand Others, and to Contribute Positively to the Group and Inspire Team Work.

Opening Circle Time

Being part of a team often means working with other people's ideas, needs, and interests—all of which are sometimes different from your own.

If we look at this one inquiry challenge (show example), *what are some ideas of things we can do with the project? As we hear the ideas from everyone, we'll quickly put each one on an index card, and then we will sort the cards* (students can also put down ideas individually on a card and then collect them).

Let's sort the ideas. Which are in full conflict, which are almost the same? How could we work with these ideas that are in conflict?

Let's brainstorm some ways to work with the different ideas and interests. Which ideas are possible to combine somehow? Which are not? Let's explore those you think <u>are not</u> possible as well. Perhaps there are ways to bring the ideas together that you haven't thought of yet.

How does it strengthen a project or endeavor to have many different ideas? How can it weaken a project to have too many different ideas?

What does it take to work with another person's idea, especially if it conflicts with or is different from your own (understanding and acknowledging others, brainstorming solutions, thinking flexibly)*?*

How does it help to Step Back and Look at the Whole Picture together as you work in a group?

How does it help to settle yourself, to stay confident and excited about your own ideas, yet also be open to hearing others' ideas? Is that sometimes hard to do?

Let's see how the inquiries go today. (All work in small groups.) *How will you work with all the different ideas and interests of your team?*

Conversation and Question Possibilities for Lab Time

You all have great ideas here! Your group is on to something!

Hans, explain Murray's idea to me. Jamie, what is Nicholas's idea? Christopher, what do you see could be possible with all these ideas and approaches?

How are the ideas and approaches similar? How are they different?

How could you combine the ideas?

From *Nine Thousand Straws: Teaching Thinking Through Open-Inquiry Learning* by Jean Sausele Knodt. Westport, CT: Teacher Ideas Press. Copyright © 2008.

What is the strongest part of each idea?

Would it strengthen the project to combine the ideas?

What might each of you need to give up when you combine your ideas?

What could your project gain by combining your ideas?

Reflection Circle Prompt

Who can map out how the ideas developed in their group today?

Did any ideas come into conflict? How did you work with the ideas? How did you resolve the conflict?

Writing Prompt

What challenge did your inquiry team have today? Were there any conflict(s) of ideas or interests? How did you work out the conflict(s)?

29. WHAT SKILLS DOES IT TAKE TO BE PART OF A TEAM?

Objective

Children reflect on their experience together as a group and establish a personalized listing of positive team skills and attitudes. Listings are then employed by the group for ongoing reference. This Focus Theme highlights the dispositions to Contribute Positively to the Group and Inspire Team Work, and Understand Others.

Examples of Team Skill Lists Written by Children

A First-Grade Class:
Take Turns
Use Self-Control
Be Responsible
Encourage Others
Give Positive Messages
Share Ideas
Be Friendly
Listen
Persevere
Forgive

A Sixth-Grade Class:
Share Leadership
Share Ideas
Listen
Speak Clearly
Strategize Together
Think About the Whole Group
Give Positive Messages
Stay Focused
Deal With Frustration
Really Fast Persevere

Opening Circle Time

How is your class a team?

What skills does your team need to be an industrious, happy working group?

We have talked about what it takes to engage the habits of mind to Understand Others and to Contribute Positively to the Group and Inspire Teamwork. Now let's get some specific ideas on paper. Let's make your own personalized class poster of team skills.

Note: The lead instructor helps combine similar skills and keeps the list as close to ten as possible. Posters and bookmarks can be made for students. If working in a centralized lab, posters from all attending classes can be up on walls for all to see. Posters can also be mounted in the lobby of the school or children's hospital or become a great bulletin board.

Who is going to put their class team skill list on the refrigerator at home?

Would anyone like a bookmark of their team skill listing?

Let's practice some team skills with challenges.

Conversation and Question Possibilities for Lab Time

One team skill you added to your list today is . . .

How are you working with that skill now?

Right, it's one thing to know what the skill is, and another to actually use it!

Reflection Circle Prompts

Which team skills from your list did you put into practice today?

What skill was hard to work with today? How?

Are there any other skills you would add to your list?

Writing Prompt

What was the challenge your group had today? In which ways did you work together to meet your goals? What skills from your Class Team Skill List did you put into practice? How did getting that skill into action make a difference and help you reach your goals?

30. WHAT ACTION STEPS COULD YOU TAKE TO MEET YOUR GOAL?

Objective

The group acknowledges that a goal can sometimes be overwhelming and sees that taking time to plan their actions helps to manage the meeting of a challenge or pursuit of an inquiry. Students take responsibility for the goal at hand and brainstorm strategy steps. The group sees that designing and taking steps requires flexibility and that sometimes steps need to change as one moves through the process of meeting a challenge or goal. This Focus Theme highlights the dispositions to Set Goals and Make Plans and to Think Independently.

Opening Circle Time

Sometimes a goal can seem impossible to meet. Overwhelming!

Have you ever seen a project or challenge in front of you, froze, and thought, "Yikes! This is too much! No way! I won't be able to do this!"? The "final product" or goal seems unobtainable, too much to handle, and you freeze. Can you do much frozen?

How many of us have felt overwhelmed with a big goal? How many have felt they wanted to leave the goal before even getting started? Perhaps you have a class social studies project to make replica's of two American Indian tribal villages; maybe it's your challenge to try out for the traveling basketball team, and you see the "big guys" out practicing looking "too good"; perhaps you are wanting to improve your handwriting and see your teacher make these perfect letters on the chalkboard like a fine-tuned typesetting machine. How does he do that anyway?!

Any big class assignments coming up? Any personal quests? Let's select one of these goals and brainstorm how we might meet the challenge. Let's take some time and see if we can come up with action ideas that make sense for meeting the goal at hand.

Let's think before we act and figure out our strategy to meet this goal!

Looks good! What does it feel like to have ideas and strategies in mind to meet our goals? Do you feel like you are more in control? Setting a course? Ready to go? Even excited to get started?

Even if you are not overwhelmed with a goal, how does it pay off to plan steps? Let's take some strategy steps with our inquiry projects!

Conversation and Question Possibilities for Lab Time

What steps have you taken so far with this project?

Did the steps need to be in that order?

Did you need to change your steps as you went along?

Reflection Circle Prompt

Imagine you are giving someone advice. What actions could they take to meet the challenge you had today?

Who found thinking about taking strategy steps helpful to meet their challenge? How? Where else could you stop and take some time to plan action steps to meet a goal?

Writing Prompt

What is a goal you have? What are some action steps that will help that goal become a success?

Note: This Focus Theme is based on an idea presented by Jeanette Aydlette, Counselor, Haycock Elementary School, McLean, Virginia.

31. PLAYING AROUND WITH THINKING

Objective

The group reflects on the innovative process, and the productive use of "playing around" with things and ideas. To tinker and to work toward experiencing "ah-ha!" moments. This Focus Theme highlights the dispositions to be Adventurous and Open-Minded; to Wonder, Explore, and Ask Questions; and to Think Independently.

Opening Circle Time

> *All sorts of things can happen when you're open to new ideas and playing around with things.*
> —Stephanie Kwolek, Inventor of Kevlar (Kevlar is a material invented by Kwolek
>   and produced by Dupont that pound for pound is five times stronger than steel.)

Has anyone here ever had an "ah-ha!" moment? When? What are some examples?

What do you think Ms. Kwolek is saying about ah-ha moments?

Many problem solvers, from artists to doctors, find time to "play around" with their ideas and thinking. Many find it essential.

What are some times when it would be helpful to play around with ideas (book report, painting, plan for winning a soccer game . . .)? *How would it help?*

How can taking time to play around with ideas make for some serious thinking? How can it be a productive part of the process of meeting a challenge or pursuing a project?

Have you ever played around with your ideas? Give some examples. What happened? What thinking are you doing when you play around with ideas (exploring alternatives, brainstorming, weighing pros and cons)?

When you play around with ideas, you are relaxed, but ready for a breakthrough to happen. You're looking, open, perched—ready and waiting for the surprises and the ah-ha's to start to happen.

Do you need to be open and flexible when you are "playing around" with ideas? Right, you need to settle in, enjoy, and let the time unfold.

Playing around with ideas is part of the inventive and innovative process!

Who wants to play around and think about thinking with some inquiry challenges?

Conversation and Question Possibilities for Lab Time

Who is playing around with ideas today?

Has anyone had an ah-ha moment while tinkering?

Are you able to play around with ideas as a team? How?

From *Nine Thousand Straws: Teaching Thinking Through Open-Inquiry Learning* by Jean Sausele Knodt. Westport, CT: Teacher Ideas Press. Copyright © 2008.

Reflection Circle Prompt

Who was surprised with something they came up with today? Who had an ah-ha moment? Did playing around with things bring you to any breakthroughs?

Writing Prompt

Imagine you were the person who invented the paper clip, Velcro, kite, swing sets, Band-Aids, ice cream, or row boats. How might you have played around with ideas to figure things out? What might you have been doing before the ah-ha moment arrived?

(or) Describe your project today. How did you find yourself playing around with ideas? Did you have an ah-ha moment? What was it? What did you discover?

32. MAKING MISTAKES

Objective

Children consider how making mistakes can provide information. This Focus Theme supports the habit of mind to Think Independently and helps support students to take responsible risks with their thinking and doing.

Opening Circle Time

I've heard that it took Thomas Edison one thousand tries before he was able to meet the challenge of making the lightbulb work. Would he have succeeded and finally engineered the lightbulb if he was afraid of making mistakes?

What can you imagine he gained from his many "mistakes"?

Edison knew that mistakes were part of the process of giving something a try. He knew that mistakes were going to happen when he tried a new approach—when he attempted or tested a new idea. But he also knew he would gain important information and learn from the "mistakes."

How can making a mistake lead to an ah-ha moment? How can an ah-ha moment happen even when answering something clear cut, like offering an answer to a three-digit multiplication problem? What can you learn if you should make a mistake here? What information can you collect? What new insights can happen?

Have you ever had (or heard) an idea that seemed silly at first and then said to yourself—Wait, actually, this isn't such a silly idea, we could. . . ?

When someone says, "Have courage, trust yourself," what are they saying?

What makes it hard to try something new, say something not already said, or offer an answer?

Where should we see how mistakes can be part of the process of meeting our goals and challenges? Where are the inquiries in the lab today?

Conversation and Question Possibilities for Lab Time

How does it feel risky sometimes to offer a new idea?

Why are we all sometimes afraid to make mistakes?

Reflection Circle Prompt

Where did some mistakes pop up today? What did you learn from your mistakes today?

Writing Prompt

Describe a mistake experience you had. What information did you gain from it? What did you learn from the mistake?

From *Nine Thousand Straws: Teaching Thinking Through Open-Inquiry Learning* by Jean Sausele Knodt. Westport, CT: Teacher Ideas Press. Copyright © 2008.

33. PROBLEM FINDERS AND QUESTION MAKERS ARE BIG THINKERS

Objective

Children consider how *problem finding* and asking questions are key aspects of developing industrious thinking and doing. Students see that they actually ask many questions to themselves as they work, perhaps not even aware they are doing so. They consider how becoming more aware of our many questions can help us frame up more interesting and focused inquiries. This Focus Theme highlights the habits of mind to Think Independently and to Wonder, Explore, and Ask Questions.

Opening Circle Time

You really have questions in your mind.
—Lab student

What do you think this student is saying?

Asking questions and problem finding is a big part of being an industrious thinker. What might we call a person who asks a lot of questions? Curious, right!

How does curiosity build stronger thinking and doing?

Many of you have heard of the term "problem solving." How many of you have heard of the term "problem finding"? Are some of you thinking, "Wait a minute, who would want to find a problem?!"

Who are some big problem finders in our world and history? What are some problems that intrigued them (the wheel, paper, lightbulbs, zippers, Velcro, telephones, the Internet, paper clips)? Problem finders are big thinkers! Certainly inventors are often problem finders.

Problem finders ask a lot of questions.

Have you ever heard yourself asking, "I wonder if . . ."?

Just like the boy I just quoted, we really ask a lot of questions as we work. Sometimes we don't even know we are asking a question as we work.

Do you think becoming more mindful of the questions we ask ourselves as we work could make our inquiries more interesting or successful? How?

What is that big word again? It begins with an M (metacognitive)!

People love challenges and finding and solving problems.

Why do you think that might be so? Why do people like to find a challenge?

Where are the inquiries today? What are your questions? What great problems or challenges do you think you could find for yourself?

Conversation and Question Possibilities for Lab Time

What questions do you hear yourself asking today?

What challenges or problems have you found here today to work on?

How are your questions helping you develop your inquiry?

What other ideas do you have for new challenge possibilities?

How could you combine this project with some other inquiry project for other interesting challenge possibilities?

Reflection Circle Prompts

What questions did you hear yourself asking as you worked on your inquiries today?

What problem and challenge finding did we have going on here today?

Writing Prompt

Why do you think people like to find and solve problems, or to find and meet a great challenge? What inquiry project have you especially loved working with? Why? What new questions and challenges did you find for yourself with that project?

Your mind opens up and you want to do all these different things.
—Lab student

Chapter Five
Inquiry Project Design

AT THE HEART OF INQUIRY

With fifteen children busily exploring during an open-inquiry lab time, seven or eight projects are likely out and underway. For one team of students, it may be that wires, batteries, tin foil, rubber bands, a small lightbulb, and a couple of pennies have become the precious objects of the day. The children appear mostly oblivious to the other action in the room as they discuss (sometimes loudly) their many ideas and new configurations for getting their lightbulb to work. The conversation moves from excitement to frustration, and even anger, as they run into trouble. *It must be a dud. We must be missing something.* And finally, *It's on! I see it! Look!*

At the same time that this group works with electric circuits, across the room a student works independently at the Story Board Center. The child first moves various photo cards around to get a better sense of the resources he has to work with before placing the cards on a mounted wall rack. Carefully and quietly, he establishes a series of sequential relationships with the pictures that mean something to him, that feel right, or that help tell a specific story he has in mind. Once ready, he sits facing the cards, and, with a microphone in hand, makes an audio taping of his story.

In the Think Tank you can pretend you are an inventor.
—Lab student

Two other children work to set up and balance a mobile in the corner of the room. They weigh out large hardware bolts and fill containers with various combinations of bolts. The containers are then carefully placed on the arms of the mobile as the children attempt to achieve a perfect balance using different portions of weight. Four feet away from the mobile, working on the floor, are three children pursuing yet another classic lab challenge, the making of a suspension bridge with the coveted "Kapla Blocks." *How far apart can you make your two towers and still suspend a bridge of blocks between them with no support underneath?*

The children are eager to record the span between their towers on the Challenge Chalkboard in both centimeters and inches, and to see whether their number will beat the current record. Just like those at Batteries and Bulbs, Story Board, or the Mobile project centers, these children are absorbed in their inquiries, undistracted by the action going on in other parts of the room. There are also groups working to identify the bones of an upright model skeleton, those performing a lab survey and graphing their results, two children trying to figure out how to make a geodesic dome out of straws, and those at the invention building station, called "Think It! Do It!" with this day's challenge of creating something that moves using wind generation.

What Makes a Great Inquiry Project?

In all the project scenarios just described, children have found places to explore openly and constructively. To them, the projects are full of innovative and industrious possibilities. This potential is what inspires their inquiry action to get underway, thereby *setting the stage* for instructors to engage questioning and use the projects as teaching mediums (see Chapter Two: "Project as Medium, Teacher as Coach").

Most projects are made up of simple items, many made of wood, and depend on an individual's energy to make "sensational" things happen. Even computer technologies that are present usually are combined with hands-on manipulatives, such as Claymation or Lego structures that are programmed to move. As children brainstorm and produce products, they clearly see that *their thinking* is the fuel that makes exciting things happen. It is this feeling of empowerment that drives their inquiries, that creates the spirit of the lab time, and that becomes what many love most about the program.

Essential Elements

There are key ingredients to successful project design that lead to rich and purposeful inquiries and mediums through which to teach. In a nutshell, a successful open-inquiry project will likely embody a healthy handful of the following:

- is primarily student led and directed; students can get started and be well on their way without a lot of upfront teacher direction and instruction

- requires the employment of various thinking skills and dispositions

- establishes potential for children to extend the challenge and uncover related inquiries

- employs hands-on materials

- is constructivist and problem-based in nature

- lends itself to developing a rich process

- avoids mindless busy work

- establishes research and investigation opportunities
- is multi-age friendly
- lends itself to progressive skill-level development
- can be used by either a group or an individual working alone
- can be revisited often by individuals to build sustained interests
- connects to unfolding curriculum content and offers transfer of learning opportunities
- makes abstract concepts more clear, concrete, and tangible
- links a curriculum content with complex higher-level thinking
- displays thinking that can also be seen in action in professional and vocational real-world domains
- is made up of parts and pieces that can be easily replaced
- can be handled and worked on by many children, many times
- is presented in strong portable containers or at a clearly defined center area; packaging materials are removed, and objects are arranged for handy use, storage, easy access, and visibility
- presents directions and other accompanying graphics simply
- cleans up easily by children; inquiries can be immediately ready for the next group of students

Enriching the Process

Project designers first think through the process that students will likely experience while working at that center and then set elements in place to enrich that process. With this process-based orientation, a lead instructor or committee reviews an existing or new inquiry project for pitfalls of unnecessary busy work, while ensuring that it has the potential to meet a number of instructional goals. Wearing their project design hat and keeping in mind objectives such as those just listed, educators ask: *What do we see or imagine that children will actually be doing with their time at this center? To what thinking skills and dispositions does it link? Which intelligences? What are the transfer of learning opportunities? What could enrich this project further?*

Project Collaborations

No one educator, or even a team of project designers, will likely have all the necessary skills to develop a wide array of inquiry projects to their full potential. A great way to build the process and content potential of a project is to enlist folks with relevant expertise. A variety of individuals can be engaged, from a school's faculty and parents to other community members, such as those from a nearby college or business. Especially for a program that highlights Multiple Intelligences, many vocations and specialty skill sets are represented in the various projects. Review project ideas or existing centers with folks who know! Enlisting help from various school specialists, as well as from college instructors, attorneys, chefs, mechanics, builders, botanists, music specialists, or architects will generate important ideas to incorporate into an inquiry project, help work out technical issues, and inspire altogether new project ideas.

The project design team or individual begins by interviewing specialists for general ideas. What makes their content or domain area tick? Projects at various stages of development are also brought along to review and develop further. One might hear the domain professional say things such as, *This project hasn't hit one very important way in which I think when working with my carpentry. To make this project more engaging, add an activity in your wood-building center that requires a child to move from a two-dimensional image to actually building the object in three dimensions. I spend a lot of time working to understand what a spec or drawing is saying, and how it translates into three dimensions, to get my job done.* Ask if the professional or specialist can visit during lab time, see the projects in action, and work alongside the children. Overall, the project designer or team is always on the lookout to see where a challenge might be missing the essence of the relevant content or skills, how to enrich the process, and how to incorporate a higher level of complex thinking.

An engineer might suggest eliminating tape as a tool from the invention center, Think It! Do It! (see Chapter Six: "Inquiry Project Sampler"). This simple move significantly changes the working process and automatically moves the project to a higher level of thinking. *How will you attach things successfully without using tape?*

The art educator providing advice might see clearly that when building a Triangle Truss Toothpick Bridge (see Chapter Six: "Inquiry Project Sampler"), it is not going to work if the students butt the sticks together edge to edge and think the glue between them is going to hold the bridge together. The artist will know that small paper triangles used as joints might work, or that layering the sticks provides another solution. These ideas are not told to the students; rather, the children are questioned toward finding their own solutions, leaving it open for them to uncover other potential ways to solve the problem. It helps, however, if the educator is aware of possible solutions and troubles that can arise when using various materials.

A school reading specialist might look at the Rebus Story Board (see Chapter Six: "Inquiry Project Sampler") and offer suggestions to slip into the working process. Perhaps students could explore and find the different parts of speech as they pursue the inquiry. Or the specialist might observe that there are not enough magnetic strips containing certain parts of speech (nouns, articles, etc.) available for a child to successfully develop a series of sentences, leading the student to become frustrated and unnecessarily limited.

A school math specialist can help project developers become aware of the concepts with which students in that school are generally having trouble. These might include areas shown as weak in standardized testing, such as perhaps general number sense and estimation skills. This information then inspires new inquiry project possibilities for establishing a transfer experience within this area of study. The Strawberry Basket Challenge (see Chapter Six: "Inquiry Project Sampler") is an example of a project that introduces these particular skill areas following such a consultation.

As new content or curriculum elements are instructionally added to an inquiry experience, the designers maintain the initial objectives of that center. New elements and objectives added to the project can take over! An example of this would be the Magnet Mural (see Chapter Six: "Inquiry Project Sampler") with its initial purpose in the lab being to develop flexible and fluent thinking and open up a student's ability to create two-dimensional images. Asking the child to steer in a specific curriculum direction, however—perhaps asking that the shapes be used to make a representation of an Iroquois Village—might halt growth within the primary objective. The initial purpose of the project needs to be kept clear. Perhaps the Iroquois Village direction could be introduced after the student has had a full experience exploring the primary objective of the project and then weaving in the curriculum content question later: *I love what you did with these shapes today. Tell me about it. OK, I have a question for you. Do you remember the Iroquois Village we studied? Could you also make a village representation using these same shapes?* The ability to be flexible and fluent takes yet another step forward as the curriculum content transfers and becomes personalized by the child.

Avoiding Busy Work

How hard will a child need to think to perform a hands-on task? Consider a child's skill-level development. Are the hands-on skills they use when pursuing a project automatic for them, such as using tape, tying a shoe, cutting along the perimeter of a square? Or are the skills more complex and new, such as weaving a pattern at the loom or folding a complex origami pattern? The latter skills will require the student to engage in higher-level thinking employing Math-Logic and Visual-Spatial intelligences, as well as the habits of mind to Persevere and to Strive to Be Accurate and Precise. For the child at a more developed skill level, the former skills would be better defined as busy work.

Removing the tape from Think It! Do It!, as mentioned earlier, is a good example of heightening the complexity of thinking and doing. Taking away the automatic tasks from a work process and leading students to find alternative ways, as in this case binding objects together without using tape, builds thinking skills and helps avoid the dreaded busy-work syndrome. Granted, meditative time with busy work can be helpful to settle one's thoughts and for reflection. But overall, inquiry time is geared toward stretching skills.

Student Directed

Successful inquiry projects require minimal introduction so that children can begin working with centers right away. These quick starts become essential with larger groups when perhaps as many as fifteen projects are set into action at once. Educators help students move from the initial Focus Theme Circle to their chosen centers with a goal in mind, a challenge, or a quest to rally around. Yet the bulk of instruction unfolds after inquiries are already underway. The goal is to avoid acquiring projects that require a significant amount of upfront instruction or ongoing teacher direction. Students are then able to get off to a good start with their inquiries and are not left in a lurch as educators work with other groups. Some projects, of course, will require more involved skill review and guidance. This is especially true as a new center is introduced to the children, such as working with Spirit Stones or an animation program on the computer (see Chapter Six: "Inquiry Project Sampler," and Appendix I: "Additional Inquiry Possibilities"). The number of these types of projects that are out on the floor at one time then becomes a lab-time management issue for the lead instructor to keep in mind. For example, assigning a visiting specialist or Room Guide to work specifically with students at the new project that first day, before the children are better able to work on their own and assist one another, can be helpful.

Building a Project Inventory

It takes time to build a great inventory of inquiry centers. At the start, for a group of thirty students there should be at least fifteen projects available. Once a base inventory is established, efforts to find and build new ones continue. Some projects will develop after a specific need is identified, such as finding an inquiry that explores simple machines or one that develops group verbal communication. At other times, a director will see a great project idea to add to the inventory while visiting a children's museum or leafing through a catalogue or book of hands-on science projects.

Some of the new projects will be nearly ready to use in the lab simply by taking them out of the box and assembling them as a complete center (see Chapter Eight: "Setting the Open-Inquiry Stage"). Other projects will take weeks to design, construct, or obtain needed parts. In general, inquiry projects are constructivist, problem-based, and team-developmental in orientation, practices for which there are many related resource materials available for support.

Likely, a program's working budget will determine which projects will initially be developed or purchased. If you look at the collection of inquiry projects in the next chapter, some centers cost nearly nothing, such as the Habit of Mind Interview, whereas others have a minimal cost, such as the geodesic dome. A few project centers will require the director to run around collecting items, such as with Think It! Do It!; others will need more significant funds, such as acquiring a good supply of Kapla Blocks. Dream projects may require applying for a grant or saving funds for purchase, such as a sound studio, a computer robotics setup, a stereo microscope, or a full-scale model skeleton.

Checklist for Project Startup

Before spending significant sums of money and time to develop a complete collection of projects, or investing in the bigger-ticket items, start first with a smaller inventory and get students working with their inquiries. As students start exploring, insights begin to unfold regarding which projects will be effective teaching mediums and exciting for the lab. As the early lab time unfolds, observe which projects make sense for the particular developing program, and which ones draw in the students. Evaluate why certain projects are successful, and which ones generate the student's spirit of inquiry. Check that all skill-level needs are sufficiently represented and addressed. Here are a few key guides for finding and developing projects:

- Visit museum discovery rooms for ideas. Observe projects in action and note why you think they work for children. Also be sure to consider maintenance and supply issues.

- Review project ideas from books, catalogs, and Internet sources (see Suggested Readings, and Appendix J: "Potential Suppliers").

- Review Chapter Six, "Inquiry Project Sampler," and Appendix I, "Additional Inquiry Possibilities."

- Look around your space or building and go on your own treasure hunt. What can you find that sparks ideas for projects? Especially in schools, there are often storage closets with items that could use a new home.

- Ask for donations and supplies from the parents, faculty, or community.

- Find a group of volunteers and possible staff collaborators to help as "project scouts." Establish the group as a project design and production team. Assign responsibilities to gather needed items, create graphics and accompanying questioning, and to handle display and shelving needs.

- Start with a collection of projects that allows for many possible challenges, such as Kapla Blocks (see Chapter Six: "Inquiry Project Sampler").

Settling into Project Design and Development

Once an initial inventory is put together and available to students, the next stage of project development begins. Where are the gaps? Do you find you have some children who just don't seem to settle? This problem can be due to a child's inability to self-structure (see Chapter Two: "Project as Medium, Teacher as Coach"), but it may also indicate a gap in the lab's inventory. Making sure there is something for everyone can be as simple as getting out the Multiple Intelligences list and seeing how the program's project inventory supports all the intelligences. Math/logic-oriented children love to see chess, those more verbal are delighted with a dictionary game, a visual-oriented child is drawn to the Magnet Mural, and highly kinetic children love Think It! Do It! All have a place to get started, show their stuff, and generate spirit for the lab. A well-stocked inventory also relieves other lab management issues, including class disruption and maintaining a serious work ethic.

Some intelligences are more difficult to engage in a traditional grade-level classroom, or even in a central lab setup, such as gross motor kinesthetic. However, an instructor can head outside with a small group of students (assuming there is enough coverage in the lab and sufficient adult expertise, as well as a safe environment, to pursue kinesthetic movement). Certainly one can engage fine motor Kinesthetic Intelligence easily in the classroom setting. Another area that is sometimes difficult to support is Musical-Rhythmic Intelligence, because sounds can become too loud and take over the working energy of the lab time. However, there are ways to arrange things, such as using areas of the lab that are a bit removed or that do not project instrument sounds as much.

Students as Project Designers

> *You can make your challenges.*
> —Lab student

Students working in a thinking skills program soon learn that a project must work hard to earn its keep. If it doesn't build a little frustration and demand tough work, it's out of there! Even with the best intentions, some projects simply do not pan out. However, before rejecting the project, open it up for examination with a group of children to see whether it could be the basis for new challenge possibilities. Often the project can be saved with some creative brainstorming.

Positioning students to review projects in this way is good instructional lab practice in general, because it provides students with a greater level of ownership for the lab as they become project designers and innovators. Reviewing a project with the students might proceed as follows:

What skills or thinking dispositions do you feel are developed with this project?

Which ones could it develop? What have you learned here?

Remember lab projects have to earn their keep! I'm not sure about this one!

What could be added or changed with this inquiry to make it more challenging or purposeful?

Is there a way this project could be combined with other inquiries in the lab?

Great! Could you develop those ideas for us! Maybe this project has a chance after all.

The Project Inventory: A Pile of Gold

To the lead lab instructor, the inquiry projects are well known, and a healthy collection of instructional possibilities have been identified for each one. However, for a visiting parent or faculty member hoping to work with the children, the challenges can easily appear overwhelming. They may think to themselves, *What are all these projects? What do you do with this one? What are the content connections? How can I contribute? What questions will I ask?*

A Project Inventory is a valuable resource—a handbook of sorts. It allows the inquiry time to be used successfully by more than just one educator, especially helping those who attend the lab only occasionally, to become more meaningful contributors to the program. Having a developed list of inquiry projects, as in the next chapter's "Inquiry Project Sampler," that displays objectives and goals, major dispositions in action, curriculum links, as well as suggested questioning and conversational ideas, can become an essential lab-time tool.

Visiting parents, staff, and teachers will benefit from a handy resource that helps them to see more quickly the purpose and possibilities of each project. They can sit for a moment with the project listing and gain some quick instructional ideas, or make a curriculum connection, before heading off to work with students. Such guidance can also help folks to switch gears from their other daily responsibilities and instructional formats, thereby allowing them to take part more immediately in the inquiry scene. The project inventory also aids in sending the inquiry program out the door, with those inspired taking project ideas with them and creating centers in their own classrooms or homes.

Inventory Journal for Educators

Extending the project inventory listing into an interactive journal that welcomes ongoing contributions helps involve visiting educators with project design and development. They can add insights and offer ideas, curriculum connections, and new project challenge ideas as the possibilities occur to them. New ideas can be reviewed, and additional comments added, as each educator visits the inquiry room. For programs not in a centralized lab format, ideas can be generated by passing along the journal as the projects are used throughout the school or organization.

Inquiry Project Cards

Another way to employ the inquiry project listing is to take the information for each project and make individualized laminated cards that are then placed with each developed lab center. Students and educators can then easily refer to the cards for basic startup and questioning ideas (see Chapter Eight: "Setting the Open-Inquiry Stage").

The Project as a Place to Start

*When it's raining it would be nice to come to the lab
and explore. It's like being outside.*

— Lab student

In general, as educators observe children working with inquiry projects, they should always be asking themselves the following questions: *What are children experiencing as they explore? What does the time mean to them? How might the experience lead them to learn something new? How can I employ this project, and the students' experience with it, to support the objectives of the inquiry program?* A mindful instructor is on the lookout for opportunities to jump into the inquiry process with dialog and questioning, such as:

This reminds me of something we just studied yesterday in our classroom. Who sees it?

Right, this is all about fractions! Show me how. What learning can you transfer to meet the challenge of this project?

Did you really hear what your partner was saying? Which habit of mind could be helpful to get into action here? I agree, Active Listening! Where else does it make a difference to be an active listener?

What intelligences does this project put into action?

Compare and contrast the process of playing a game of chess and thinking through and designing a wind-generated machine at Think It! Do It! What are the similarities and differences?

Can you combine these two inquiry projects in some way to create a new challenge idea for the lab? Evaluate your effort. What would people likely experience as they work here? What thinking skills and habits of mind will they need to put into action?

OK, I would also like to build a Kapla bridge. Could you give me some advice? Explain to me how your design system works.

Your interest in the geodesic dome appears strong. Let me help you investigate further and research more about Buckminster Fuller. I believe our library has his biography! We also have many books on structures and architecture!

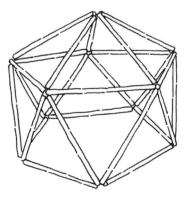

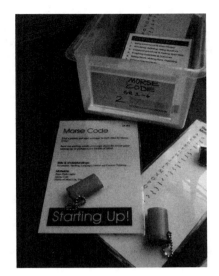

Chapter Six

Inquiry Project Sampler

NOTES ON THE FOLLOWING THIRTY-THREE INQUIRY PROJECTS

The following thirty-three inquiry projects are developed for children in kindergarten through Grade 6. General appropriate grade ranges are suggested, but are flexible, with individuals simply stepping in at their own skill levels.

Each project description provides the following:

- Inquiry Activity

- Materials needed

- Highlighted Goals for Students, including Content Understandings, Intelligences, Cognitive Skills, and Habits of Mind

- Process of working with the inquiry

- Lab-Time Dialogue Possibilities

All inquiries will bend in a variety of directions according to the students' interests, their age and skill levels, and the guidance of instructors. Other possible contents, thinking skills, and dispositions will likely surface as challenges unfold. These project listings are therefore meant as a place to get started. They are open and flexible guides and can be adapted appropriately, depending on the needs at hand. Names of students in Lab-Time Dialogue are added to animate the text and are fictitious.

These relatively short inquiries are designed for children to work on for thirty to forty-five minutes and are available to return to time and time again. For most, students will need the solid thirty to forty-five minutes to make progress and move their inquiries to higher levels. When planning for a lab period, be sure to include the time needed for an initial Opening Circle conversation, cleanup, and a group Reflection Circle.

A more complete Project Inventory of nearly one hundred possibilities, which includes the projects in this sampler (without the extensive description) is found in the Appendix I, Additional Inquiry Possibilities of this book. For easy reference, projects are organized by the dominant thinking areas engaged by each inquiry: Thinking Scientifically; Thinking Visually, Spatially, and Technically; Thinking Verbally and Linguistically; Thinking Musically and Rhythmically; Thinking Mathematically; and Thinking Through Strategy, Games, and Puzzles (see Chapter Eight, "Setting the Open-Inquiry Stage").

Keeping an Eye on Child Safety

All projects require adult supervision and judgment to ensure children's safety. Educators need to review each inquiry project challenge carefully and determine whether its general procedures, and the items included, are safe and appropriate for individual children.

1. ANIMAL TRACKS (*Grades K–6*)

Inquiry Activity

Press rubber casts of actual animal paws, claws, and webbed feet into clay or wet sand to observe, identify, and classify tracks.

Materials

- Soft clay, Play-Doh, or wet sand

- Rubber casts: Animal Tracks Set (search Internet and see Appendix J, Potential Suppliers)

- Book or poster to identify tracks (or make a quick reference poster by printing rubber casts with India Ink onto a large sheet of poster paper and labeling them)

Highlighted Goals for Students

Content Understandings: Animal Species, Identification, Environment and Habitat

Intelligences: Naturalist, Visual-Spatial, Interpersonal, Intrapersonal

Cognitive Skills: Observation, Classify, Similarities/Differences, Synthesize/Apply

Habits of Mind

    Wonder, Explore, and Ask Questions

    Imagine Possibilities and Outcomes

    Use What You Know—Transfer Learning

    Look Carefully

    Support Ideas With Reasons Why

Process

- Students set rubber paw, claw, or web casts into wet sand or soft clay.
- By referring to identification chart, students identify and classify various animal tracks.

Lab-Time Dialogue Possibilities

What are some things that interest you about animal tracks?

What are you wondering about? What are you investigating?

How and why might a live animal track look different in nature (ground moisture, type of soil, age of print, movement of the animal, sticks or leaves in the soil . . .)?

Where have you seen real animal tracks out in the world?

How and why would the American Indians have observed tracks?

What important skill do you need to identify tracks well? Visual Observation! I agree!

When are other times you Look Carefully to understand and gain information?

How would you classify these different tracks? How would you group them?

What are some common characteristics? What are similarities and differences?

What clues do we get from each track about the way each animal lives?

What were the different parts of your inquiry? What steps did you take to meet your goal? What was the process of thinking things through?

What is a habitat? Visualize, put a picture in your mind of each animal's habitat.

Describe the habitat. Yes, you are describing . . .

Where have you learned about habitats before? What understandings can you transfer?

Let's see where I can help you research more about various habitats . . .

2. DRAW WHAT YOU FEEL *(Grades K–6)*

Inquiry Activity

Draw an object by feeling the contours and edges of forms rather than by looking at them.

Materials

- Feel It or Whatzit Box (make or purchase)

    To make: Find a large box or build one out of wood. For both the homemade or purchased box, secure a small chalk board on its top.

    To purchase: Search Internet and see Appendix J, Potential Suppliers.

- Chalk

- Simple to more complex wood shapes, three-dimensional "Find and Feel Shapes" (search Internet and see Appendix J, Potential Suppliers)

Highlighted Goals for Students

Content Understandings: Shapes and Forms, Contour Edge

Intelligences: Naturalist, Visual-Spatial, Intrapersonal

Cognitive Skills: Sensory, Fine Motor, Identification, Analyze, Evaluate

Habits of Mind

> Be Adventurous and Open-Minded
>
> Strive to Be Accurate and Precise
>
> Look Carefully

Process

- One student at a time works with the "Feel It" or "Whatzit Box." Students reach a hand into the box, find an item, and explore carefully the *contour edge* of the shape.

- While the students slowly move the finger of one hand along the contour edge of the object, the line drawn by the other hand moves along at the exact same spot.

- After students draw the shape, they take the item out of the box and compare their drawing to its actual shape.

Lab-Time Dialogue Possibilities

What are ways you collect information (sense of smell, sight, sound, touch . . .)? *Usually when you draw something, you look at the object.*

How are you collecting your information <u>here</u> *to draw the object in the box?*

This is certainly a different way to draw! What does it mean to be open-minded and flexible? How were you open-minded and flexible as you gave this project a try?

To be accurate and precise with your drawing, what do you need to do? Oh, to move your finger very slowly along the edges of the form you are holding to collect the information you need to draw the object on the chalkboard.

Where else do you need to be accurate and precise with your work and activities?

What is a plane? Do you feel a shift in planes?

What is a curve? Do you feel various curves and arches?

Why do you think a person reading a book written in Braille has a well-developed sense of touch? In what other ways would one with limited eyesight depend on the sense of touch to do things?

Perhaps I can help you find some resources about Braille.

From *Nine Thousand Straws: Teaching Thinking Through Open-Inquiry Learning* by Jean Sausele Knodt. Westport, CT: Teacher Ideas Press. Copyright © 2008.

3. FELT BOARD STORY *(Grades K–4)*

Inquiry Activity

Create story ideas with felt pieces, and record the story on a tape recorder.

Materials

- Large felt board (search the Internet and see Appendix J, Potential Suppliers)
- Precut felt pieces offering various story ideas—zoo, farm, underwater or space adventure, city life, etc. (pieces can also be made by instructor or children during lab time; students would then need more time for the project)
- Tape recorder with microphone
- Clipboard
- Beginning, Middle, End Clipboard Graphic (see Appendix Q)
- Pencils

Highlighted Goals for Students

Content Understandings: Creative Writing, Oral Presentation

Intelligences: Verbal-Linguistic, Visual-Spatial, Body-Kinesthetic, Interpersonal, Intrapersonal

Cognitive Skills: Brainstorm, Organize, Plan, Vocabulary, Prewriting, Writing, Oral Communication, Listening, Synthesize, Evaluate

Habits of Mind

Be Adventurous and Open-Minded

Imagine Possibilities and Outcomes

Step Back and Look at the Whole Picture

Communicate Clearly

Process

- One or two students begin formulating ideas for their story at the Felt Board Center. As they develop a story line, they record it in writing (note form) on the clipboard sheet, a beginning, middle, and end.

- Students then refer to their notes and record their story on the tape recorder. Children take turns telling the story. They then listen back to the story they created, amend it, build ideas, and tape again.

Lab-Time Dialogue Possibilities

What are your ideas for a story? How is your brainstorming going?

What are things you can do if you run out of ideas?

How can you help the brainstorming to be more productive and imaginative?

Do you have a picture in your mind? What do you visualize? What do you imagine?

Is there a message you are trying to give in your story?

Can you record ideas for the beginning, middle, and end of your story on the clipboard graphic?

Where are other ways your story could develop? What would happen if . . .

What is the sequence of the story? What steps does it take?

How does your story work as a whole? Step back and look at how the different parts of your story relate to each other. What links could you make to help the story connect?

How have you developed ideas together as a team? How are your ideas similar or different? How do your ideas work together to make a great story?

Have you recorded your story on tape?

What are ways you can organize telling the story as a team?

Let's hear your story on tape. The way you describe . . . makes me feel/think about. . . . What do you like most about your story? Where would you like to see your story develop further?

Where on the tape is your speaking the most clear? Where is your voice the most animated, or playful, with the story? What are ways you can develop further how you tell your story and speak on the tape?

What have been the different parts of your inquiry? What steps did you take to meet your goal? What was the process of thinking things through?

How did you make parts of the process stronger?

Compare your story with (suggest a familiar book or story). *How are they similar? How are they different?*

This story reminds me a little of (suggest book idea). *Shall we see where we can find that book?*

4. FINDING BALANCE (*Grades 2-6*)

Inquiry Activity

Sort and compare various items by their weight. Explore ways to distribute weight and create balance with a tabletop mobile.

Materials

- Tabletop Mobile (see Appendix U: Mobile in Balance Building Instructions)
- Scale (a platform scale and/or a fulcrum balance scale)
- Various items to weigh (for broader range of use and for children's safety, avoid small parts)
- Baggies for placing objects
- Student Lab Project Advice Clipboard Graphic (see Appendix L)

Highlighted Goals for Students

Content Understandings: Weight, Mass, Fractions, Volume and Measurement, Simple Machines, Employ Technology

Intelligences: Math-Logic, Visual-Spatial, Body-Kinesthetic, Interpersonal, Intrapersonal

Cognitive Skills: Fine Motor, Organize, Symmetry, Predict/Hypothesize, Cause/Effect

Habits of Mind

Contribute Positively to the Group and Inspire Teamwork

Set Goals and Make Plans

Use What You Know

Strive to Be Accurate and Precise

Process

- Balance is established with arms of mobile.

- One to three students work with various materials and the scales, sorting groups into whole units and fractions of weight. Weighed items are placed in "baggies" and added to the arms of the standing mobile.

Note: Is the mobile actually balancing? The tell-tale sign is how horizontal the beams settle once the weights are placed.

Lab-Time Dialogue Possibilities

What is your team's strategy for meeting its goals?

Does everyone have a role to perform? How is each team member contributing?

What are some qualities of a great team?

What skills are you using to meet this challenge?

When have you used the skills you are using now? Somewhere else?

What skills and understandings are you "transferring"?

Oh, this mobile is a flop right now, I agree. The whole thing is dragging down.

Let's step back and look at the whole picture. What has to happen to get a mobile in balance? How do the different parts of the mobile relate to each other?

Boy, you really need to use the habit of mind to Be Accurate and Precise with this project! Do you agree? Why? How?

5. FLOOR PLAN (*Grades 3–6*)

Inquiry Activity

Design and draw the floor plan of your dream home.

Materials

- Floor plan templates such as those available with "Young Architects" (search the Internet and see Appendix J, Potential Suppliers)

- 14 × 20 inch or larger heavy white paper or graph paper to create a grid for scale

- Paper for thumbnail sketches

- Pencils

Highlighted Goals for Students

Content Understandings: Perspective, Mapping, Measurement

Intelligences: Visual-Spatial, Math-Logic, Intrapersonal

Cognitive Skills: Fine Motor, Visual Observation, Brainstorm, Spatial Reasoning, Research, Synthesize, Design, Evaluate

Habits of Mind

      Be Adventurous and Open-Minded

      Imagine Possibilities and Outcomes

      Think Independently

      Use What You Know

      Step Back and Look at the Whole Picture

From *Nine Thousand Straws: Teaching Thinking Through Open-Inquiry Learning* by Jean Sausele Knodt
Westport, CT: Teacher Ideas Press. Copyright © 2008.

Process

- Students work at the inquiry center independently or in a two-person team.

- Students brainstorm and do thumbnail sketches to explore design ideas. When ready, children begin working with templates and draw their floor plan design on the larger paper.

- Students look at architectural furniture representations and design the interior of their rooms.

- Children can easily work back into their drawing at later times, even without the templates.

Lab-Time Dialogue Possibilities

What space do you imagine? What do you visualize?

What picture do you have in your mind for your floor plan?

What steps are you taking to explore this inquiry and meet your challenge?

Are you being Open-Minded and Adventurous as you come up with ideas for your building? How? Let's hear your ideas!

Where else does it help to brainstorm and come up with flexible ideas as you work?

What sort of things do you like to do in your life? How will the living space you design include those things you like to do or that are important to you?

Who else lives with you? What are their needs? How will your home help you share times and activities together?

How do you get from space to space? How do your spaces connect and make sense in their arrangement? How are you Stepping Back and Looking at the Whole Picture of how your floor plan works?

What point of view are you taking when you make a floor plan like this?

Have you talked about perspective before? When? What is the "bird's-eye view" perspective?

What does the word "scale" mean? What is the scale of your floor plan? How does this map reference scale? (Show example).

How does the map show North, South, East, and West?

How could you position your floor plan in terms of direction?

If you added a courtyard in the middle of your floor plan, how would your design change?

How could a courtyard affect the light coming into the house?

Let's research floor plans of actual architects, and collect ideas.

6. GEODESIC DOME *(Grades 3–6)*

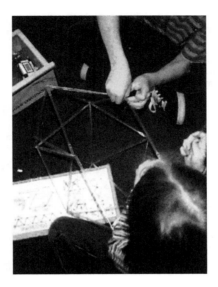

Inquiry Activity

Build a geodesic dome with straws and paperclips.

Materials

- Straws
- Paper clips
- Geodesic Dome Nonverbal Instructions (see Appendix W)
- Pictures of dome structures and triangular braces in architecture

Highlighted Goals for Students

Content Understandings: Geometry, Structures, Architecture, Inventors, Engineering Technology, Design Technology

Intelligences: Math-Logic, Visual-Spatial, Naturalist, Body-Kinesthetic, Interpersonal, Intrapersonal

Cognitive Skills: Fine Motor, Symmetry, Organize, Construction, Visualize Outcomes, Plan Strategy, Perceive Patterns, Sequence, Research

Habits of Mind

Use What You Know

Strive to Be Accurate and Precise

Support Ideas With Reasons Why

Persevere

Process

- One or two students work to look carefully at instructions and build the geodesic dome by following the clues from the instruction sheet.

Variation

Design another structure by employing triangles.

Lab-Time Dialogue Possibilities

What steps are you taking to explore this inquiry and meet the challenge? What is the process?

Why do you think triangles work so well for making a dome?

Why do you think triangles are so strong?

Try making a square with the straws and compare what happens to the shape.

How could you make the square become steady (show triangle braces in buildings)?

Everything you need to know to build the geodesic dome is in the illustration. Certainly you need to employ the habit of mind to Look Carefully!

I think you are all set to work well. I'm going to leave for a while and see how you go about this task. Take it one step at a time. See how well you can manage the effort. If you get stuck, first review what we have talked about and try again.

Have there been any frustrating parts to this challenge? How are you dealing with your frustration?

What other things can people do if they get frustrated with a project or activity?

Have you ever been on a geodesic dome (often on playgrounds)?

What advice would you give someone about building a geodesic dome?

What does it mean to be accurate? What does it mean to be precise? In what ways were you being accurate and precise as you built the dome? Where are other places you need to be accurate and precise as you work or do activities?

What if we went through nine thousand straws to make domes and other triangular structures? Let's imagine that all the structures were domes. How many domes would nine thousand straws make? I'm also curious! How many paper clips would we use? Transfer what you know, and figure it out!

What other modular structures could you make with triangles?

Could your team do some research on Buckminster Fuller, the inventor of the geodesic dome? As you research, could you explore how domes were built before the geodesic dome was invented?

You could also research the use of triangular forms in classical Roman and Greek architecture and structures. Would you give us a short report at our next lab period?

Resource

Zubrowski, B., and Fleischer, S. (1981). *Messing Around With Drinking Straw Construction.* Boston: Little, Brown & Company.

---

7. HABITS OF MIND INTERVIEW (*Grades 3–6*)

Inquiry Activity

Using a microphone and tape recorder, interview individuals to see which habits of mind are in action.

Materials

- Microphone and tape recorder
- Video camera
- Clipboard
- Pencils
- Habits of Mind Student Reference Sheet (see Appendix V)

Highlighted Goals for Students

Content Understandings: Conducting a Survey, Data Collection, Analysis, Graphing

Intelligences: Interpersonal, Intrapersonal, Verbal-Linguistic, Math-Logic

Cognitive Skills: Data Analysis, Form Relevant Questions, Organize, Vocabulary, Oral Communication, Interview, Listen, Visualize Outcomes, Predict, Brainstorm, Plan Strategy, Perceive Patterns, Analyze and Evaluate

Habits of Mind

Wonder, Explore, and Ask Questions

Imagine Possibilities and Outcomes

Set Goals and Make Plans

Listen Actively

Communicate Clearly

Understand Others

From *Nine Thousand Straws: Teaching Thinking Through Open-Inquiry Learning* by Jean Sausele Knodt
Westport, CT: Teacher Ideas Press. Copyright © 2008.

Process

- One to three students take a careful look at the Habits of Mind Student Reference Sheet or poster (see Appendix V).

- Students make a plan and brainstorm a questioning approach for their interviews that focus on the habits of mind. Students then walk around the lab while projects are underway, ask questions, and record their interviews.

- Students uncover what habits of mind other lab students feel are in action and which ones they need to put into action. Interviewers probe for elaboration.

- Students then compile information and prepare a report for Reflection Circle time. Students can also graph results.

- Students find a couple of sound clips from student recordings to illustrate findings.

Variation

Video Camera Interview

Lab-Time Dialogue Possibilities

What sorts of questions can you ask in your interview to uncover how others are aware of habits of mind and how they employ them?

Take some time to brainstorm as you develop and design your questions. How long do you think you should take? Maybe a bit longer than that! By the way, why do you think taking time to brainstorm is a worthwhile effort?

Imagine possibilities and outcomes with your questioning.

In what ways could it help to imagine the likely outcomes—what people might say or how they might respond—when designing great survey questions?

How can you design questions so that you move beyond getting "yes" or "no" answers in your survey? Analyze your list of questions before you start interviewing.

What are your plans for setting out and asking questions to the group?

How are you listening actively to others as they speak? What does it mean to be an active listener?

Now that you have some information from the lab students, how will you organize the information to give us at the Reflection Circle?

Are you finding all the habits of mind in action? Which are employed the most? Which habits are used less often?

Which sound clips do you think are most insightful? Which will you cue up for us to hear at Reflection Circle?

How will the three of you take turns presenting your report? Think about your presentation. How about practicing once or twice. What ways will you use to report and communicate your findings clearly?

(To Group) In what ways does this report, given to us by Nicholas and Fritz, help us understand each other and ourselves as a group, as a team?

What have been the different parts of your inquiry? What steps did you take to meet your goals?

8. HIEROGLYPHS HABITS OF MIND *(Grades 3–6)*

Inquiry Activity

Write out a couple of habits of mind in Hieroglyph: the habit you think you employ most often, and one you want to work on and develop.

Materials

- Habits of Mind Student Reference Sheet (see Appendix V)
- Hieroglyphs reference chart
- Brown mailing paper roll
- Pencils
- Black Sharpie pens

Highlighted Goals for Students

Content Understandings: Historic World Culture, Symbols, Language

Intelligences: Verbal-Linguistic, Visual-Spatial, Interpersonal, Intrapersonal

Cognitive Skills: Fine Motor, Compare and Contrast, Visual Observation, Analyze and Evaluate

Habits of Mind

    Think Independently

    Step Back and Look at the Whole Picture

    Look Carefully

    Understand Others

Process

- Together in a group (could be the entire class) students review the habits of mind poster. Students consider which dispositions they are most connected to, and which they feel they need to develop.
- Students then work individually.
- Referring to the hieroglyphs chart, students write out (in hieroglyphs) first the habit of mind they feel most connected to, and second the habit of mind they have chosen to develop.

- Students begin making hieroglyphs by first drawing each character with pencil onto the brown mailing paper and then drawing over the pencil with a black Sharpie pen. *Note:* It's difficult for children to draw contours of the image if they work small. Each symbol should be three to four inches high.

Variations

Communicate with sign language, Morse code, or Braille

Variation with Morse Code: Two students take turns communicating one word or phrase at a time with flashlights (use "doorbell"-like press with an easy on/off button). Possibilities include a class weekly spelling list, terms from the habits of mind, the Multiple Intelligences, or perhaps Words for Thinking and Doing (see Appendix N).

Lab-Time Dialogue Possibilities

Step back and look at the whole picture—the whole picture of you!

Which habits of mind do you find are regularly part of your thinking and doing?

Which can you usually depend on to be active?

What are some examples of how you use that habit of mind?

Which habits are you trying to build? Which do you feel you need to develop?

What are ways you can build those habits to become stronger?

How will those habits of mind help your thinking and doing? How will they make a difference?

As you work on your hieroglyphs, take it slowly and steady with the contour edge. What is a contour? Point to the contour edge on the hieroglyph you are working with.

What are the different habits of mind highlighted by the group today? Is there much diversity?

How can diversity be helpful when solving problems or working on a project together?

How does it help you understand others to know which habits of mind they feel most connected to and which they want to work on?

What have been the different parts of your inquiry? What steps did you take to meet your goal?

Variations

Children can work on papyrus with scribe pens or brushes, and red and black ink (search for nontoxic inks).

Source

Connecticut Library Consortium (Decorative Decodes—Hieroglyphics): http://www.ctlibrarians. org/events/roundtables/childrens4/wdsr/manual_activities.html

9. HOW DOES THIS DO THAT? THE FOUNTAIN CONNECTION AND CARTESIAN DIVER *(Grades K–6)*

Inquiry Activity

Take a close look and come up with ideas. How do the Fountain Connection and Cartesian Diver work? Diagram the ideas.

Materials

- "Fountain Connection" (search the Internet and see Appendix J, Potential Suppliers)
- "Cartesian Diver" (search the Internet and see Appendix J, Potential Suppliers)
- Three large soda bottles
- Hole punched 8.5 × 11 inch white drawing paper
- Notebook or clipboard to display student work records
- Pencils
- Clipboard and graphic, Analyze It! How Does This Do That?! (see Appendix M3)

Highlighted Goals for Students

Content Understandings: Physical Properties and Phenomenon, Technology

Intelligences: Naturalist, Visual-Spatial, Verbal-Linguistic, Intrapersonal, Interpersonal

Cognitive Skills: Spatial Reasoning, Brainstorm, Investigate, Visual Observation, Oral Communication, Form Concepts, Diagram Findings, Observe and Record a System, Form Relevant Questions, Analyze and Evaluate, Research

Be Adventurous and Open-Minded

Wonder, Explore, and Ask Questions

Think Independently

Look Carefully

Support Ideas With Reasons Why

Persevere

Process

- One or two students observe the action of the Fountain Connection and the Cartesian Diver. Students then document what they think is going on through diagrams and written notation.

- Students offer their ideas to the project's challenge clipboard or notebook.

Lab-Time Dialogue Possibilities

When you put pressure on the Cartesian Diver bottle, what do you see happen? Describe what you see. What could that pressure be doing to the small bottle inside?

How and why does the small bottle inside submerge? I hear you saying . . .

What would happen if the small bottle inside was closed at the end instead of open as it is?

Describe what you see happening with the Fountain Connection.

When you turn over the Fountain Connection bottle, how do you think the water moves up the straw and spurts out? What do you see in the straw with the water going up?

Stick with it, this thinking will take Perseverance!

Compare and contrast the Fountain Connection with the Cartesian Diver. How are these two things similar? How are they different?

How can you support your ideas and findings with facts and reasons? Here are some resources about the Cartesian Diver and the Fountain Connection. Let's research this.

How does it help your thinking when you search for and support your ideas with facts and reasons?

Add your ideas to the project notebook/clipboard!

10. HOW MUCH IS THAT VEGETABLE IN THE WINDOW? *(Grades K–3)*

Inquiry Activity

Set up the store, establish a price list, get some bags, and sell some groceries!

Materials

- Store Front Center (search the Internet and see Appendix J, Potential Suppliers)
- Assortment of plastic or wooden vegetables, fruit, and other store items
- Play money
- Price lists of various skill levels, or help students create their own list (see Appendix R)
- Store Sum Student Worksheet clipboard graphic to compute sums (see Appendix R)

Highlighted Goals for Students

Content Understandings: Math Computation, Percent, Fractions, Food Groups

Intelligences: Math-Logic, Interpersonal, Naturalist

Cognitive Skills: Number Sense, Organize a System, Classify, Analyze and Evaluate

Habits of Mind

    Set Goals and Make Plans

    Use What You Know

    Strive to Be Accurate and Precise

Process

- Two or three students work at this center.

- Objects are organized and a price list is established. The educator helps children develop an appropriate price list or has previously created a series of different lists appropriate to various skill levels.

- One child works as the cashier and the other(s) as the customer(s). Children start by buying no more than five items at one time (or fewer as necessary).

- To advance the math further, students work with multiplication (three for $2.35), or finding percent off of the final sum (5%, 10%, 25%).

- After the customers have selected their items, the teller and the customers work together to compute the sums due. The customer then gives the exact sum of money due or gets change back from teller.

Variations

- Include a review of the food groups. Have containers available to sort the different foods.

- Select the ripest apple! Provide digital photos of various fruits and vegetables in various forms of freshness. Place photos in sequential order. *Which apple would you buy, and why?*

- Work with fractions using parts of the fruits, vegetables, or pizza.

Note: This center requires a close watch by the lab educator. Children often want to get to the store, but not necessarily to add sums and exchange money precisely.

Lab-Time Dialogue Possibilities

What do you like most about working at the store? Oh, organizing things. Making lists! Where else do you work in that way?

What are the needs here? Oh, I know everything is a mess!

You both want to be the store teller? What are ways in which you can work this out?

What are ways you are organizing the buying and selling of grocery items?

Who is adding the sums? Perhaps you should both check to see if you get the same sum!

Are you offering the exact amount due or getting back change?

How are you being accurate and precise at the store today?

How could you classify or sort these different items at our store (examples: by food groups, things processed and packaged, items grown)?

11. "IMPOSSIBLE" SPIRAL! *(Grades 2–6)*

Inquiry Activity

Solve the puzzle of the Kapla Block Complex Spiral.

Materials

- Kapla Blocks (search the Internet and see Appendix J, Potential Suppliers)
- Picture of Complex Kapla Block Spiral (in Kapla project pamphlet)

Highlighted Goals for Students

Content Understandings: Systems, Structures, Number Sense, Unit Measurement, Two and Three Dimensions, Design Technology

Intelligences: Visual-Spatial, Math-Logic, Body-Kinesthetic, Intrapersonal, Interpersonal

Cognitive Skills: Spatial Reasoning, Design, Fine Motor, Symmetry, Estimation, Computation, Visual Observation, Construction, Brainstorm, Predict, Plan Strategy, Perceive Patterns, Visualize Outcomes, Research

Habits of Mind

Be Adventurous and Open-Minded

Think Independently

Step Back and Look at the Whole Picture

Look Carefully

Process

- One student or a team of two students begins working by first observing carefully the photo of the Complex Spiral, as seen in the Kapla Blocks introductory project pamphlet.

- With no written instructions and by just looking at the picture, students begin to solve the problem of how to build the structure.

- Students are told there is a system to understand and that they will build with a series of "units."

- Students can start by observing the Single Spiral (one block rotating in spiral) and how it might give clues to building the Complex Spiral (four blocks rotating in spiral).

- Students research spiral formations in nature.

Lab-Time Dialogue Possibilities

No, it's not impossible! Would we send you off to do the impossible?!

Glad you asked for help instead of leaving the project! This is a good challenge, a good place to deal with frustration and persevere.

Let's Step Back and Look at the Whole Picture. Perhaps you can uncover a system.

Look at the Single Spiral (in which one block on each level rotates up in spiral).

What are the parts of the spiral? How do the parts connect—what do they do?

What is a unit? Right, it is a single measure of something.

Well, in the Single Spiral we have made, what is the unit (a single Kapla Block)?

Let's look at the Complex Spiral. Compare and contrast it to the Single Spiral. What is the same, and what is different? Let's be open-minded and adventurous and use brainstorming skills!

Who has an idea to offer? Can you restate your idea, Sharon? It sounds like a new way for us to look at this challenge. I hear you saying . . .

Who can add to that idea or offer a new one?

Boy, this challenge certainly demands one to Look Carefully!

In the photograph of the Complex Spiral, how many blocks do you observe in one level?

The Complex Spiral is also made of one unit, repeating for each level. It is different however, in that there are more blocks on each level, in each unit.

What if we could look on the other side, which, in a way we can because of the spiral. Do you see shifts in the way the blocks appear in each level? Do the blocks all run along flat, or do they shift?

I'm going to leave you for a while. Let's see what you can come up with for your unit design on the Complex Spiral.

Looks good! (Or) Still struggling? Let's take another look, and review.

Right! That's it! Now how are you going to build your Complex Spiral with this unit?

Well, how did you do it with the Single Spiral?

There you go! You ought to add your names to the project's Challenge Clipboard!

Sure feels good to meet a challenge like this!

Could you apply these ideas and design another Kapla unit that repeats in a spiral?

Where in nature do we see spirals? Where could we find some possible resources to explore?

12. MAGNET MURAL *(Grades K–6)*

Inquiry Activity

Create images with a variety of colorful freeform (Calder-, Miró-, or Matisse-like) magnetic mural shapes.

Materials

- Sheets or rolls of flexible, white, vinyl magnet (can be found at a sign company—like the material that magnetic poetry is made of; search the Internet and see Appendix J, Potential Suppliers)

(Or) Sheets of various colored magnetic vinyl (primary and secondary colors, and black)

- Large magnetic board (at least 20 × 30 inches, a magnetic dry erase board or chalkboard works well)

- Set of magnetic shapes in variety of sizes and colors (see Appendix S)

Making Magnetic Shapes

- See illustration of magnet shapes (see Appendix S).

- Draw outlines of various shapes on the magnet sheet. Organic shapes should vary in size, from three to twelve inches. Paint shapes with various colors of acrylic paint. Keep the painting loose and brushy, but not thick. When paint is fully dry, cut out shapes. Or, draw and cut shapes out of colored vinyl magnetic sheets.

Highlighted Goals for Students

Content Understandings: Creating Images, Abstract and Representational, Properties of Color, Positive and Negative Space

Intelligences: Visual-Spatial, Intrapersonal, Interpersonal

Cognitive Skills: Organize, Brainstorm, Fluency and Flexibility, Visualize Possibilities, Spatial Reasoning, Synthesize Ideas and Information, Design, Evaluate

Habits of Mind

    Be Adventurous and Open-Minded

    Imagine Possibilities and Outcomes

    Think Independently

Process

One or two students begin making a mural with magnetic pieces. As they work, educators interact and ask questions.

Lab-Time Dialogue Possibilities

Do you love to draw and paint? Do you love to create images? I can tell.

Tell me about your mural. Tell me about your ideas.

Before you started working on the mural, did you have a picture in your mind? Did you visualize an image? What possibilities did you imagine?

In what ways did your ideas grow as you worked? What new possibilities did you discover?

Does your mural tell a story?

What other mural images can you imagine and create with the same pieces?

How flexible is your thinking today? Is it like a rubber band?

Where else do you need to be flexible with your thinking and doing?

Is your mural image "representational"? Does it show forms that look like familiar things, such as a human shape, chair, or flower?

Is your mural image "abstract"? Are these designs that don't look representational, but have shapes and color in various patterns or formations?

Does your abstract image give a feeling? What do you feel?

When I look at your image, I think of . . .

Where are the negative spaces in your mural? Where are the positive spaces?

How could you sort the pieces? What common groups are there?

What was your process for creating different mural images?

From *Nine Thousand Straws: Teaching Thinking Through Open-Inquiry Learning* by Jean Sausele Knodt
Westport, CT: Teacher Ideas Press. Copyright © 2008.

13. MULTIPLE INTELLIGENCES PHOTO JOURNALISTS *(Grades 3–6)*

Inquiry Activity

Interview your partner. How are they developing *all* their intelligences? Take their picture with the digital camera to add to your interview sheet.

Materials

- Polaroid or digital camera and printer
- Clipboard
- Pencils
- MI Student Interview Clipboard Graphic (see Appendix T)

Highlighted Goals for Students

Content Understandings: Human Behavior and Intelligence, Digital and Computer Technology

Intelligences: Verbal-Linguistic, Visual-Spatial, Interpersonal, Intrapersonal

Cognitive Skills: Organize, Collect Data, Interview, Oral Communication, Listening, Form Relevant Questions, Record Information, Analyze and Evaluate

Habits of Mind

Wonder, Explore, and Ask Questions

Think Independently

Communicate Clearly

Understand Others

Process

- Students pair up, take each other's digital photos, and gain help as needed to print out the photos. Each photo is then mounted on an interview sheet.

- Students begin interviewing each other and record specific examples of how multiple intelligences are in action in their lives (examples: swimming class every Tuesday, writing in class journal, listening, drawing, nature walk with family, piano lessons on Saturday with practice every day).

Variation

This can be an individual self-reflection project. The students would need help having their photos taken.

Lab-Time Dialogue Possibilities

How do you see the intelligences in action on these mind map sheets?

Any surprises? Did you know James loves to draw? What other things about James have you learned?

Which of your intelligences are you interested in helping to grow?

What activities can you think of to help develop that intelligence?

How do different intelligences work together to get something done? Example: If you are making a book report and designing a new cover to go with the report, which intelligences will you put into action?

What is something you love to do? What intelligences work together when you pursue that activity?

Look at both your Multiple Intelligences interviews. What are the similarities and differences?

Are there any intelligences not in action? It looks to me like you are both using and developing all of them!

Source

The New City School. (1994). *Celebrating With Multiple Intelligences: Teaching for Success.* St. Louis, MO: The New City School.

14. MIRROR SYMMETRY *(Grades K–6)*

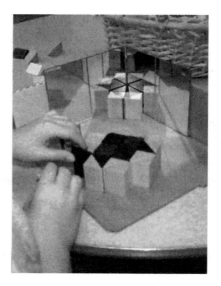

Inquiry Activity

Build block patterns while looking at them in an angled mirror.

Materials

For the Corner of the Room

- Two large safety mirrors, Plexiglas, approximately 2 × 4 feet (mount against wall in a corner)
- Large floor color pattern blocks (available from various suppliers, or it can be made of foam or carpet)

Tabletop Version

- Haba Mirror Project (or two tabletop size, Plexiglas mirrors, hinged)
- Haba Pattern Blocks or other colored wooden geometric blocks (search the Internet and see Appendix J, Potential Suppliers)
- New Lab Challenge Idea! Clipboard Graphic (see Appendix K)

Highlighted Goals for Students

Content Understandings: Symmetry, Geometry

Intelligences: Visual-Spatial, Math-Logic, Intrapersonal, Interpersonal

Cognitive Skills: Fine Motor, Visual Observation, Spatial Reasoning, Design, Visualize Outcomes, Analyze

Habits of Mind

Use What You Know

Strive to Be Accurate and Precise

Look Carefully

Persevere

Process

This project can be developed on a smaller scale for tabletop use, or larger for work on the floor.

Tabletop: Using colored pattern blocks and two small Plexiglas mirrors
Floor: Using large Plexiglas mirrors mounted at right angles in the corner of a room, and large colored pattern blocks

- Students work at center in groups of two to three. A student can also work individually.

- Students first create a pattern by placing geometric shapes that they can observe in the angled mirror (move up to edge of mirror with shapes). Pattern should be only one layer deep with pieces. It's best if the shapes fit in against a right-angled mirror (the size of the pieces determines the angle at which the mirror should be set). Younger children can start with making patterns against just one mirror.

- After the challenge pattern is designed, students then build the pattern they see in the angled mirror (with separate identical pieces) on the floor or the tabletop while referring back to the mirror image as they work.

Note: Be sure to obtain enough pattern pieces. If you place one blue piece in the right-angled mirror, then four additional identical blue pieces will be needed to build the entire reflected pattern. Also, the size of the pattern pieces will change the angle at which the mirrors need to be set because the pieces need to fit directly up against the edge and into the corner of the two joined mirrors.

Lab-Time Dialogue Possibilities

What do you see in the mirrors' reflection?

Look at this one piece again. What colors do you see on the right side of the piece?

Now look again at the pattern you are building. Does it look the same? Yes, I see a different shape there, as well . . .

This project is a real test for critical observation!

Where else is Looking Carefully important? Where else do you use the skill of seeing critically and observing visually in school, at home, in the community, and in other things you do?

What are some adult jobs where Looking Carefully is important?

What do Looking Carefully and Listening Actively have in common?

At what angle are the mirrors set?

What is "symmetry"?

Where have you worked with the concept of symmetry before? How about sports and symmetry? How are our bodies symmetrical?

Where else in nature do you see symmetry? Where in nature do you not see symmetry?

15. NAIL CHALLENGE *(Grades 2–6)*

Inquiry Activity

Solve the puzzle: suspend six nails on the head of one mounted vertical nail. None of the six suspended nails can touch the wood base.

Materials

- Seven large, eight-pound nails with no sharp points (filed down)
- Wood cutting board, 12 × 9 inch thick
- Or find a wood alternative for the Wooden Nail Challenge puzzle (search the Internet and see Appendix J, Potential Suppliers)
- Sketch paper
- Pencils

Highlighted Goals for Students

Content Understandings: Structures, Physics, Balance

Intelligences: Intrapersonal, Math-Logic, Body-Kinesthetic, Interpersonal, Visual-Spatial

Cognitive Skills: Fine Motor, Spatial Reasoning, Visualize Possibilities, Brainstorm

Habits of Mind

Be Adventurous and Open-Minded

Wonder, Explore, and Ask Questions

Contribute Positively to the Group and Inspire Teamwork

Persevere

Communicate Clearly

Understand Others

Process

- Students work on one of two versions:

1. Large eight-pound nails (with points well filed down)

2. Wooden Nail Challenge Puzzle, found from a supply company

- One to three students discuss ideas and draw possibilities on a clipboard. The teacher aids by giving leading questions, but not the solution. It's OK if the solution takes a few inquiry visits to accomplish.

Lab-Time Dialogue Possibilities

It's not impossible?! We've seen it done! I can't show or tell you, but there are a few guiding ideas and questions to offer. This is a worthwhile project to stick with—to deal with frustration and Persevere.

First of all, you certainly need to brainstorm ideas and be Open-Minded.

How flexible can you be with your thinking?

This project requires rubber-band thinking for sure! Ready? Here we go.

What is the head of the nail designed to do? What is its traditional purpose?

With this puzzle, you have to brainstorm about what else the head of a nail can be used for other than for what it was intended. Any ideas? Why don't you fiddle with this question for a while?

Imagine what might happen if you use the nails in another way.

What did you come up with? Hmmm. You have some ideas that are headed in the right direction.

Review those ideas again. Try communicating the ideas as clearly as you can.

I'm curious, what are the different ways in which you see each of your team partners think through ideas? Oh, Kyle likes to draw out concepts, which makes the ideas clear for all to see. Nicholas is quiet but then adds an important idea just at the right moment.

What do the words "system" and "structure" mean to you? This puzzle requires you to think about creating a structure with the nails. It's not going to work if you try to just balance one nail on top of the other like pancakes. That system won't work. If you do this puzzle correctly, you will be able to wiggle the wood board a bit, but the structure will not fall. Maybe you could think about that and the idea about the head of the nail a bit more, and possibly make some drawings. Try again.

What does the word "cradle" mean to you? In this puzzle, one nail ends up looking as if it's being cradled by the other five. Try again. Sketch again. Think of a system, think of structure, and certainly think of what the head of the nail can do!

Have you explored the idea of an X formation? How could you balance two X formations on either side of one horizontal nail? Now that's a big clue. I have to go before I say more!

How did brainstorming and working together help you stay with this project and persevere?

What else helps you to stick with a tough challenge?

Note: First graders have solved this puzzle without the above questioning, and some sixth graders needed more help. This is a big eye-opener for educators to observe students' spatial reasoning capacity and stamina.

Safety Note: The puzzle base needs to be bolted onto a working table or counter surface so that it is not carried around the room by children. The vertical nail is a hazard. Use the actual nail version of project only with children capable of handling nails responsibly and safely.

16. NAME THAT BONE! BUILD THAT BONE! *(Grades 2–6)*

Inquiry Activity

Label the bones of the life-size plastic skeleton with identification tags.

Materials

- Full-scale plastic human skeleton on standing base (search the Internet and see Appendix J, Potential Suppliers)
- Reference chart of names of bones
- Laminated labels of names of bones with punched holes at top, or add another dimension by having children write the words out themselves and make their own labels
- Pipe cleaners to twist labels on the identified bone
- Clay
- Cardboard or trays
- Dictionary
- *Name That Bone! Clipboard Graphic* (see Appendix Y)

Highlighted Goals for Students

Content Understandings: Living Systems, Working in Three Dimensions

Intelligences: Verbal-Linguistic, Naturalist, Visual-Spatial, Body-Kinesthetic, Interpersonal, Intrapersonal

Cognitive Skills: Organize, Phonics, Vocabulary, Reference, Identification, Perceive Patterns, Visual Observation, Fine Motor, Spatial Reasoning, Analyze and Evaluate

Habits of Mind

Use What You Know

Strive to be Accurate and Precise

Look Carefully

Listen Actively

Communicate Clearly

Process

- One to three students refer to the chart of a human skeleton and label the bones of a standing skeleton with identification tags (attached by pipe cleaners).

Variation

- Students build a bone, or a series of bones, in clay, mount bones on corrugated cardboard, and then identify bones by writing names directly on cardboard. Hand and feet bones are best to work with. Some bones, especially the skull bones, are too complicated or involved for one period.

- This variation builds on direct observation. Students are encouraged to slow down, look closely, and build the subtle shifts and changes in planes of bones. They should look at how the bones get narrower and then wider in places. No rolling clay into tubes for fingers and feet!

Lab-Time Dialogue Possibilities

Boy, I agree these are tough words to say. We don't see words like this every day! This will certainly employ your knowledge of phonetics!

What are ways to sound out a word like this? What parts of the word do you see?

Let's check the phonetic pronunciation in the dictionary.

How many bones can you identify on our plastic skeleton?

As you build the hand bones with clay, what helps make your work more successful? Oh, take just one section at a time . . .

By the way, what is a plane? Can you point to the shifts in planes on the bone?

Imagine your eye is traveling the surface like an ant, moving up, and down, and over the edges and planes. Look and build slowly.

Compare the human skeleton with this picture of a (bird, dog, or horse) skeleton. How are they similar. How are they different?

Which part of the human skeleton has the most parts?

What do the different parts of the skeleton help us do? How do the parts function?

How do different parts protect us? What if we did not have joints?

As you work with this project, which habits of mind do you think you have in action, and how? Certainly I agree, you are Looking Carefully and Striving to Be Accurate and Precise!

How can looking slowly and carefully and being precise, such as you are doing here, help your other work or activities?

What professions require careful and exact work with observation skills like the ones you used here? Yes, my dentist is good at visual observation, too! Thank goodness for that!

What could be another goal for this center?

Note: When students first come into the lab and see the skeleton, be sure to let them know that the skeleton is made out of plastic. Many children will think it's real.

17. PEOPLE AND PIPES *(Grades 2–6)*

Inquiry Activity

In a group of five to ten people, find a way to get one golfball through each of the provided pipes in sequential order, while each person holds only one pipe. Pipes and hands cannot touch one another!

Materials

- Fifteen or more PVC pipes of various lengths (diameter should easily allow a golf ball to roll though; PVC pipes are available in hardware stores, and many will cut the lengths for you; file and smooth pipe edges)

- Golf ball

- Metal bucket (so that it makes a ding! sound)

Highlighted Goals for Students

Content Understandings: Force, Motion, Energy, Citizenship, Simple Machines, Design Technology

Intelligences: Interpersonal, Math-Logic, Verbal-Linguistic, Visual-Spatial, Intrapersonal

Cognitive Skills: Fine Motor, Spatial Reasoning, Organization, Brainstorm, Fluency and Flexibility, Oral Communication, Listening, Visualize Outcomes, Plan Strategy, Synthesize Ideas, Analyze and Evaluate

Habits of Mind

Be Adventurous and Open-Minded

Contribute Positively to the Group and Inspire Teamwork

Think Independently

Listen Actively

Communicate Clearly

Process

- Five to ten students are given guidance by the educator about the specifics of the challenge. Stress to children that no pipes or hands can touch each other. Golf ball must get through every pipe in sequential order. (Start with smaller groups of students.)

- At first, group problem solving is likely to be disorganized, confusing, and frustrating for students. Students experience the struggle for a while, then the educator steps in to gear discussions toward uncovering how listening and sharing ideas and leadership will help the working dynamic. Teachers do not organize the group but rather guide its members to organize themselves. The goal is for the students to discover ways "to get their own act together" and have success finding solutions.

Lab-Time Dialogue Possibilities

Well, how is it going? (Terrible! No one is listening! It's a disaster!)

Yes, I see a lot of frustration!

Where are the problems? What is working here so far?

What are some things that help team members work well together?

What are aspects of good team work?

Have you taken time to brainstorm together? Are you aware of each other's ideas?

Is everyone able to present his or her ideas clearly?

Is everyone open to others' ideas and interests?

Are you Listening Actively to each other?

Is everyone committed to solving the problem? How can you become committed? How can you help others to become committed?

Are you willing to share leadership? How will you share tasks?

What are ways you can come up with a group plan?

Good luck! Let's see if you can solve the problem now!

Source

Sikes, S. (1995). *Feeding the Zircon Gorilla and Other Team Building Activities.* Tulsa, OK: Learning Unlimited.

18. REBUS STORY BOARD *(Grades K–6)*

Inquiry Activity

Create a story using both pictures and words. Make a Rebus story.

Materials

- Magnetic words (search the Internet and see Appendix J, Potential Suppliers)

- Rebus pictures are made of photographs of people, places, pets, and things that are mounted on stiff cards and then laminated. Magnetic strips are then put on the back of the cards. Instructors can also make Rebus pictures by drawing images directly on magnetic vinyl material with a Sharpie pen and then cutting around the contour of the image (blank magnetic sheets are available through sign companies and other suppliers). Students can also create and draw their own Rebus images on white construction paper or illustration board, which are then cut out and mounted by the instructor (as needed) onto the surface of a larger-sized flat magnet with double-sided tape. A student resource bin of images can be established.

- Large magnetic surface, like a chalkboard or dry erase board

Highlighted Goals for Students

Content Understandings: Creative Writing, Parts of Speech

Intelligences: Verbal-Linguistic, Visual-Spatial, Interpersonal, Intrapersonal

Cognitive Skills: Organize, Vocabulary, Listening, Brainstorm, Oral Presentation, Speech, Synthesize Information, Analyze and Evaluate

Habits of Mind

Be Adventurous and Open-Minded

Wonder, Explore, and Ask Questions

Imagine Possibilities and Outcomes

Think Independently

Step Back and Look at the Whole Picture

Communicate Clearly

Process

- Students work at the center alone or in groups of up to three.

- Children explore Rebus pictures available and create stories with the pictures and magnetic words on the large surface.

- Children tell their developing stories from the board and revise as desired.

Lab-Time Dialogue Possibilities

Let's hear your story! What ideas have you come up with?

What steps have you taken to meet your goals? How could you strengthen your process of working and building the story?

What does it mean to be adventurous with story writing?

What does it mean to come up with flexible ideas?

Read through your story one more time. Let's first practice loosening up a bit . . . try speaking a little louder/softer . . . . Think how to communicate your great story clearly and effectively!

Let's step back and look at your story as a whole. How do the different parts connect? How could you work with and build those connections? What other action would you like to add? How can you elaborate your ideas?

Try again. I'll be back to hear the revised edition!

Great! And you read that so clearly and with a new pizzazz!

When I hear your story I think of . . .

How would you compare your story to . . . . How is it similar? How is it different?

Imagine what would happen with your story line if the plot changed a bit to . . . .

With these same pictures, what other story possibilities can you come up with?

Be flexible and brainstorm!

What parts of speech do we see with the magnetic words?

19. ROCK AND MINERAL SLEUTHS *(Grades K–6)*

Inquiry Activity

Take a close look and identify rocks and minerals under the stereo microscope.

Materials

- Stereo Microscope
- Rock and mineral specimen identification poster or book
- Larger (two- to three-inch) rocks and mineral specimens (search the Internet and see Appendix J, Potential Suppliers)
- Container to properly store various specimens
- Clipboard
- Hole-punched blank paper
- Pencils
- Notebook to display students' Venn diagrams

Highlighted Goals for Students

Content Understandings: Rocks and Minerals, Scientific Technology

Intelligences: Naturalist, Visual-Spatial, Interpersonal, Intrapersonal

Cognitive Skills: Visual Observation, Identify, Compare and Contrast, Classify, Organize, Form Relevant Questions, Research, Evaluate Findings

Habits of Mind

Wonder, Explore, and Ask Questions

Use What You Know

Step Back and Look at the Whole Picture

Look Carefully

Process

- Students work at this center individually or in groups of up to three.

- Children work with reference chart and identify a group of rock and mineral specimens.

- Children produce Venn diagrams to compare and contrast two or more different specimens.

Lab-Time Dialogue Possibilities

Identifying these rocks and minerals takes careful visual observation! I see you are definitely developing your habit of mind to Look Carefully!

Where else do you find you need to employ careful and critical observation? What does the word "critical" refer to when used in this context, as I did just now?

Where have you studied rocks and minerals before? Tell me what you know!

Transfer some understandings!

How do you think this rock/mineral was formed? Let's look at the whole picture! Think about the environment where it developed.

How would you classify these different rocks and minerals?

Where could we find more information about rocks and minerals?

Safety Note: Keep an eye on rocks and mineral specimens for loose parts and sharp edges.

From *Nine Thousand Straws: Teaching Thinking Through Open-Inquiry Learning* by Jean Sausele Knodt. Westport, CT: Teacher Ideas Press. Copyright © 2008.

20. RUBBER-BAND CAR DERBY *(Grades 3–6)*

Inquiry Activity

Using Lego parts, how can you design a car that will run on the energy from a rubber band? How could you design and test three unique rubber-band cars and perform time trials with your fleet?

Materials

- Good supply of various Lego parts, including wheels and rods to be made into axles (do not include completed Lego premade axles)
- Rubber bands of various widths and lengths
- Wooden rubber-band car as an example model (available through various suppliers), or show the following illustration

- Centimeter/inch yardstick
- Timers, graph paper, pencils

Highlighted Goals for Students

Content Understandings: Technology and Design, Motion, Data, Simple Machines, Measurement, Time, Estimation, Graphing

Intelligences: Visual-Spatial, Math-Logic, Body-Kinesthetic, Intrapersonal, Interpersonal

Cognitive Skills: Spatial Reasoning, Visualize Outcomes, Construction, Fine Motor, Brainstorm, Plan Strategy, Form Relevant Questions, Synthesize, Evaluate

Habits of Mind

Be Adventurous and Open-Minded

Wonder, Explore, and Ask Questions

Imagine Possibilities and Outcomes

Contribute Positively to the Group and Inspire Teamwork

Use What You Know

Set Goals and Make Plans

Strive to be Accurate and Precise

Process

- Students set off to the center in groups of two or three. A single child can also pursue this challenge.

- The question is how to build a car, and possibly a fleet of cars, with functioning wheels and axles that harness rubber-band power.

- As they are working, educator asks questions to stimulate and refine design concepts and directions and to help set up time trials and graphing collected information.

Lab-Time Dialogue Possibilities

How are you engineering your rubber-band car?

What are the main design elements of your vehicle?

What have been the different ideas of your group?

How could you refine your design?

What do you predict would happen if . . .

What simple machines do you see in your car(s)?

How do the different simple machines function?

What could be the criteria of a study of your various car designs?

How could you measure and chart the distances that your cars travel?

How could you include the element of time in your trials?

What does the word "inertia" mean?

Can you visualize another way to make a rubber band car? Another design?

Safety Note: Keep in mind that there are potential small parts. Keep an eye out to ensure that Lego parts and rubber bands don't fly around, especially among younger children.

21. SEEING AND BUILDING PRECISELY *(Grades K–6)*

Inquiry Activity

Build a three-dimensional structure by carefully observing a two-dimensional drawing or photograph.

Materials

- Kapla Blocks and Anchor Stone (search the Internet and see Appendix J, Potential Suppliers)

- Kapla Block or Anchor Stone pictures showing building possibilities (come with product)

- New Lab Challenge Idea! Clipboard Graphic (see Appendix K)

Highlighted Goals for Students

Content Understandings: Two and Three Dimensions, Structures, Negative and Positive Space

Intelligences: Visual-Spatial, Math-Logic, Body-Kinesthetic, Intrapersonal, Interpersonal

Cognitive Skills: Spatial Reasoning, Visual Observation, Construction, Fine Motor, Brainstorm, Plan Strategy, Perceive Patterns and Sequence

Habits of Mind

Set Goals and Make Plans

Think Independently

Step Back and Look at the Whole Picture

Strive to Be Accurate and Precise

Look Carefully

Listen Actively

Persevere

Process

- Students work at the center alone or in small teams.

- Students select a photo or illustration of a structure built with Kapla Blocks or Anchor Stones, gather needed blocks or stones, and begin working.

Variation

- Go the other way around. Students create a three-dimensional structure or building from Kapla Blocks or Anchor Stones and draw what they built, accurately and precisely and add the drawing to a "Designer Challenge Notebook" for this project.

- The notebook is then available for other students to follow and make what was drawn in three dimensions. Students can sign their names in the notebook as "Designers" and then as "Builders."

Lab-Time Dialogue Possibilities

What is your plan for building this structure as a team?

What is your idea about planning a team strategy? That's a great idea, I haven't thought of that approach. Who has been an active listener as your teammates have been describing their thoughts? Who has built on those ideas? How?

What are two and three dimensions?

What dimension does this photo or illustration represent?

In what dimension is the structure you are building?

Let's step back and look at the whole picture here. How does each side of your building work with the others? What brings all the sides together? How do the parts become a whole?

What does it mean to be accurate and precise?

How are you being accurate and precise with what you see and build?

Why is observing carefully important with this challenge?

What is negative space? What is positive space? Can you point out some examples?

When you look at the diagram instructions, what is the size of that negative space in relation to the two blocks next to it? Does it seem off in your structure?

What about this row of blocks, how many do you see in the photograph? Look closely here—I see something else going on.

Where else is visual accuracy or looking carefully important with things you do in school or in other activities?

What adults find visual observation an important skill in their work or profession?

Yes, this project takes a lot of patience. Your group has already worked well through some tough spots. Now you want to leave the project? I'm glad I found you just in time! Let's talk about it. What are things you can do when you are about to give up on a good, positive project or effort? What are things you can do to help yourself stick with this challenge? How can you manage your frustration and persevere?

Safety Note: Some building systems such as Anchor Stones have small parts.

---

22. SPIRIT STONES *(Grades 3–6)*

Inquiry Activity

Make your own Spirit Stone by observing a variety of Native American animal symbols and choosing a characteristic that represents something about you. Draw your selected image on a stone.

Materials

- American Indian Spirit Symbol examples: "Animals as Symbols," The Sacramento Zoo EFeature: Draw a Totem: http://www.saczoo.com/3_kids/7_symbols/_symbols_totem.htm and/or "Spirit Stone Designs:" http://ca.geocities.com/nunavut_guide/spirit_designs.htm

- Pencils, Sharpie pens

Highlighted Goals for Students

Content Understandings: American Indian Culture, Language, Citizenship, Animal Behavior, Contour

Intelligences: Naturalist, Intrapersonal, Verbal-Linguistic, Visual Spatial, Interpersonal

Cognitive Skills: Fine Motor, Visual Observation, Oral Communication, Drawing, Analyze and Evaluate

Habits of Mind

Contribute Positively to the Group and Inspire Teamwork

Think Independently

Look Carefully

Communicate Clearly

Understand Others

Process

- Students review American Indian symbols and their meanings.

- Students select an American Indian symbol that they feel represents an important characteristic of themselves. For example, the symbol of the Wolf means perseverance, the Young Fawn means gentleness, the Beaver represents the love and skill of building.

- Students draw their symbol on a stone, as large as possible, lightly with pencil. They then refine the drawing by looking carefully at the symbol.

- Students then take a black Sharpie pen and go over the pencil drawing and make things permanent.

- During Reflection Circle, students share and explain why they selected the symbol and how it represents something important about them. They describe the characteristic in action in their lives. The class discusses who else relates to that characteristic, and who would have selected another symbol. *How does a tribe, class, or team need and depend on this personality trait or characteristic?*

Variations

- Students design their own symbols.

- Students consider making a Totem of a group of characteristics.

Lab-Time Dialogue Possibilities

What is a characteristic?

What is a symbol? Why are you selecting this symbol for your Spirit Stone?

What does the symbol you chose tell us about you? How does it show us one of your characteristics?

Are you having a difficult time selecting a symbol?

I have seen that you love to build with Kapla Blocks. What animal symbol represents that characteristic (Beaver)?

How is this characteristic important for a group? What does it contribute? Yes, we all often see how your skill and ability to build helps a team meet its challenges. Who else can describe what the characteristic they selected would offer to a group?

Do you think it is important to have a team or tribe with many different interests, abilities, and characteristics? Why?

How do you think American Indians learned the behavior and characteristics of animals?

In what ways did the American Indians use the symbols? Let's research more on this. . .

American Indian symbols are simple and clear. Do you agree? Why do you think it was important for the American Indians to make the symbols simple, direct, and clear?

Note: This project needs the educator to keep a close eye on students as they work. They tend to draw symbols too small or to hurry and get to the Sharpie pen before working out their designs on stone.

Source

The Nature Company (original source)

The Sacramento Zoo, "Kids World": http://www.saczoo.com/3_kids/kids.htm

Blue Bunny Northern Guide, Spirit Stones: http://ca.geocities.com/nunavut_guide/spirit_stones.htm

23. STORYBOARD SEQUENCE *(Grades K–6)*

Inquiry Activity

Create story concepts and ideas with photo cards by arranging and rearranging photo images. How can the same cards, ordered in a different sequence, create a new story line?

Materials

- 9 × 12 inch photo images—a wide variety of genres, things, scenes, people, animals, food, etc.

- Tape recorder and microphone

Highlighted Goals for Students

Content Understandings: Creative Writing, Enriching Plot

Intelligences: Verbal-Linguistic, Visual-Spatial, Body-Kinesthetic, Interpersonal, Intrapersonal

Cognitive Skills: Organize, Vocabulary, Oral Communication, Verbal Description, Sequence, Listening, Writing, Recall Ideas and Information, Visualize Outcomes, Make Connections, Brainstorm, Synthesize Information, Analyze/Evaluate

Habits of Mind

Be Adventurous and Open-Minded

Contribute Positively to the Group and Inspire Teamwork

Imagine Possibilities and Outcomes

Listen Actively

Communicate Clearly

Understand Others

Process

- Students go off to the center individually or in a group of up to three.

- Students sift through various photo cards and think of story possibilities.

- Children develop sequences with cards and establish a story. Cards can lie out on floor, a table, propped up against a wall, or stand on a chalkboard ledge. By adding magnetic strips on the back, the cards can be mounted on magnetic boards or other metallic surfaces.

- Students take turns (card by card) and record a story together on a tape recorder. Children then listen to and review their story. Children revise and enrich the story line and record again.

Variations

- Create a chain story. A group of three to six students starts with the stack of pictures upside down.

- The first child takes a picture and places it in view on the board and begins a spontaneous story. The next child finds a card, places it on the storyboard for all to see, and adds to the story, and so on. Students can tape record their story as they go along. After hearing the final recording and when the inquiry period is over, students can write a story on their own based on their group exploration, perhaps taking off into new directions.

Lab-Time Dialogue Possibilities

Let's listen to the story that you recorded.

When I hear your story I feel/think of . . .

What can you imagine could help the story grow? Brainstorm.

How can you enrich and develop the ideas? What could be added?

How do the parts of your story relate to one another? How do they connect?

What are ways in which you could build connections?

In what ways could you make your reading of the story stronger or more exciting?

Could you speak a bit louder? Softer? More clearly? More slowly? In a more animated, or more lively, way?

With these same cards, what could be an entirely different idea for a story? What possibilities can you imagine?

What does the word "sequence" mean to you? Can you create another sequence of events or actions?

What were the different contributions from each person in the group for this story?

Are the contributions different? Oh, some are funny, some are more like poems, some are descriptive . . .

What do the different contributions add to the story?

How do the individual contributions help you understand each other?

---

24. STRAWBERRY BASKET NUMBER SENSE *(Grades K–6)*

Inquiry Activity

Build translucent green towers and other structures with strawberry baskets.

Materials

- Five hundred to one thousand green strawberry baskets (Aim to get square shaped, not rectangular, for stacking ease. Gather from stores or purchase from a supplier. Search the Internet and see Appendix J, Potential Suppliers.)

- Wood or plastic strawberries for questioning (not needed, but animates questioning)

- Clipboard and graphic, Strawberry Baskets Number Sense (see Appendix X)

Highlighted Goals for Students

Content Understandings: Structures, Number Sense, Multiple Unit Measure, Percent, Recycle and Reuse, Spatial Reasoning

Intelligences: Math-Logic, Visual-Spatial, Body-Kinesthetic, Interpersonal, Intrapersonal

Cognitive Skills: Fine Motor, Estimation, Computation, Organize, Design and Apply, Systems, Visualize Outcomes, Brainstorm, Plan Strategy, Analyze, Evaluate

Habits of Mind:

Wonder, Explore, Ask Questions

Contribute Positively to the Group and Inspire Teamwork

Set Goals and Make Plans

Use What You Know

Strive to Be Accurate and Precise

Understand Others

Process

- Up to five or six students can work at this center as they build a structure (such as a circular tower) with the baskets. Usually one lucky student gets in the middle of a tower that is forming. (Curiously, it is usually the most active students who want to be the center builder!)

- After students build a structure (often a circular tower), the educator asks questions to focus the inquiry on number sense and estimation. Multiplication computations are pursued. Children record all information on a clipboard, and numbers are compared and examined.

- Additional questions are asked depending on grade level, such as:

  Imagine you are at a store and about to buy all these baskets (full of strawberries).
  If each unit costs $2.36, how much would someone have paid for the strawberries?
  If there was a 20% discount sale, how much would someone owe then?
  If there are nine strawberries in each basket, how many strawberries would be here?

- Finally, for speedy clean up (of possibly five hundred to eight hundred sprawled baskets), a timely question is delivered:

  This is essential! We need an exact count number! How many stacks of twenty-five baskets do you think we will have? Let's stack and see! What is the remainder? What is the final number? How close are the number hunches?

Variation

Take pictures of baskets in a variety of formations for children then to build what they see. One great challenge is to try to create an arch with the baskets. Students investigate possibilities and come up with new ideas and add to the resource of photo challenges.

Lab-Time Dialogue Possibilities

What is your group plan for working at this center today? What is your team goal? What steps have you planned for reaching your goal?

Does everyone have a way to contribute to the goal?

I see you have built a really great tower! OK, let's generate some questions!

What is a unit? Could one strawberry basket be seen as a unit of measure in your tower?

How many strawberry basket units do you think are in your tower?

Take a guess. What is your hunch (before estimating)*?*

Let's record everyone's number hunch on the clipboard .

When can it be helpful to have a hunch, or sense, for the amount of something?

OK, how could you as a group perhaps gain a more precise idea of how many strawberry basket units are in your tower? That's a good idea! Multiply! Multiply what?

What math skills and understandings are you transferring? Ah, yes—estimation!

Are there other ways you could estimate a number?

Let's record the estimated number on your sheet. How does that number compare with each person's number hunch?

OK, we need an exact count. Do you know why?

We have to clean up this pile of baskets! Besides that, it will be interesting to see how close your number hunch and estimated number are to the actual count.

What could be an efficient way to get an exact count? What system could you organize?

Oh, that's a good idea! Stacking groups of twenty units in sets of one hundred!

Is there a remainder number?

Now let's compare your three numbers: the number hunch, estimation, and exact count!

How do you need to employ the habit of mind of being Accurate and Precise with this center? Yes, with the math computations. How about as you build?

What other explorations could you pursue with these baskets? I have seen a great arch system made out of the baskets that looks like a Roman aqueduct!

Let's review all the various contributions from each of you to making this tower exploration such a great success! How are those contributions the same. How are they different?

Note: This project is always a big hit and worth the effort of finding a supply of strawberry baskets. Often green square strawberry baskets are available in grocery produce sections, where, after placing berries into a large selection bin, many baskets will be thrown away. Ask the produce department to save them. Baskets can also be ordered directly from a produce container supplier.

25. SUSPEND A BRIDGE *(Grades K–6)*

Inquiry Activity

Build a bridge with Kapla Blocks to span across two towers (also made of Kapla Blocks). There can be no support beyond the two towers. How far apart can the towers be?

Materials

- Kapla Blocks (search the Internet and see Appendix J, Potential Suppliers)
- Sketch pad and pencils
- Analyze It! Moving from Three to Two Dimensions Clipboard Graphic (see Appendix M1)
- Student Lab Project Advice Clipboard Graphic (see Appendix L)

Highlighted Goals for Students

Content Understandings: Structures, Design Technology, Perspective, Measurement, Weight and Balance, Spatial Reasoning

Intelligences: Visual-Spatial, Math-Logic, Body-Kinesthetic, Intrapersonal, Interpersonal

Cognitive Skills: Fine Motor, Construction, Oral Communication, Brainstorm, Plan Strategy, Perceive Patterns, Visualize Outcomes, Cause and Effect, Form Relevant Questions, Research, Synthesize Ideas and Information, Design, Analyze and Evaluate

Habits of Mind

Be Adventurous and Open-Minded

Contribute Positively to the Group and Inspire Teamwork

Imagine Possibilities and Outcomes

Set Goals and Make Plans

Strive to Be Accurate and Precise

Look Carefully

Persevere

Understand Others

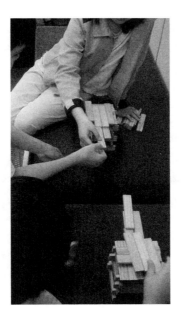

Process

- Students move to the center in groups of two or three and work together to meet the challenge of building two towers and spanning a bridge between them.

- After achieving one bridge, students can extend inquiry by thinking up an entirely different system for another bridge.

Variation

Two groups make a "Bridge X," with one group's bridge going over the other.

Lab-Time Dialogue Possibilities

There are different ways to get this bridge to span between the towers. What picture do you have in your mind to do it? What do you imagine? What do you visualize?

What is your team's plan? Do you have a group strategy?

Now, is this a single bridge the two of you are building? I see you working on this side, and your partner working on the other side, but you're not talking to each other and thinking together. Hmmm. Do you see a problem here?

Yes, I see it fell again! They fall all the time. I know it's frustrating.

What helps you stick with a tough challenge? What are things that work for you (step back, look at the whole picture, look for ideas, take a quick break, laugh a little, draw out ideas . . .)*?*

When should you ask for help? Right, a person can handle some frustration, but not a whole big armful of it! You can hold three dictionaries, but not eight! You need to know when to ask for help. So let's see how we can work this out. How might I be of assistance to you?

What does the word "counterbalance" mean to you? Look at this scale. How do you balance it? Where is the point of balance on the scale? What is a fulcrum? Where is the point of balance for your bridge? Where should the weight go to counterbalance the weight placed on this side?

Let's analyze this area of your construction compared with this other area. Which design seems the most stable? Which system is the sturdiest? Which has the most potential to make a longer bridge?

What do you predict would happen if . . .

How far apart are your towers? (Measure from inside edge to inside edge.) *What is your first feeling or "number hunch" of that space? How many centimeters? How many inches? Let's check.*

You should record your bridge distance on the Challenge Board (or in Student Challenge Journals)*. Better hurry, this bridge is looking a bit unstable! It needs to be standing when you record your number in the challenge notebook!*

You made it! By the way, what could be another goal for this center? What can you imagine?

26. TANGRAM TANGO *(Grades 2–6)*

Inquiry Activity

Two individuals sit on either side of a large board or other partition. One individual (the "communicator") carefully observes a tangram pattern and gives his or her partner (the "builder"), on the other side of the partition, the exact pieces needed to build the pattern. The communicator talks to the builder, who cannot see the pattern, and describes exactly how to build the tangram design. The partners can use only words to describe the positioning of the pieces and the building of the tangram pattern.

Materials

- Set of tangram or pattern blocks that include at least two of each shape (search the Internet and see Appendix J, Potential Suppliers)

- Partition made of wood or foam core or purchased (A standing felt board, coming up from the floor, works well)

- New Lab Challenge Idea! and Student Lab Project Advice Clipboard Graphics (see Appendices K and L)

Highlighted Goals for Students

Content Understandings: Geometry, Spatial Reasoning

Intelligences: Math-Logic, Visual-Spatial, Verbal-Linguistic, Interpersonal, Intrapersonal

Cognitive Skills: Oral Communication, Verbal Description, Organization, Visualize, Plan Strategy, Perceive Patterns, Synthesize Information, Restate, Analyze and Evaluate

Habits of Mind

Strive to Be Accurate and Precise

Look Carefully

Listen Actively

Persevere

Communicate Clearly

Understand Others

Process

- Two students work at the challenge, or there can be two teams of two to three students, each sitting on opposite sides of the partition. Students then take turns as builders and communicators of tangram patterns.

- The communicator builds a pattern with pattern blocks. With the partition, the builder cannot see the communicator's pattern.

- The communicator observes the pattern and *describes verbally* how to build the pattern to the builders' group (who has been given the necessary pieces).

Note: Students, especially younger age levels, need to be guided to start with simple designs and to keep with one level (no layers) of pattern pieces.

Lab-Time Dialogue Possibilities

Take a look at our habits of mind poster. Which habits of mind or thinking dispositions do you think need to be in action when working at this center? For starters, this project certainly highlights the habits of mind to Communicate Clearly, Look Carefully, and Listen Actively! Not to mention to Strive to Be Accurate and Precise and to Persevere! Tell me how. Where else do you use these habits of mind?

What is working? What is not working? Oh, one person is taking over? Oh, you say no one is listening to the others—everyone is talking at the same time! That can be a disaster when trying to meet this challenge!

Well yes, I think you are right, it's not as simple as that. She didn't want to take over, things had just gotten desperate. Right, he would have liked to be more involved, but there was no room for him to step in! You say James tends to be thoughtful and takes time to offer ideas. Yes, I agree! You need to be patient. You need his ideas here to help out!

What are other ways you can help with your team dynamic?

Source

Sikes, S. (1995). *Feeding the Zircon Gorilla and Other Team Building Activities.* Tulsa, OK: Learning Unlimited.

27. THINK IT! DO IT! *(Grades 2–6)*

Inquiry Activity

An invention station. Design and build with found objects. Develop an individual quest, or take on a lab-time challenge.

Materials

- Found items, such as . . .

paper towel tubes	strawberry baskets	yarn spools
straws	spools	pipe cleaners
cardboard pieces	onion or lemon	mesh bags
tin foil	paper cups	rubber strips
brass fasteners	corks	twisties

- Establish a large table as a working area, with materials nearby where a group of students can work. Have handy the tools that students will need to assemble the projects, such as pliers, hole punch, safety scissors, and clamps.

- New Lab Challenge Idea! and Student Lab Project Advice Clipboard Graphics (see Appendices K and L)

Highlighted Goals for Students

Content Understandings: Design Technology, Simple Machines, Recycle and Reuse, Force, Motion, Energy

Intelligences: Math Logic, Visual-Spatial, Body-Kinesthetic, Intrapersonal, Interpersonal

Cognitive Skills: Fine Motor, Visualize, Brainstorm, Construction, Organize, Strategy, Spatial Reasoning, Cause and Effect, Synthesize Ideas and Understandings, Design, Analyze and Evaluate

Habits of Mind

Be Adventurous and Open-Minded

Wonder, Explore, and Ask Questions

Imagine Possibilities and Outcomes

Look Carefully

Listen Actively

Support Ideas With Reasons Why

Communicate Clearly

Process

- One to six students start exploring challenge ideas (see below) and make a series of "thumbnail" sketches. If working as a team (no more than two or three), students discuss plans with partners and organize a work process. As children work, educators help extend thinking and refinement of ideas.

- Variations for handing out materials:

  1. Students choose what they want to work with by taking items from supply bins (supplies easily get disorganized).

  2. Students ask for specific items (things stay better ordered, but teachers need to cover "the store").

  3. Educator bags up a preselected group of materials (this is an "egg drop" type of direction; you get what you get and make things work).

- Weekly or biweekly challenge themes:

  Wind-Generated Machines. Make something that moves in front of a fan.

  Wheels That Really Work. Make a vehicle with wheels and axles that *truly* rolls.

  Mobile Mania! Make a mobile with at least three levels.

  Motor Boat. Design a boat that floats and moves on its own, but not by wind.

  Rube Goldberg-Like Chain Reaction Machine. Design and build a structure that establishes a series of connected and sequential movements.

  Open Clipboard Session. Students come up with a new Think It! Do It! challenge, add it to the clipboard, and then give the challenge a try. Educators review challenge ideas and help to refine and simplify.

Variation

Do not provide the tape and stapler, or other "easy binders." Changes everything!

Lab-Time Dialogue Possibilities

Do you have a picture in your mind? What do you imagine your car will be like?

What questions do you have right now for developing your car?

You want your car to really roll? Certainly! Let's take a look.

What steps do you think you need to take to make this car roll?

Do you know what an axle is?

Here is our wooden car example. What do you see that allows this car to roll?

Where is the axle on the wooden car?

What is stopping your car from rolling freely?

What is the most essential part(s) of your design with this project?

What are the "must have" part or parts of your object?

Explain that one more time. The idea could be clearer. I see that you are on to something!

What is your main reason for thinking that way? How can you support your idea with a fact or by what you see happening? You are practicing the habit of mind to Support Ideas With Reasons Why. How can it help your thinking to uncover reasons why something is working or is not working?

Let's research this . . . . Of the facts and ideas you have gathered, which are the strongest? Which will most help to develop your design ideas?

How can you make your idea stronger? How can you refine your design?

What would happen if . . .

What if you combine these two ideas/constructions? How could they work together to become one thing or meet one purpose?

Oh, yes I see, this is just falling apart on you. You have a great idea here, however, so don't give up! I've actually never seen this approach for a wind-generated machine.

OK, what are some options? How can you bind your sections together in a more permanent way? What tools do you have here? What are some potential materials to work with? Oh, right! The hole punch and the twisties can be a great binder concept! Let's see what you can do! Great brainstorming!

What is the energy source for your object? An inclined plane? Wind from a fan?

You want to quit!? Does it feel like you saw your concept through? Did you reach your goal? Is this car really rolling, or do you have to scoot it along? What momentum does it get on the ramp? How can you improve its performance? How can you engineer things differently to get a better roll?

What have been some of the strongest parts of your thinking and working process?

Do you have a new challenge to add to the Think It! Do It! Challenge Clipboard?

Safety Note: Depending on the supplies provided for construction, the educator may need to keep a closer eye on children to ensure safety.

28. TOWER OF PATTERNS (*Grades K–6*)

Inquiry Activity

How many different patterns can be included in one Kapla Block Tower?

Materials

- Kapla Blocks (search the Internet and see Appendix J, Potential Suppliers)
- Centimeter/inch yard stick
- New Lab Challenge Idea! and Student Lab Project Advice Clipboard Graphics (see Appendices K and L)
- Analyze It! Moving From Three to Two Dimensions Clipboard Graphic (see Appendix M1)

Highlighted Goals for Students

Content Understandings: Patterns, Sequence, Symmetry, Structures, Number Sense, Estimation, Computation

Intelligences: Visual-Spatial, Math-Logic, Body-Kinesthetic, Intrapersonal, Interpersonal

Cognitive Skills: Fine Motor, Construction, Symmetry, Spatial Reasoning, Brainstorm, Visualize Possibilities and Outcomes, Predict, Hypothesize, Plan Strategy, Compare and Contrast, Cause and Effect, Synthesize Ideas and Understandings, Design, Analyze and Evaluate

Habits of Mind

Be Adventurous and Open-Minded

Wonder, Explore, and Ask Questions

Think Independently

Use What You Know

Strive to be Accurate and Precise

Look Carefully

Listen Actively

Process

- Students work together in groups of two or three. A child can also pursue the challenge independently.

- Children begin with one (AB or ABC) pattern and build it by repeating the pattern at least twice. Students then design a *different* pattern and build it on top of the first. Students continue adding as many patterns as possible.

- The tower needs to be standing to record the number of patterns achieved on the Challenge Chalkboard, clipboard, or project notebook.

- Students record their number sense of how many Kapla Blocks are in their tower before they begin a system for estimation and then organize a way to make an exact count.

Lab-Time Dialogue Possibilities

You are having trouble coming up with another pattern possibility?

It's tough when generating new ideas becomes difficult. This project depends on ideas!

What are things you can do when you have "run out" of possibilities?

Do you remember when we talked about "popcorn brainstorming" (see Chapter Four: "Focus Theme Sampler")? One kernel pops, then you hear the next, then the kernels pop faster and faster. That's how brainstorming goes. Get some ideas started, then they come faster.

How can you work as a team to build ideas?

Does it help to get ideas from photos of buildings, structures, other Kapla constructions? Let's find some resources. Who has a new idea we haven't tried yet? Could you restate that idea, Michael?

Who can add to that idea?

In what other situations does it help to come up with a lot of ideas? When do you find yourself brainstorming?

Let's imagine for a moment what would happen if this tower fell. Which way do you think it would go?

How can you engineer or design things so the tower will not fall? As you add more patterns, what can you do?

It took precision building to get a tower this high! What are other times when you need to be so exact, careful, and precise?

Describe the structure of your pattern. What makes this particular pattern stable and this other one more delicate and unstable?

From *Nine Thousand Straws: Teaching Thinking Through Open-Inquiry Learning* by Jean Sausele Knodt
Westport, CT: Teacher Ideas Press. Copyright © 2008.

Where do you see patterns in your life? Where might we see patterns in nature?

Let's find some resources for patterns in nature. It could be a way to generate more ideas!

So you have twenty patterns in a standing tower. Why not add your success in the student challenge journal! Add some advice for another team that might work with this inquiry!

Let's explore an analogy. How is a tower of patterns like a story?

Let's explore sequence. Describe the sequence of pattern in your tower.

How many blocks do you think are in your tower right now?

What is your number hunch?

How would you estimate the number of blocks in the tower?

How can you get an exact count of the blocks in your tower?

Oh, grouping in stacks of twenty? Is there a remainder number?

29 . TRIANGLE TRUSS BRIDGE (*Grades 3–6*)

Inquiry Activity

Build triangle truss bridges with balsa wood or blunt-end toothpicks.

Materials

- Blunt-end toothpicks, Structure Sticks, or balsa strips (1/8 × 1/8 × 24 inches; search the Internet and see Appendix J, Potential Suppliers)

- Timber Cutter, a plastic-encased safety blade cutter (search the Internet and see Appendix J, Potential Suppliers) or blunt but effective scissors

- A triangle truss bridge illustration or guide, such as *Building Toothpick Bridges* by Jeanne Pollard; *Toothpick Bridges, Getting Started* by Robert Stokes; and *Balsa Wood Bridges, Getting Started* by Dana Cochran

- Water-based nontoxic paper or wood glue that is safe for children's use

- Plastic or cardboard trays, wax paper

- Student Lab Project Advice Clipboard Graphics (see Appendix L)

Highlighted Goals for Students

Content Understandings: Structures, Engineering Technology, Symmetry, Geometry, Two and Three Dimensions, Perspective

Intelligences: Math-Logic, Visual-Spatial, Body-Kinesthetic, Interpersonal, Intrapersonal

Cognitive Skills: Fine Motor, Visual Observation, Analyze and Evaluate

Habits of Mind

Think Independently

Strive to Be Accurate and Precise

Look Carefully

Communicate Clearly

Process

- Students work individually or in two-person teams.
- While referring to a diagram or drawing of a triangle truss bridge structure, students make a balsa wood or toothpick model.
- Student work is mounted on wax paper and on a tray for support.
- Students are guided in how to bond joints effectively.

Lab-Time Dialogue Possibilities

Again, triangles in structures!

Have you ever seen a real triangle truss bridge?

What are some ways you could strengthen the way these sticks join together? What are some options? Gluing small triangular pieces of construction paper at each joint could work. Oh yes, layering one stick just on top of the other at each joint could also work. I agree, just butting edges together with glue would be the weakest bonding method.

What steps will you take to meet this goal? What is your plan? How are you going to manage your work and see this task through? What are the different parts of the process?

Which part of the process needs the most strengthening?

As you work with such concentration you are practicing the habit of mind to Be Accurate and Precise. Where else do you find yourself practicing that habit of mind?

Why do you think triangles are so strong? We see them in the geodesic dome as well. They are often used in building and construction.

Could you repeat what you just said? Try clarifying your statement, I think you're on to a great idea!

Where might we find some resources about bridges? Let's see . . .

30. WHAT CAN A THUMBPRINT BECOME? *(Grades K–4)*

Inquiry Activity

Create a variety of images using thumbprints and simple drawn lines. Be a detective! Use the magnifier, and find the three different thumbprints on the master sheet.

Materials

- Thumbprint identification sheet of three individuals
- Thumbprint sheet with randomly placed thumbprints of thee individuals (see Appendix B3)
- White paper
- Black Sharpie pens
- Handheld magnifying glass

Highlighted Goals for Students

Content Understandings: Magnification, Scale

Intelligences: Visual-Spatial, Naturalist, Math-Logic, Interpersonal, Intrapersonal

Cognitive Skills: Fine Motor, Brainstorm, Fluency and Flexibility, Visualize Possibilities, Investigation, Direct Observation, Identification, Perceive Patterns, Compare and Contrast, Synthesize Ideas, Draw, Analyze and Evaluate

Habits of Mind

Be Adventurous and Open-Minded

Wonder, Explore, and Ask Questions

Look Carefully

Support Ideas with Reasons Why

Process

- Students work individually at a group table. Educator shows a few examples of thumbprint pictures.

- Children are given an 8.5 × 11 inch photocopy of thumbprints from three people (perhaps the music specialist, the principal, and the media specialist).

- Thumbprints are scattered randomly over the copy but with enough room so children can make various creative drawings and images out of the thumbprints by adding pen lines (see Appendix B3).

- Students also try to identify the three individuals' prints. Students refer to a chart that shows the individual's name next to his or her print. Students use a handheld magnifier.

- Students consider the scale change of the print while using the magnifier.

Lab-Time Dialogue Possibilities

You can't think of another image you can make out of a thumbprint!?

I see you have made quite a few images out of the thumbprints. You have a teapot, a bee, a car, a flower, and even a submarine. Your drawings are (unique, creative, specific . . .).

Do you remember when we talked about "popcorn brainstorming"? One kernel pops, then you hear the next, then the kernels pop faster and faster. That's how brainstorming goes. Get some ideas started, and more will come faster.

What are other times you need to generate a lot of ideas?

Can you take the magnifying glass and find out whose thumbprints are on your sheet?

Amazing—those fine parallel lines! What is a parallel line?

What do ridges on our fingers help us do? Why do we need them?

It will take careful observation to find three distinctly different prints. But they are there!

You have a match?! Support your case and show the proof with facts! How are you sure you found the right match with the prints?

Compare and contrast these different thumbprints. How are they alike? How are they different?

How much bigger is the print when you view it with the microscope? Two times bigger? Three?

What is the change in scale?

Variation

With a stamp pad and paper, students fill a sheet of paper with their own thumbprints. Students then make drawings with the Sharpie pen (this is a bit messy; stamp-pad ink travels).

Source

Ed Emberley's Great Thumbprint Drawing Book. New York: Little, Brown and Company.

31. WHY IS ORIGAMI PAPER SQUARE? *(Grades 1–6)*

Inquiry Activity

Make a variety of origami paper constructions.

Materials

- 9 × 9 inch origami paper
- Origami books or guiding illustrations
- Paper and pencils to tally geometric shapes found
- New Lab Challenge Idea! and Student Lab Project Advice Clipboard Graphics (see Appendices K and L)

Highlighted Goals for Students

Content Understandings: Geometry, Two and Three Dimensions

Intelligences: Math-Logic, Visual-Spatial, Body-Kinesthetic, Verbal Linguistic, Interpersonal, Intrapersonal

Cognitive Skills: Fine Motor, Visual Observation, Visualize Outcomes, Synthesize Ideas, Design, Analyze and Evaluate, Verbal Description and Oral Communication, Organize, Teach

Habits of Mind:

Set Goals, Make Plans, Organize

Use What You Know

Strive to Be Accurate and Precise

Look Carefully

Listen Actively

Persevere

Communicate Clearly

Process

- Students move off to their center alone or in a group. Students work individually but support each other in their efforts. Perhaps they all work on one pattern at the same time and do not move to the next one until everyone has "got it."

- Students look for and record the geometric shapes they see as they develop their origami patterns. They draw columns on a sheet with each shape at the top, then tally how many of each shape they find. This can be done individually or as a group.

- Students are instructed to work only on origami patterns they have never done before. (Some children know the patterns well.) As a result, they need to observe the two-dimensional illustrations carefully, rather than relying on memory.

Inquiry Extensions

A student, who knows a pattern well by memory plans and organizes steps to lead other children to make the design. Or students design, build, and document the folding instructions for their own origami pattern.

Lab-Time Dialogue Possibilities

Do you like to look closely at something to figure it out? Origami can be very complex and challenging. It can take great visual focus and perseverance.

Let's see what has gotten you stuck with your pattern. Let's review the steps you have taken so far.

Where do you think things went wrong? Ah, I agree this might be your trouble area. What do you see happening here?

Do the instructions show to make the new fold toward or away from you?

What geometric shapes do you see as you fold?

How many geometric shapes have you recorded on your tally sheet?

Why do you think origami paper is square in shape?

It appears you have been making patterns for years! Since you were three?! Since you know this pattern by heart, will you instruct the others how to make the pattern? How will you organize the steps they need to take? How will you communicate clearly what needs to be done? How can you describe to the others how to make the crane you know so well?

How well are you actively listening as Sharon gives instructions to fold the crane?

Has anyone ever tried designing their own origami pattern? What steps would you take to do that (rough sketch to start, clarify, try folding, unfold, document)? How will you record your system clearly so others can successfully fold your origami pattern?

32. YOUR MISSION: UNDERSTAND THE TOWER *(Grades 1–6)*

Inquiry Activity

Work to solve the Tower of Hanoi puzzle and draw a diagram of how you think the puzzle is solved.

Materials

- Tower of Hanoi Puzzle (search the Internet and see Appendix J, Potential Suppliers)
- Clipboard
- Pencils
- 8.5 × 11 inch white drawing paper (three-hole punched)
- Analyze It! What System Are You Using to Solve This Challenge? Clipboard Graphic (see Appendix M2)

Highlighted Goals for Students

Content Understandings: Sequence, Pattern Recognition

Intelligences: Math-Logic, Visual-Spatial, Interpersonal, Intrapersonal

Cognitive Skills: Spatial Reasoning, Systems Analysis, Record System, Diagram, Predict, Perceive Patterns, Plan Strategy, Synthesize Ideas and Understandings, Analyze and Evaluate

Habits of Mind

Be Adventurous and Open-Minded

Imagine Possibilities and Outcomes

Think Independently

Step Back and Look at the Whole Picture

Persevere

Process

- One or two students work with the project. As they explore strategies to solve the puzzle, educators lead them to become aware of an emerging system.

- The puzzle: Move the tower from one post to another. Only one disk can be moved at a time. A larger disk may not be placed on top of a smaller disk

- Students record how they are solving the puzzle with diagrams and written notations.

- Students can place their ideas in the project challenge notebook or clipboard.

Variation

Find other appropriate strategy games or puzzles for students to analyze carefully and then document their thinking as they work through their ideas.

Lab-Time Dialogue Possibilities

Do you feel yourself taking a ride with this puzzle—trying this or that? Sometimes that sort of playfulness really pays off. All of a sudden, the puzzle is solved! You are relaxed, ideas are generating, there's no real pressure. However, sometimes it is also helpful to be more mindful and try to perceive whether there is a system unfolding.

It takes discipline to be more mindful.

Do you see hints of a pattern emerging as you work to solve this puzzle?

Is there a procedure or set of steps underway?

Now that you are well on your way or have even solved the Tower of Hanoi puzzle, will you document your thinking process? Can you draw a diagram of the system?

Add your ideas to the Understand the Tower Challenge Notebook/Clipboard.

To come up with ideas and solve problems, why do you think scientists and inventors rely on both tinkering and a more mindful study of systems?

What do both offer?

33. ZOETROPE ANIMATIONS *(Grades 3–6)*

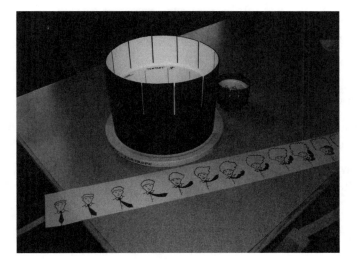

Inquiry Activity

Visualize, design, and create "moving pictures" with a Zoetrope, an early form of animation.

Materials

- Scrap sketch paper
- Paper strips to fit Zoetrope
- Pencils
- Sharpie markers
- A Zoetrope (search the Internet and see Appendix J, Potential Suppliers)
- Or build your own Zoetrope, see: Hayes, R. 2005. How to Make a Zoetrope. *Random Motion.* Retrieved May 10, 2007, from http://randommotion.com/html/zoe2.html.

Highlighted Goals for Students

Content Understandings: Sequence, Animation, Design Technology, Computer and Digital Animation Technology

Intelligences: Math-Logic, Visual-Spatial, Body-Kinesthetic, Intrapersonal

Cognitive Skills: Fine Motor, Brainstorm, Visualize Outcomes, Synthesize Ideas, Design, Draw, Analyze and Evaluate

Habits of Mind

Be Adventurous and Open-Minded

Wonder, Explore, and Ask Questions

Imagine Possibilities and Outcomes

Step Back and Look at the Whole Picture

Strive to Be Accurate and Precise

Look Carefully

Process

- Students first observe examples of Zoetrope animations as a group.

- They then brainstorm ideas for animations and sketch out plans for the significant sequential parts of the animations.

- Students draw animation sequences on provided paper strips—first lightly in pencil, then with black Sharpie pen.

- Students mount the paper strip in the Zoetrope and spin the device.

Variation

Project can extend at a later inquiry session toward digital computer animations (various programs are available).

Lab-Time Dialogue Possibilities

What are some ideas you have for an animation?

Let's look at some examples of Zoetrope animations.

Put a picture in your mind. How do you visualize the animation will go? Imagine the possibilities!

What are the essential movements you need to communicate this idea visually?

What are the main parts you need to get across?

Let's look at some examples: umbrella going up and down, tadpole turning into a frog, a caterpillar changing into a butterfly.

How do you move from frame to frame to make the animation flow?

What would happen if you added a small flower about to bloom, then showed it blooming in your frames?

How could you put together these two ideas into one Zoetrope animation?

What does the word "sequence" mean?

What frames are needed to make this animation work well?

How do you need to be careful and precise to get the animation to work well?

By the way, where else do you need to be careful and precise with your work or activities?

Let's take a moment to critique our work. Do you remember what the word "critique" means? What is a positive critique? What is a negative critique? Can someone critique Nicholas's animation?

Review your process of working here today. What were the different parts or steps of the process? How did you strengthen your process of working? How did you strengthen each part or step?

Let's research and see what ideas might surface by finding some Eadweard Muybridge Stop-Action Sequence Photographs (look for resources of horses and other animals in motion. *Note:* human figure studies are unclothed).

How do you think someone came up with the idea of the Zoetrope?

What did Zoetrope Animation perhaps help to inspire? Let's look at a filmstrip!

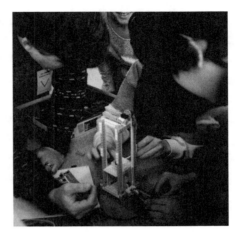

If you work together, you can think together.
—Lab student

Chapter Seven

Finding Parents as Partners and Sending Inquiry Home

An inquiry lab in action is a fantastic place to share with parents and the entire family. It is rare to find such an open instructional arena where parents can drop by at any time and work together with faculty or other teaching specialists as co-educators. The instructional format presented in this book is purposefully designed to welcome parents and other family members (ages three and up) to walk in at any moment and become comfortably part of the scene. Indeed, an open-inquiry lab program is in an ideal position to build a School-to-Home (or other organization-to-home) learning and thinking community.

With the many projects in action, all ages get into the spirit of inquiry, inspiring each other, facing frustrations, and meeting their challenges. Children find working together with others to be exciting and respond eagerly by telling their stories and showing their successes. *Come see what I did, Mom—you won't believe it!* or *Mr. Reynolds, take a picture of this!* Their energy sets the inquiry pace and inspires everyone. They even become teachers themselves as they help someone's father or their own younger sibling work through a tough part of a challenge.

> *At the Think Tank, it was my preschool child who visiting the lab with me was first to pick up on what the new word "inquiry" means. One evening at dinner he exclaimed, "Inquiry means to search and discover!" As the director quizzed the class the following session by asking who remembered what inquiry means, it was my youngest son who remembered first and told everyone. Not only is he teaching us at home, he is teaching the older children at the Think Tank!*
> —Volunteer lab parent

While participating in the lab action and the Focus Theme and Reflection Circles, family members see children from a different perspective and learn new ways to interact with them and their unfolding interests and abilities. Conversations continue to roll along after the lab period as parents and children discuss their time together, the projects they saw in action, and ideas related to the day's theme.

> *One day as a soccer coach out on the field with my little league*
> *players (many who attend the lab at school), I reminded the kids of*
> *how, during lab time, we considered why triangles are so strong. As*
> *we went over ideas, I then asked how a triangle formation could be*
> *an advantage while playing soccer.*
>
> —Volunteer lab parent

Adults can help with teaching at lab time even before attending an orientation meeting for the program. With that day's Focus Theme leading and prompting lab-time conversations and possible question ideas always handy (see Appendix D: Quick Link: Lab-Time Conversations to Build Habits of Mind), interested adults easily pick up the beat and become part of the instructional scene. The inquiry program thus builds an active teaching partnership and broadens the scope of its pedagogy through its policy of easy access to family members.

Multigenerational Learning

All ages can relate to and practice the habits of mind together. During a Focus Theme conversation, parents often present examples of how a particular thinking disposition affects different parts of their lives. All within the circle become curious when parents shake their heads and smile, amazed to see that a habit of mind—one so critical to them—is being highlighted.

> *I just had a meeting on this very discussion—on the lack of active*
> *listening skills in our office! Guys, you wouldn't believe how*
> *essential this habit of mind is in my workplace!*
>
> —Volunteer lab parent

The parent then explains how the lack of active listening played out, and what their company did to develop that habit of mind. As adults share their experiences of working to develop these same thinking skills and dispositions, students become aware that lab time is putting real-life thinking into practice.

Simply by walking in the door, the presence of a parent or other family member in the lab helps connect the child's important worlds, such as the home and school or the home and children's hospital. This connection helps children to see their learning in the lab program, as well as in the school or organization as a whole, applied to other arenas in their lives and as part of the bigger picture. A child sees (even if the visiting parent is not their own mom or dad) that what he or she learns at school is also used at home and out in the world.

Inquiry Thinking at Home

She's making a Discovery Room in our basement!
—Volunteer lab parent

As parents see children fully engaged in building a dome with straws and paper clips, constructing a tower with strawberry baskets, or perhaps brainstorming a new felt-board story, they consider what hands-on, minds-on materials they may have for such explorations at home. Parents spending time in the lab can directly relate to children spending more time with inquiry at home.

My son now has a stash of 350 strawberry baskets, all his own.
Perhaps not as many as in the lab, but still a lot! Look at this photo
of a recent new arch system that my child designed!
—Volunteer lab parent

As they visit a lab in action, become a regular Room Guide volunteer, or attend a program orientation, parents are gaining ideas and teaching skills that they can put into practice at home. All parents receive a list of the habits of mind and Multiple Intelligences to put on the refrigerator. They are offered guidance for creating hands-on inquiries with their children at home and for questioning ideas to help generate investigations with these projects. Soon lab directors are asked, *Where can I find those Kapla Blocks? And how did you ever get hold of all those strawberry baskets?!*

Parent Orientations to the Lab

Orientations are offered to all parents in the school or organization, both to those who are able to work at lab time as regularly scheduled volunteers and those who are not. Orientations are titled something such as "Building Your Child's Innovative and Industrious Thinking!" and are offered both during the day and in the evening. The goal of the orientation is for parents to:

- gain a clear view of what a lab time looks like in action

- understand the mission and objectives of the open-inquiry center

- be aware of the program's foundational theories and methods, such as Multiple Intelligences, flow, teaching for transfer, and divergent questioning

- know what will unfold instructionally for their children throughout the year

- be presented with the Focus Theme lineup, complete with the year's timetable

- receive a take-home information packet with the basic theories and methods

- know their child's inquiry time schedule and that they are always welcome to join in

- be encouraged to sign up as a consistently attending lab volunteer, or Room Guide

- get started with some concrete ideas about working with children to build thinking skills and dispositions through inquiry, both at home and in the lab

One way to get things started at the first lab orientation session is to ask the group of adults, *What do you think it takes to meet a challenge?* With an easel board handy, have someone list the results of the group's brainstorming. Then highlight, with actual examples, how children have answered that same question. Adults are usually surprised that children frequently offer the same points and insights, as well as ones they themselves had not considered. The listing also often contains many of the generalized thinking skills and dispositions already imbedded in the inquiry program's teaching agenda. The orientation then moves into talking about the program's mission and its expanded listing of thinking skills and dispositions.

The orientation makes it clear, early on, that parents do not need a teaching background to make a significant difference to children's inquiry experiences—either at home or in the lab program. Adults are led to see that simply working alongside the children as a fellow discoverer and as someone who listens meets essential objectives of the lab time. Through this involvement children receive messages of affirmation for their choices and see that the learning objectives at hand are relevant for individuals of all ages. With this comfortable starting place established in their minds, parents then receive the same review of the relevant theories and methods as do the faculty and staff (see Chapter Two: "Project as Medium, Teacher as Coach"). Special focus is placed on the art of questioning and the etiquette of the inquiry setting.

To gain a clear view of the lab and its teaching mission in action, the lead instructor or inquiry team shows slides of students working with various centers. Each slide and its accompanying discussion reveals conversation and question possibilities that parents can engage with the children at their inquiries. Emphasis is placed on the art of open and divergent questioning that parents can employ right away, in both the lab and the home environment.

The essential goal of the orientation is to establish a common understanding and vocabulary to strengthen the delivery of the ideas to the children. Whatever terms, theories, and methods are employed, the idea is to pull concepts into a unified focus that children, faculty, parents, and the family can share. A packet that reviews all the major components of the presentation then goes home for further reflection. Following the initial orientation, newsletters or e-mails keep parents aware of the current Focus Theme and perhaps a few new questioning ideas, related articles, or supportive lab graphic aids (such as those in Appendix E, Quick Link: Target Inquiry Lab Skills; Appendix G, Lab Rubric: Inquiry in Action; or Appendix N, Words for Thinking and Doing) to use at home.

Room Guides

Although projects are designed to be primarily student-directed, the inquiry lab is all about developing children's thinking by interacting with them and coaching their inquiry experiences. The title of Room Guide identifies a parent volunteer who works alongside the children to help the lab time meet its teaching objectives. Room Guides help make it possible for multiple learning stations to unfold at the same time with the students truly focused on the inquiry-based learning objectives.

> *Room Guides can run the show.*
> —Grade-level teacher

In a true coteaching partnership, Room Guides help maintain the flow, make connections to the outside world, offer one-on-one time with children, present essential questioning, and set sparks for new inquiry experiences to unfold. In addition, Room Guides often become caretakers and ambassadors of the lab, collecting needed items for projects and sharing with visitors their understanding of how students are learning in this instructional format. From fundraising for projects to helping out in the lab, and with their great enthusiasm and support, Room Guides make essential contributions to any inquiry lab program.

Finding Room Guides

> *Mom, the Halloween party sounds nice, but I'd rather you come to the Think Tank and be a Room Guide!*
>
> —Lab student

Success in finding Room Guides will generally follow the volunteer climate found within the broader school or organization. For many programs, creating a consistent volunteer group presents a challenge. Some will experience a great amount of help at the beginning of the year or at the start of a program, then see it taper off later. Yet with ongoing efforts to nurture a volunteer staff, true and devoted folks will become a regular part of the scene.

Establishing a Room Guide group is a significant management task, one that requires many hours for cultivating a consistent effort. Of great help is to enlist an especially devoted parent (or small team) as "Volunteer Coordinator," one who keeps track of all active Room Guides, helps recruit new volunteers, and sends out schedules of lab times.

The exercise of identifying parent volunteers starts fresh at the beginning of each school year or, in the case of a museum, children's hospital, or community center program, at other similarly appropriate times. In the school setting, a short informational session about the lab, as part of a whole school function such as Back-to-School Night, aims to deliver information to a large number of assembled parents. Slides or a short video of the lab in action helps bring the learning format to life for the parents. Also valuable is for parents to know the date when the first full lab orientation will take place, perhaps indicated on a flyer placed on each chair. In a quick presentation to the group, list a few major objectives of the program and extend an invitation for all to come to the orientation/seminar while highlighting what they gain by attending. *Learn how to develop your children's thinking. Explore the theory of Multiple Intelligences. Discover ways to strengthen your child's learning in school. Help your family build productive habits of mind!* In other words, sell it! Make sure everyone feels welcome, both those thinking of becoming regular Room Guides and those who are just curious and would like to learn more about the program. Also, alert parents to watch for inquiry lab newsletters, articles, and flyers throughout the year.

Just as you said, ideas from the lab really do trickle into the home. We'll be working together on a puzzle or building something and we hear ourselves asking questions much like in the lab. We have great thinkers in our home.

—Volunteer lab parent

Developing a working relationship with parents not only supports the program but also becomes a joyful shared experience. Yet beyond that, for some open-inquiry learning programs, parent volunteers' contributions—from fundraising to assembling the projects, from establishing lab-time staffing to daily maintenance—may be what make the entire effort possible. Regardless of the level of need, helping parents and family to become part of the program changes the learning dynamic for children in both the lab and the home in many potentially positive ways.

LAB-TIME ESSENTIALS FOR ROOM GUIDE VOLUNTEERS

- Lab-Time Caution! Only children over three years old may attend a lab session because of the small parts present in some lab projects.

- Make sure that parents know their times working as a Room Guide *are not* the time for consultations with their child's teacher or hospital therapist! As a golden rule, there are no discussions in the lab about an individual child or related classroom issues. The school faculty and specialists follow this rule as well.

- Be sure parents know that student behavioral issues or problems during lab time are treated respectfully and privately. They should always report any troubles to the program director or lead teacher.

- Parents working in the lab need to be familiar with all health and safety procedures, including fire drill routines, bathroom trips, contacting the school nurse when necessary, dealing with cuts, and so on.

- Make sure volunteers know where to find project materials and the graphic aids that support their questioning and inquiry dialogues.

- Include parent volunteers in the Focus Theme Circle conversations. Make sure that introductions to the students are made.

- Make sure the Focus Theme conversation has stimulated dialogue and questioning ideas that parent volunteers can then employ during the inquiry lab time.

Chapter Eight
Setting the Open-Inquiry Stage

The goal was to establish a critical and creative thinking lab for all students of the school and offer an exploratory time that would "take the lid off children's thinking." In those early days I was still trying to get a handle on how to make the Think Tank work beyond a free-for-all. I found myself feeling crazed as I simultaneously looked for missing paper clips for one group of children, while giving a project review to another, all while trying to extend thinking with divergent questioning for everyone. Certainly I was in new territory for myself—not teaching one lesson to a group, but many lessons to various groups at one time. Yet what then unfolded that year was a terrific creative experience. Through the spirit and action of the children working—it was as if the lab just started talking and led the way to reveal what it could all be about. As class after class arrived, it became clear how to establish an open yet manageable inquiry format, as well as one clearly focused on thinking about thinking. With all set in place, lab time would just hum.

—Jean Sausele Knodt

FIRST STEPS

Even before inquiry projects are put together, volunteers are called and lab times are scheduled. When it comes to teaching children thinking skills and dispositions, there are many ways to get a program immediately underway. For example:

- A grade-level teacher can get things started by reviewing with the students the classroom's new habit of mind poster.

- A health professional can ask a circle of children, *So, what do you think it takes to meet a challenge?*

- Parents can ask while driving with their children, *By the way, what are different ways we are smart? How are you developing the ones you mentioned?*

- A librarian can help students transfer their learning and understandings of the habits of mind by asking them, regarding the novel they are reading together, to consider what thinking dispositions are being displayed.

- Educators can engage questioning to heighten, enrich, and personalize children's thinking with any unfolding life experience or curriculum content.

Regardless of the type of program being established—from a centralized school or children's hospital lab to grade-level classroom or homeschool lab times—putting together an open-inquiry format begins by establishing initial goals, getting the action underway with students, and then building from there as new insights unfold.

For the grade-level teacher or librarian who already has a good collection of project centers, getting ready for a whole-class inquiry lab period will likely include finding a few new projects, establishing parent volunteer help, and outlining a starting lineup for Focus Themes and writing prompts. For a school, hospital, or community center aiming to develop a centralized lab program, the first steps may involve establishing the necessary personnel, finding space, and securing funding.

Checklist

Wherever the starting point, the following checklist offers help in organizing the tasks at hand:

- Determine the primary goals and interests for the specific inquiry program. How will the program help the children, class, school, or organization? What is the purpose of developing such a program approach? Keep the program simple, especially at first.

- Find potential partners who might offer various talents to the effort. Are there possible collaborations that would help strengthen and integrate the program into the school or organization? Would a grade level be interested in developing a collection of projects to rotate among classrooms?

- Locate space for the program.

- Schedule teaching time.

- Outline instructional methods. How will you teach? What will you emphasize?

- Determine who will teach.

- Locate any available resources. Find hidden closets, look for stray materials and projects. Locate catalogs and other resources for project ideas.

- Determine what funds are available for the program. Is there a budget for materials? Is it time to write grant proposals or establish a fundraiser?

- Once a budget is set, firm up ideas for an initial list of lab projects.

- Determine a start date for lab times to begin and then schedule volunteers.

- Determine a starting list of Focus Themes.

- Assign tasks to the right folks for the jobs at hand. Include the following: project building and related carpentry, procurement of supportive instructional materials, graphic design tasks, lab preparation and cleanup, inquiry project development, talent scouting, miscellaneous shopping needs for materials, and volunteer recruiting, scheduling, and in-servicing.

- Lead orientations for parents, faculty, and staff who will be working with the children. Get everyone on the same page with the program's goals and methods.

FINDING AND WORKING WITH SPACE

Grade-Level Classroom

Most grade-level teachers will be asking themselves, *What? Find space in my classroom?* Likely the task will be easier than one might think. For starters, many educators already have in-house projects and materials for Center Time, when children work primarily on self-directed projects in between their other work, during indoor recess, or in the morning as the class filters into the room. For many, organizing the Center Time space to accommodate more projects, possibly with stacking containers, might be a first step. In most classrooms, a space is also set aside for a whole-group circle discussion, which would be the ideal site for the initial Focus Theme and Reflection conversations. The rest of the classroom (desks, floor, and even the hallway if volunteers can help) is then employed to spread out during the students' inquiry lab time.

A Central Lab Setting

Perhaps the reader is headed toward developing a program with one centralized lab, housed in a school, children's hospital, or rehabilitation center, as part of a school or public library, museum, community center, or homeschool network. Depending on the given institution, the job of finding a space for the lab often requires some administrative juggling. Sometimes the central lab will find itself moving from year to year. Such programs have been housed in a regular-sized classroom, a trailer, or a school's larger "multiuse" room. You take what you can find and just make it work. Ideally, the space needed is determined by the number of children who will attend the lab at one time. A group of fifteen to twenty students working with a mix of portable hands-on projects, with a scattering of larger inquiry stations, works well in the space of a regular classroom.

Cart or Takeout Program

Successful cart or takeout inquiry programs also need a dependable and accessible space to work well. A place where projects can be lined up on shelves for easy viewing needs to be found so educators can see which ones are available. A cart or two are standing by, ready to be loaded up with items that then will move out to the classrooms.

Certainly an inquiry cart program complements, and can be housed in, a school library. Additionally, a librarian can be called in to consult with *any* developing cart program (as well as a centralized lab, and single classroom lab time) and help with storage, circulation, and display. A natural co-instructional relationship can develop as the librarian sees how children's work with the projects can easily be developed into research opportunities. The librarian can cross-reference the program's inquiry projects with the library's available resources and offer them for the outgoing carts, or deliver them directly to the lab. These may include books, magazines, or computer resources.

Design and Organization of Lab Space

The way to start designing the lab space is to draw a series of possible floor plans and consider various alternatives for organizing the use of the available space. In general, the types of space needed to make a successful lab time are as follows:

- a large circle area for meeting with children during Focus Theme conversations, and later Reflection, perhaps with a rug and low seating or pillows

- a shelving area to house the various inquiry projects that children can easily approach to gather projects and take to a work area

- a standing-height tabletop work area, especially good for projects that need to remain stationary, such as a stereo microscope or the Nail Challenge (see Chapter Six, "Inquiry Project Sampler")

- a tabletop workspace for projects such as origami, thumbprint art, or animal footprints

- a workbench-like space, with handy nearby shelving, for projects such as the invention station, Think It!, Do It!

- an open floor workspace (can include the hallway), for block construction projects such as bridge building with Kapla Blocks

- floor space to place larger projects such as the Standing Loom, Store, or Flannel Story Board

- a wall surface area for projects such as the Magnet Mural or Corner-of-the-Room Mirror Symmetry

- a wall surface area to display students' work, new challenge records, new question and challenge ideas, students' writing samples of lab experiences, research links uncovered, advice for others, or digital photos of inquiries in action

- ample tabletop space for computer and related projects, such as the Lego Dacta Control Lab (making motorized Lego objects and then computer programing their movements)

- a storage space for supplies (such as straws and paper clips)

- a professional resource area—a place to display articles, books, and theory reviews and where visitors can contribute to an interactive journal of lab teaching experiences or new challenge and questioning ideas

- a work station for the lead instructor or lab director

Also helpful, as space allows, would be:

- low platforms for working on projects and for alternative seating; these can be large plywood boxes wrapped in carpet (just position them carefully so that people don't trip over them)

- a somewhat isolated area where sounds, rhythm, and music can be explored

- a quieter, more reflective area where students can work, read, draw, or write

PRESENTING PROJECTS FOR INQUIRY

All Have a Place

Each project needs its own distinct home in a handy wooden box, basket, or plastic container. Likewise, each larger stationary center, such as the invention station, needs its own distinct and identified storage and work space. For various reasons, it works well to have all containers be of the same type, in different sizes as needed. This helps the central lab, an area within the classroom, or a cart program maintain continuity and an overall identity. It also avoids the lab or project storage space becoming visually demanding and cluttered in appearance. If the project was purchased, all original packaging materials are removed, and the item is set up in its new container, along with any other materials or clipboard graphics.

Use simple graphics where needed with the projects and larger stationary centers, such as for labeling, signage, and opening guidance; also, stay as consistent and unified as possible with the typeface and design. The idea is not only to keep communication direct and clear, but also to establish consistent program tools and continuity. As a result, the program will develop a "trademark" appearance and identity. As an additional benefit, if a project wanders off within the school or organization, people will know where to return it. For this purpose, project labels should have the same design, font selection, and type size, as do any other supportive program materials. Try to keep any illustrations consistent in style, such as all being simple line illustrations or antique engravings.

In terms of displaying graphics related to the overall lab space, keep them simple and clean. Use wall space effectively and make changes periodically. Uncluttered walls give visual relief for the room and highlight the essential messages presented.

Instructions and Question Cards

Each project needs direct, open, and simple startup ideas that are written for students (third-grade level and up) or visiting educators to quickly grasp the basic possibilities of the inquiry and be able to get started on their own. Project cards also list the necessary materials to see whether something is missing. On the back side of these laminated project cards are a list of questions to help students extend their thinking while working with the particular project. It is worthwhile, if not essential, to create cards or some other guiding method for each project. By doing so, the program greatly extends the ability of the children to self-structure their work and helps visiting parents and teachers to tap more quickly into the possibilities for each inquiry. Once again, the graphic design and headings of each card are consistent: individuals see one and immediately know its purpose (see Appendix P, Project Card Master Example). Accompanying each project card can be another card that lists all the habits of mind for easy reference, or students can refer to a listing on the wall.

What system are you employing to move the tower from one disk to another?

What is your "number hunch" of how many baskets are in your tower?

How would you estimate the number of units?

What is the exact count of strawberry baskets?

Clipboard Graphics

Various supportive graphics are presented in this book, such as a sheet for students to work with and record estimates in the Strawberry Basket Number Sense challenge or for them to record the process they perceive while solving the Tower of Hanoi puzzle (see Appendix X, Strawberry Basket Clipboard Graphic, and Appendix B1 and B2, Student Lab Work, Analyzing and Recording a System). In both cases, working with the graphic sheet stimulates the inquiry experience toward making connections to curriculum content and complex thinking. These graphics are presented on a clipboard right in the project container. Not only do children love working with the official-looking clipboards, they also readily have something to write on while standing or working on the floor.

Students' Inquiries on Display

Throughout the host school, hospital, or community library, there should be places available to record and display students' experiences and success stories. Exhibiting their involvement cultivates interest and encourages a wider use of the program, giving other children ideas for their future work at lab time and showing educators the possibilities of the instructional format. Displays help establish focus on selected lab objectives, such as leading children to develop their own questions and new inquiry challenges. Many students are eager to document their success with an inquiry by either drawing or writing about it and are happy to record publicly their having pursued an inquiry or met a particular challenge. *Your work with the Rubber-Band Car Derby has been so successful. Could you write about your experience and offer some advice to others? We'll put this up on the hallway display board with a digital picture of your car.* (For examples of student lab writings, drawings, and records, see Appendices A and B.) Here are a variety of possibilities for promoting objectives, illustrating instruction in action, and displaying student work:

- an inquiry center bulletin board that shows recent action at lab time through photos, along with samples of questions that were asked

- a "Challenge Chalkboard" or lab notebook where students add their names after having worked with a particular listed inquiry; example: Bridge Span, Michael and Leslie—26 inches

- a "Student Lab Advice" notebook or bulletin board: this could be one lab journal listing various projects or a clipboard at each project where students offer advice to others working on that challenge

- a "New Inquiry Challenge Idea" clipboard or bulletin board

- a "Questions in Our Minds" listing: ask students to add to a list of unfolding questions that have been generated through their work with the inquiries

LAB MANAGEMENT

Organizing the Project Inventory

Once an inquiry project inventory grows, it helps to organize it into different categories for easy reference. The following suggested project categories are based on which intelligences and types of thinking tend to dominate in each grouping:

SCI: Thinking Scientifically *(Naturalist, Visual-Spatial, and Math-Logic intelligences)*

VIS: Thinking Visually, Spatially, and Technically *(Visual-Spatial and Math-Logic intelligences)*

LA: Thinking Verbally and Linguistically*(Verbal-Linguistic intelligence)*

MU: Thinking Musically and Rhythmically *(Music-Rhythmic intelligence)*

MA: Thinking Mathematically *(Math-Logic and Visual-Spatial intelligences)*

STR: Thinking Strategically Through Games and Puzzles *(Math-Logic and Visual-Spatial intelligences)*

Interpersonal and Intrapersonal intelligences lace throughout all inquiry projects, and Body-Kinesthetic intelligence (primarily fine motor), to more or lesser degrees, will be part of most hands-on projects.

The projects in each category are then numbered for reference purposes, and the list grows as projects in that thinking area are added to the lab. In this way, a developing program can also keep an eye on maintaining a balance between projects within the various categories. If it is of interest, the listing can also identify the curriculum contents and cognitive skills that each project highlights. Specific standards presented by the inquiry can also be identified and listed. Following are a few examples of projects in the categories of Thinking Mathematically and Thinking Visually, Spatially, and Technically:

Thinking Mathematically

MA1 Strawberry Basket Number Sense (Kindergarten through Grade 6)

> *Content Understandings:* Structures, Number Sense, Unit Measure, Percent, Recycle and Reuse

> *Cognitive Skills:* Fine Motor, Estimating, Calculating, Organizing, Designing, Spatial Reasoning, Visualizing Outcomes, Brainstorming, Planning Strategy, Analyzing, Evaluating

MA 2 Geodesic Dome (Grades 3 through 6)

> *Content Understandings:* Geometry, Structures, Architecture, Inventors, Engineering Technology, Design Technology

> *Cognitive Skills:* Fine Motor, Observing Symmetry, Organizing, Constructing, Visualizing Outcomes, Planning Strategy, Perceiving Patterns, Sequencing, Researching

Thinking Visually, Spatially, and Technically

VIS 1 Magnet Mural (Kindergarten through Grade 6)

> *Content Understandings:* Abstract and Representational Images, Properties of Color, Positive and Negative Space

> *Cognitive Skills:* Organizing, Brainstorming, Fluency and Flexibility, Visualizing Possibilities, Spatial Reasoning, Synthesizing Ideas and Information, Designing, Evaluating

VIS 2 Floor Plan (Grades 3 through 6)

> *Content Understandings:* Perspective, Mapping, Measurement

> *Cognitive Skills:* Fine Motor, Visual Observation, Brainstorming, Spatial Reasoning, Researching, Synthesizing, Designing, Evaluating

Takeout Methods

In the case of a takeout program with no centralized lab and in which a whole class experiences the lab time in its own grade-level classroom, it may be seen as important to keep the available inventory together and not have projects randomly taken out of the collection. Educators may want to have access to *all* projects at one time. A takeout method that meets this need is to have the faculty or staff member sign up for the *entire inventory* of projects for full or partial day use. Selected projects are then taken out on the cart or carried to the classroom at the scheduled time and returned by the end of the reserved period. In this way, the educator will not be disappointed: *Oh no, where are Rocks and Minerals?!* A calendar is mounted on the wall near the inquiry projects, and people simply sign up for desired time slots. Again, a library can be the ideal resource center to display, catalog, maintain, and circulate the inquiry program's inventory. And if the library space is available, a grade-level class could work with the inquiries there, instead of taking projects to the classroom.

As the program grows and develops a fuller inventory, it can afford to have grade-level teachers or specialists take out individual projects, much like books in a library. If so, a takeout sheet is made readily available. Classes might take an inquiry or two along with them as they go out the door. Projects can be due within a certain amount of time or collected as needed. Following is an example of the heading and first listing on a sample takeout form:

Project Number	Project Name	Teacher	Date Taken	Date Returned
LA #2	MORSE CODE	Rodgers	April 16	April 23

Time Needed for and Scheduling of Lab Sessions

Most students work well with projects for a period of forty-five minutes to a solid hour. For the most part, any time under thirty minutes is too short to cultivate a rich inquiry experience. To establish the overall time needed for a complete inquiry lab period, add in the time (ten to twenty minutes) for the initial Focus Theme and closing Reflection Circle conversation. If children are to write in their journals about their lab experience, include an additional ten to twenty minutes.

> *During the summer, at 11:50 on Wednesday, I think about the Think*
> *Tank and my time going there.*
> —Lab student

An open-inquiry lab period could be scheduled as often as once a day, or as infrequently as once every other week. Certainly, the more often that children pursue inquiry projects, the better the program sets its pedagogy and meets instructional objectives. Whatever the lab schedule becomes, make sure children are aware of it so they can anticipate and prepare for that time. In addition, foster ways for children, parents, and faculty to expand on and employ the ideas and concepts outside the inquiry project period. This way, reports of children applying ideas, researching, thinking about thinking, and building ideas for new inquiry possibilities will come back to the lab. The scheduled time in the lab should then act as a springboard.

For the centralized lab in a school or hospital, classes can be set up as part of a master or block schedule, or educators and staff can sign up at the beginning of the year for a regular time slot of their choice. In addition to educators taking the entire class to the lab, another alternative is to schedule inquiry lab times in which half the class visits the lab and the other half remains in the classroom in a smaller instructional format. The groups then switch for the next full lab period. This format has the advantages of offering more individualized attention to children, in both the lab and the classroom.

Lab Cautions

Putting together hands-on projects requires a sharp eye on keeping the inquiry experience safe for the children. All materials that students use must be initially evaluated for safety and then continually reviewed. Things to be especially mindful of include toxic substances, sharp edges, poles or sticks, magnets, chains, batteries, and ropes. Be cautious with any visitor to the lab under age three or with other children who might ingest small parts such as marbles, Lego pieces, beans, or small rocks and mineral samples that present a hazard. Many wonderful inquiry projects contain small parts; however, depending on the type of program and how it is monitored, it might pay to stay away from small parts altogether. The bottom line is that all instructors who use the inquiry projects are responsible for knowing the needs and limitations of the children they work with to keep things safe.

All who work at lab time, including parent volunteer Room Guides, need to be well aware of the safety regulations and procedures of the building at large. For instance, all should know the emergency exit procedures and the protocol for making trips to the lavatory, nurse, or office.

Project Maintenance

All projects are specifically designed to be student directed, including returning the projects back to their storage area. When watching an inquiry lab in action, many are surprised to see how, in just a few minutes, the place is ready for the next group to step in the door. Still, continual review and effort by the managing team or lead instructor are necessary to keep the inquiries supplied, clean, and generally in good shape. Keeping a handy list of where projects or supplies were purchased helps to find missing parts and supplies as needed.

Personnel Needs: Jacks of All Trades

Administrators looking to find the right mix of talent for developing and maintaining a centralized inquiry lab program should take a careful look at the checklist found at the beginning of this chapter. From establishing a project inventory to leading orientation sessions for parents, faculty, and staff, meeting the needs of the program will require one individual to wear several hats, or a diverse, focused team that works well together.

A single educator establishing an inquiry program for his or her own classroom or a homeschool family should also consider the checklist. For which areas would it be great to find a partner and establish a working relationship? Perhaps nearby classroom teachers, the school media specialist, art instructor, or other homeschool families would be interested in working together to develop a program and share the needed expertise. Also, volunteer parents, school librarians, art instructors, or technology specialists are usually happy to help out in the areas of graphic design, project development and construction, or communications.

LAB INSTRUCTION

What simple machines are in action here?

How would you measure the angles of your ramps?

How does the angle of the ramp change velocity?

Instead of using the traditional set of chess pieces, how could you use these found objects to set up a chess game?

How will you establish a reference listing of your chosen pieces?

What is it like to play a game of chess with these pieces instead of the traditional ones?

When might it be helpful to shake things up and try a new approach with a task or project? How can that change things for thinking and doing?

Classic Co-Teaching

If thirty students are working at the same time during a lab period, there could be fifteen separate inquiry projects underway. For a single lab instructor, it can be challenging to help all these students keep their project inquiries functioning at high levels. Students may drift away from a center if they become frustrated, a project may be missing an essential part, or essential thinking skills and dispositions may need to be set into practice. Where one inquiry session might run like a dream with everyone productively "on task" and stretching into new, exciting possibilities, another might miss valuable instructional extensions or be very challenged.

The inquiry project alone will not move program objectives into reality. For children to learn through inquiry, as represented by this book, interaction between students and teachers is vital. Without a strong teaching element, the program can spiral down and lose its footing for meeting learning objectives. Certainly, for a larger group of attending children, an essential element of a successful program is establishing a strong co-teaching team for each lab class. For a group of thirty children, this will mean at least two committed lab-time educators who are both well aware of the goals, methods, and possibilities of the program. They need to be ready to get down on the floor with the children and actively engage in dialogue and divergent questioning, get vitally involved in circle conversations, and transfer lab objectives to other learning arenas. Those who regularly become involved with lab instruction need to know that they are part of the mix in making an inquiry lab session work effectively.

Instructional teams could be a grade-level teacher leading a lab session in his or her classroom with one or two parent Room Guides; a director of a centralized lab program working with the classroom teacher or parent volunteers; or the lab director and a permanent lab assistant. Certainly, any interested visitor is always welcome to contribute and interact with the students, as long as essential core instruction remains established, predictable, and consistent.

Customizing Lab Times and Becoming Part of the Fabric

An open-inquiry program serves best when it finds ways to become part of the broader teaching community. The goal is to customize instruction to support the needs and interests of visiting grade-level teachers, specialists, and staff members, while maintaining the instructional plan of the open-inquiry program.

Along with the use of Focus Themes, Project Inventory Listings, and other suggestions already presented, here are a few ways to develop connections, nurture co-teaching experiences, and form new collaborations:

- Consult with each participating classroom teacher or specialist. What aspects of the program interest them most? On which lab objectives, skills, or habits of mind do teachers feel their students need to focus? Inquiry time, circle conversations, and writing prompts can be customized to meet those needs (see Appendix F: Co-Educator Questionnaire).

- Prepare for various teaching styles and interests, and present participating educators with a variety of instructional tools and methods. Make all aware of supportive lab graphic aids such as, the project cards mentioned earlier or the others found in the appendices of this book, for example, Lab Time Rubric, Lab Assessment, Student Question Cards, or Words for Thinking and Doing.

- As suggested in Chapter Two, welcome area specialists, such as the school counselor, Speech or ESOL teacher, and the Learning Disability or Gifted and Talented Itinerants to visit and work with children during lab time so they can see how students are processing, some of the specialists' instructional objectives in a different setting. New common grounds and collaborations can develop as such experiences unfold.

Helping the Wary Co-Educator

It is important to know that not everyone finds this instructional format easy to work with. Although many enter the inquiry teaching arena like a fish to water, for those to whom the format is less natural, the following ideas, in addition to customizing the program as suggested earlier, may also be helpful to keep in mind:

- Some teachers miss seeing the projects display their specific grade-level curriculum contents. During in-services, outline and emphasize the skill-based orientation of the lab program and how it connects to the grade-level learning objectives and curriculum standards (see Chapter Two and Appendix E: Quick Link: Target Inquiry Lab Skills).

- It can be challenging for some to experience this high degree of children's open explorative energy. Teachers may wonder, *If we open things up so much, how will I get children back to a whole-class and teacher-led instructional format?* Here a closing Reflection Circle after lab time can be additionally appreciated, as can a journal-writing session, to help the class transition back to whole-group instruction.

FOUNDATIONS AND STEPPING OUT

Administrative Support and Guidance

Especially as larger-scale inquiry programs are first developing, with tasks ranging from securing funds to finding a lab space, guidance and support from the administration make the lab program possible. Big questions arise that need to be grappled with, such as the best way to engage and support the grade-level teachers, how to maintain a consistent teaching ratio, setting up program scheduling, how best to engage parental interest and support, and how to infuse program methodologies throughout the school, community library, or children's hospital community. The idea for starting up an open-inquiry program might arise from the administration, or it may be presented to the administration by a group of interested educators, parents, or staff members within the organization. However it first comes about, establishing an open and supportive relationship among all parties involved—administration, program directors, parents, faculty, and staff—is critical to the success of the program as it develops.

Corporations and the Working Community

Developing relationships with the local working community, colleges or universities, and area corporations can often be a natural extension of an inquiry learning program. Corporations are often looking for ways to support and contribute to schools and children's centers, by both providing funding as well as interacting directly with children. For the local college or university, the lab can provide an interesting field study for seeing various educational theories and methods in action. Lab time is open for members of these working and higher-education communities to join in and take part, even to become mentoring Room Guides. Lab students love involvement with the outside world and are intrigued with the responses from such visitors relating to the ageless "thinking about thinking" that goes on in the lab. Learning exchanges in which the lab program director provides adult-level sessions that focus on experiential team-building within the workplace and engage the same habits of mind and skills as those in the children's program can also be organized.

All on the Same Page

Whatever the setting—be it a central lab, a single classroom, a hospital, or a homeschool learning program—meeting the instructional objectives of the program requires getting all parents, staff, and grade-level teachers who work with the children to tune into the mission and objectives of the program. Generally, this means presenting a longer overview initial orientation and then a series of shorter ongoing follow-up presentations, usually shorter in duration, at faculty or staff meetings. Getting everyone on the same page establishes continuity, transfer of program objectives, and stronger inquiry experiences for the children.

Finding Their Place to Start

A primary goal for the initial orientation is to help each individual lab-time educator make a personal connection to some element of the program that he or she finds inspiring and purposeful. Will it be to establish one-on-one time with children? To uncover gifted behavior in an open setting? To help students transfer and de-compartmentalize their learning? To reveal curriculum understandings in a different environment? To have an instructional time to follow rather than lead?

Once educators find a place to start, their teaching efforts have a chance to expand in unique ways and tap into all of that youthful curiosity and energy.

Building a Community for Thinking through Inquiry

I have come increasingly to recognize that most learning in most settings is a communal activity, a sharing of the culture. It is not just that the child must make his knowledge his own, but that he must make it his own in a community of those who share his sense of belonging to a culture. It is this that leads me to emphasize not only discovery and invention but the importance of negotiating and sharing. (Bruner 1986, p. 127)

The gift of open-inquiry instruction is that it provides opportunity for a child's inquisitive energy to be both engaged and guided; indeed, it provides an open time and place for it to thrive. It is a time and place that young minds intuitively seek and welcome with delight. When a lab time is in full gear and children are taking charge with their thinking and doing, the place also becomes uplifting for adults. As we watch a group of children moving together through a complex problem with confidence and industriousness, we smile and let out a sigh of relief—we see them on their way.

Find the questions.
—Lab student

Zest for finding inquiries and pursuing innovative and industrious thinking is catching. Excitement and purpose to follow and trust such impulses is something one can learn and build over time. The open-inquiry environment is a dynamic and intriguing place for children to see possibilities and offers educators a dynamic turn-on-the-heels creative experience as well. Finding challenges, thinking about thinking, and cultivating inspired minds are out in the open in constructive, joyful ways, developed in a community that is shared by all.

REFERENCE

Bruner, J. (1986). *Actual Minds, Possible Worlds*. Cambridge, MA: Harvard University Press.

Think Tank Journal

In Think Tank on November 21, 2000 our classes third graders went to Think Tank. The first thing we talked about was a word called ... I am not sure what it is called but I know it begins with a m. After that we went and talked about what Challenge we were going to do today. I decided that I would go and do the thing were you put two paperclips together than you stick a straw in it then they will stick together it is very cool. I worked with my classmate Lina it was fun but it Challenge me a lot it would get loose once in a while. I also used people smarts for doing this. I used people smarts because you would have to cooparate with the person you worked with.

About the Think Tank
I think the Think Tank is
a cool place. You can never
run out of things to
do. I really like the
Think Tank they have all
Kind of stuff like
caplablock and chess. I did
a challenge. William and I
had to make a road
that went in three
ways. It was hard but
but we never gave up.
We met the challenge
head on. We took tons
of steps. We keep on
fixing it. It took us
about 30 minutes. It
Keeped on falling off
it got frustrating. I
would do the same
next time if I car
I relly liked it becau
it was a challenge,
think we used math
The first step we
was to get t.

November 22, 2000

In tinktank Chris, Kyle and me did magnet marbles. We rolled marbles down a pathway we made. Our objective was to get the marble to the floor. Not by droping by useing some marble blocks. It we kept trying diffrent angles for the speep of the marbles. For the marble slope we changed the place of the blocks were the marble hit. We kept doing that for the hole think tank. Then we tried it again and bounced on the floor and went down the slope. Then it was the end of thinktank and went back to our classroom.

THINK TANK

At the Think Tank, I did the Zigguart Puzzle. The object was to move the pyramid from one pole to the other. But, you could only lift one block at a time and you couldn't put one block on top of a block that was smaller than it. ①

This was a hard puzzle. My strategy was to always have two little pyramids. One of the pyramids was the one that I was building and the other one was the one that I was taking blocks off of. It sounds easy, right? Wrong! The reason it was hard was because the block that I wanted to put on the pyramid was on the bottom of the other blocks. I had to put each block on a certain pole. Then, I had to guess which pole to start off with. This is where it got hard. Once I got going, I couldn't tell if I did it right or not until I was pretty far into it. So, I totally lost my train of thought because I couldn't remember what pole I started on. And, then I had to go back and guess again and again and again, but I was really just repeating myself a million times. The challenge was that I had to think about more than one thing at a time. What helps me in situations like this is to either go slow and think through it hard or mark the pole that I just did with something to help me remember. *well,*

good idea

Things may get tough sometimes, but one thing is for sure. I never give up and neither should you!

You don't + thats real perserverance that will carry you far in life!

From *Nine Thousand Straws: Teaching Thinking Through Open-Inquiry Learning* by Jean Sausele Knodt. Westport, CT: Teacher Ideas Press. Copyright © 2008.

I went to the Think Tank. My challenge was to balance all the nails on one nail hammered on a piece of wood. Everybody was given a question in the Think Tank. My question was 'What advice would you give to someone just starting this challenge?'

I would tell someone just starting this challenge to think of an X and not this X but this ⅄ . And I want to tell that the way to start is put a nail across on the top of the middle one like this picture tells you.

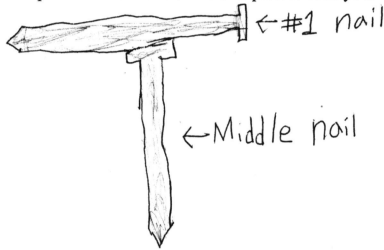

←#1 nail

←Middle nail

I have written the advice to someone just starting to challenge this challenge. I hope it's a lot of help!

January 24, 2001
Think Task Journal

I took a challenge with Strawberry baskets. I meet the Chalenge by making a nice tower of Piza. The steps I took were first to make a base and then build up and up. We used math smart, People smart, and picture smart. Atif worked with me and he was a great help. I liked best of this chalenge is that it uses arcitecture and skill It was frustrating because I didn't like when it started to fall and we had to start again. Next time I want to work with while wings.

What system have you used to move the tower over?

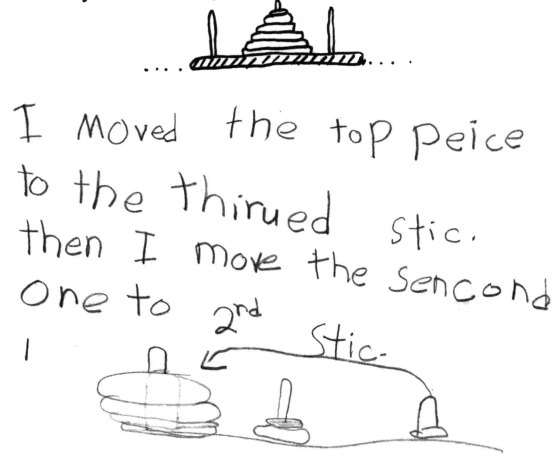

I Moved the top peice
to the thirued stic.
then I move the sencond
one to 2rd
1

What system have you used to move the tower over?

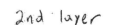

Each layer of the tower has a symtamic way to move it to another peg. Once you figure out the systamatic way to move each layer you symply move the tower layer by layer to another peg

2nd layer

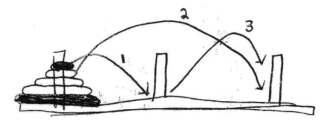

3rd layer

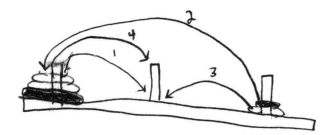

To figure out the systematic way for each layer. First you count in the part of the tower you want to move. Then you alternate between the two pegs remaining starting on the place you want to move it. You alternate the number you got and the beginning, The peg you end start with is the one you shoull

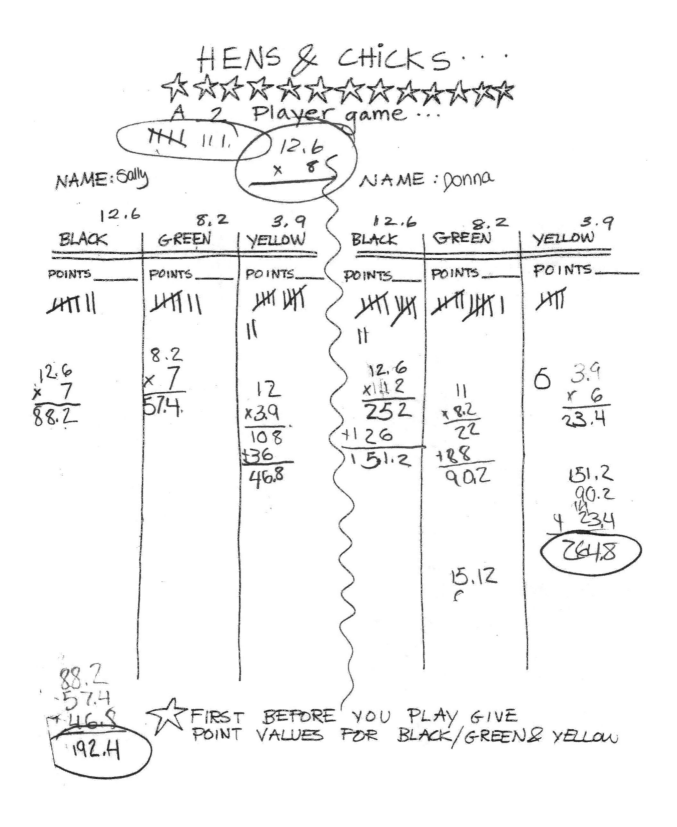

HENS & CHICKS...
☆☆☆☆☆☆☆☆☆☆☆☆
A 2 Player game...

HHL III,   12.6
                × 8 5

NAME: Sally   NAME: Donna

12.6	8.2	3.9	12.6	8.2	3.9
BLACK	GREEN	YELLOW	BLACK	GREEN	YELLOW
POINTS	POINTS	POINTS	POINTS	POINTS	POINTS

HHT II   HHT II   HH HHT   HHT HHT   HHT HHT I   HHT
                             II   II

              8.2   12.6   3.9
12.6   × 7   12   × 12   11   6 × 6
× 7   57.4   × 3.9   252   × 8.2   23.4
88.2   108   +126   22
                            +36   151.2   +88
                            46.8   902

                                                                        151.2
                                                                        90.2
                                                                      4   23.4
                                                                        264.8

                                          15.12

88.2
57.4
+46.8
192.4

☆ FIRST BEFORE YOU PLAY GIVE
POINT VALUES FOR BLACK/GREEN & YELLOW

234   From *Nine Thousand Straws: Teaching Thinking Through Open-Inquiry Learning* by Jean Sausele Knodt.
Westport, CT: Teacher Ideas Press. Copyright © 2008.

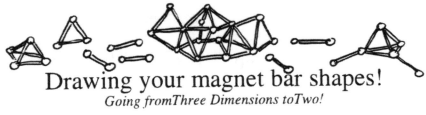

Drawing your magnet bar shapes!

Going from Three Dimensions to Two!

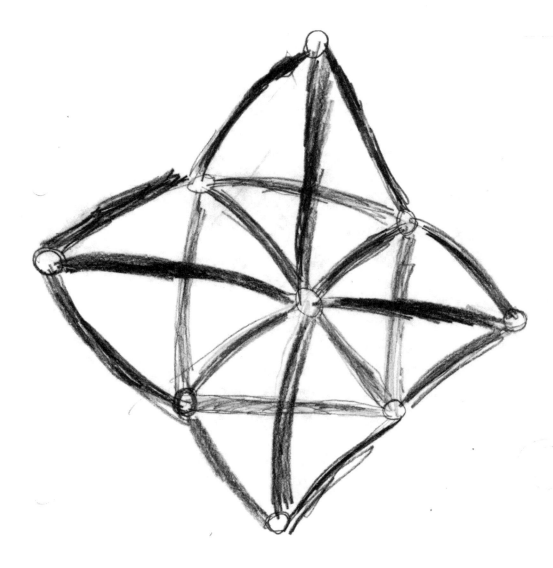

A new challenge for marble skip.

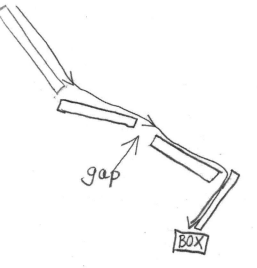

gap

BOX

The goal is to try and skip the gap. There are acutually two goals to try and achieve. The first goal is to skip the gap and land into the next runway. The other goal is to skip the gap go into the next runway and not to not bounce off the last runway and to land in the box. It took me 6 or 7 minutes to achieve these goals. Their not that easy and not that hard either. Have fun!!

A new challenge for marble skip.

This mant sid
is a tiagl sap.
We pot los ov
pesz. The mrbs
wit in to the
box. We tatd
a bed. to. som tim
the bed dost wrc.
We wtr vre hrd.

Frigts

Analyze It!
The Water Fountain
How does this work?
Draw a diagram and write an explanation.

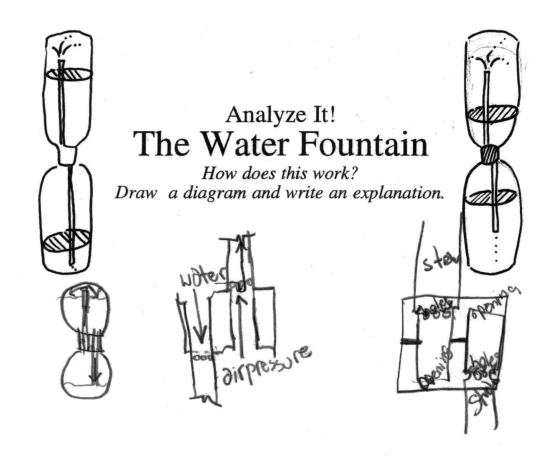

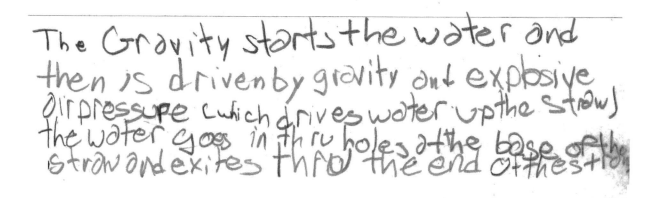

The Gravity starts the water and then is driven by gravity ont explosive airpressure (which drives water up the straw) the water goes in thru holes at the base of the straw and exites thru the end of the st..

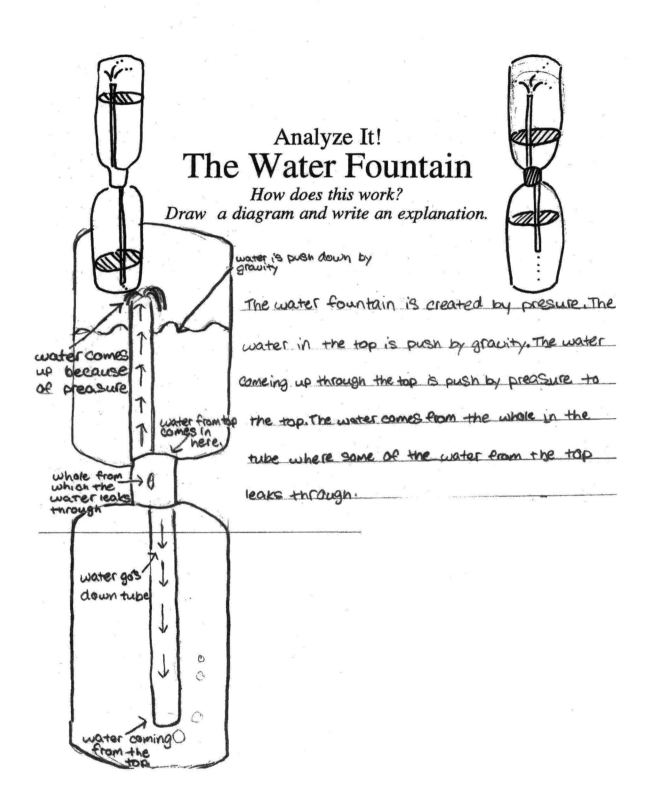

Analyze It!
The Water Fountain

How does this work?
Draw a diagram and write an explanation.

water is push down by gravity

water comes up because of preasure

water from top comes in here.

whole from which the water leaks through

water gos down tube

water coming from the top

The water fountain is created by presure. The water in the top is push by gravity. The water comeing up through the top is push by preasure to the top. The water comes from the whole in the tube where same of the water from the top leaks through.

Quick Link:
Focus Theme Conversations to Build Habits of Mind

1. Be Adventurous and Open-Minded

What does it mean to be adventurous? What does it mean to be open-minded?

How are you being adventurous and open-minded when you brainstorm ideas?

What does it mean to be flexible in your thinking?

Where can you use the habit of mind to Be Adventurous and Open-Minded? Which activities? What kind of thinking? What kind of learning?

How do you see this habit of mind in action in something we are now reading about or studying? Where do you see this habit of mind in action in adults' work?

How does being adventurous and open-minded help our thinking and doing become stronger?

2. Wonder, Explore, and Ask Questions

Most people love to explore and investigate. Why?

What things do you love to explore and investigate?

How many of you hear yourselves asking questions as you work? Questions move inquiries!

Can it sometimes feel like taking a risk to ask a question? How? Why?

Where can you use the habit of mind to Wonder, Explore, and Ask Questions? For which activities? What kind of thinking? What kind of learning?

How do you see this habit of mind in action in something we are now reading about or studying? Where do you see this habit of mind in action in adults' work?

How does wondering, exploring, and asking questions help our thinking to become stronger?

3. Contribute Positively to the Group and Inspire Teamwork

What are some examples of a team working well together?

What are some examples of a team not working well together?

What are ways to help teamwork grow?

What do you like to offer a team?

Where can you use the habit of mind to Contribute Positively to the Group and Inspire Teamwork? For which activities? What kinds of thinking? What kinds of learning?

How do you see this habit of mind in action in something we are now reading about or studying? Where do you see this habit of mind in action in adults' work?

How does contributing positively to the group and inspiring teamwork help our thinking and doing to become stronger?

4. Imagine Possibilities and Outcomes

What does it mean to put a picture in your mind?

What does the word" "visualize" mean to you?

How can it be helpful to imagine how things might go as you work on a project or activity?

Where can you use the habit of mind to Imagine Possibilities and Outcomes? For which activities? What kinds of thinking? What kinds of learning?

How do you see this habit of mind in action in something we are now reading about or studying? Where do you see this habit of mind in action in adults' work?

How does imagining possibilities and outcomes help our thinking and doing to become stronger?

5. Set Goals and Make Plans

(Start by displaying a project or lesson.) *What might be some goals for this project?*

What plans could you make to meet one of those goals?

What does the word" "strategy" mean?

Where can you use the habit of mind to Set Goals and Make Plans? For which activities? What kinds of thinking? What kinds of learning?

How do you see this habit of mind in action in something we are now reading about or studying? Where do you see this habit of mind in action in adults' work?

How does setting goals and making plans help our thinking and doing to become stronger?

6. Think Independently

What are some examples of thinking for yourself?

Why is it sometimes hard to think independently?

When do you reflect on how you think things through?

How can Thinking Independently help a group?

Where can you use the habit of mind to Think Independently? For which activities? What kinds of thinking? What kinds of learning?

How do you see this habit of mind in action in something we are now reading about or studying? Where do you see this habit of mind in action in adults' work?

How does thinking independently help our thinking and doing become stronger?

7. Use What We Know—Transfer Learning

When you" "transfer" something (teacher uses a hand gesture, picks something up, arches it over, and places it down) *from one learning activity to another, you really know your stuff!*

When you transfer a skill or understanding you show how well you know the learning. You are using your learning!

From *Nine Thousand Straws: Teaching Thinking Through Open-Inquiry Learning* by Jean Sausele Knodt
Westport, CT: Teacher Ideas Press. Copyright © 2008.

What does the word transfer mean? What does transfer of learning mean?

When do you see yourself using what you know with Reading? Math? . . .

Where else do you find yourself Using What You Know? With which activities? Which kinds of thinking? Which kinds of learning?

How do you see this habit of mind in action in something we are now reading about or studying? Where do you see this habit of mind in action in adults' work?

How does using what you know help your thinking and doing to become stronger?

8. Step Back and Look at the Whole Picture

Let's look at this project/assignment. (Teacher displays a project.)

What are the different parts of the project or challenge?

How do the parts connect or link? What parts are essential?

Where can you use the habit of mind to Step Back and Look at the Whole Picture? With which activities? Which kinds of thinking? Which kinds of learning?

How do you see this habit of mind in action in something we are now reading about or studying? Where do you see this habit of mind in action in adults' work?

How does stepping back and looking at the whole picture help our thinking and doing become stronger?

9. Strive to Be Accurate and Precise

How is it sometimes essential to be accurate and precise with your thinking and doing?

What are some examples (Math, soccer kick, taking a test, building a bridge . . .)?

How do you see this habit of mind in action in something we are now reading about or studying? Where do you see this habit of mind in action in adults' work?

How does striving to be accurate and precise help our thinking and doing to become stronger?

10. Look Carefully

What are some examples of someone looking carefully?

What does it mean to observe critically?

Where can you use the habit of mind to Look Carefully? With which activities? Which kinds of thinking? Which kinds of learning?

How do you see this habit of mind in action in something we are now reading about or studying? Where do you see this habit of mind in action in adults' work?

How does looking carefully help our thinking and doing become stronger?

11. Listen Actively

What are some examples of someone listening actively?

How does it feel when someone is listening to you?

Is it always easy to listen actively?

What can get in the way?

Where can you use the habit of mind to Listen Actively? With which activities? Which kinds of thinking? Which kinds of learning?

How do you see this habit of mind in action in something we are now reading about or studying? Where do you see this habit of mind in action in adults' work?

How does listening actively help our thinking and doing to become stronger?

12. Support Ideas With Reasons Why

What does it mean to find and show evidence?

Do all reasons or facts that we find have the same weight? Explain your answer.

Where can you use the habit of mind to Support Ideas With Reasons Why? With which activities? Which kinds of thinking? Which kinds of learning?

How do you see this habit of mind in action in something we are now reading about or studying? Where do you see this habit of mind in action in adults' work?

How does supporting ideas with reasons why help our thinking and doing to become stronger?

13. Persevere

What does it mean to persevere?

What helps us to persevere?

What helps you deal with frustration?

What can frustration be a sign of (new learning or skill acquisition)*? Right! New levels of learning are underway! A good sign! Worth persevering for!*

What do you do if things get too tough? Right! You ask for help!

Where can you use the habit of mind to Persevere? For which activities? Which kinds of thinking? Which kinds of learning?

How do you see this habit of mind in action in something we are now reading about or studying? Where do you see this habit of mind in action in adults' work?

How does persevering help our thinking and doing to become stronger?

14. Communicate Clearly

What does it mean to communicate clearly?

Where is it especially helpful to communicate clearly (Speak, write, draw, music. . .)*?*

What does it take to communicate clearly?

Where can you use the habit of mind to Communicate Clearly? With which activities? Which kinds of thinking? Which kinds of learning?

How do you see this habit of mind in action in something we are now reading about or studying? Where do you see this habit of mind in action in adults' work?

How does communicating clearly help our thinking and doing to become stronger?

15. Understand Others

What are ways in which we understand others?

How do we perceive what others are thinking or feeling?

What does it mean to be perceptive?

What does it mean to be sensitive to others?

Where can you use the habit of mind to Understand Others? With which activities? Which kinds of thinking? Which kinds of learning?

How do you see this habit of mind in action in something we are now reading about or studying? Where do you see this habit of mind in action in adults' work?

How does understanding others help our thinking and doing become stronger?

Resources

Costa, A. L., & Kalick, B. (2000). *Discovery and Exploring Habits of Mind.* Alexandria, VA: Association for Supervision and Curriculum Development.

Tishman, S., Jay, E., & Perkins, D. (1992). *Teaching Thinking Dispositions: From Transmission to Enculturation.* Retrieved June 4, 2008, from http://learnweb.harvard.edu/ALPS/thinking/docs/article2.html.

Appendix D

Quick Link:
Lab-Time Conversations to Build Habits of Mind

1. Be Adventurous and Open-Minded

How flexible is your thinking and doing today?

Do your ideas feel set in stone, or are you working with them and being flexible?

Do you feel adventurous? Are you open to trying something new?

What do you do when you feel stuck with something? What skills help you be adventurous and open-minded (brainstorming, mind mapping, interviewing, researching . . .)?

Do you remember when we talked about "popcorn brainstorming"? One kernel pops, then you hear the next, then the kernels begin to pop faster and faster. That's how brainstorming works. Get things started, and then the ideas will come faster.

What are ways to cultivate brainstorming (work with a partner, look for ideas in various places, approach the situation from another viewpoint . . .)?

Other than your project here, when are times that you need to generate a lot of ideas?

Where do you see the habit of mind of Being Adventurous and Open-Minded in adults' work?

How does being adventurous and open-minded help your thinking and doing be stronger?

2. Wonder, Explore, and Ask Questions

What are you curious about? What brought you to this project? In what are ways can you build on that interest? What might be another challenge idea for this project? What else could you investigate and explore?

What other projects or challenges are similar to this center? Where else could this interest take you? How could you combine ideas or objects from other projects?

Where could you research more about this project?

What do you wonder about? What questions come to mind?

What questions can you build or cultivate?

Where do you see the habit of mind of Wondering, Exploring, and Asking Questions active in adults' work?

How does wondering, exploring, and asking questions help your thinking and doing become stronger?

3. Contribute Positively to the Group and Inspire Teamwork

Well, how is it going? (Terrible! No one is listening! It's a disaster!) *So let's think. How can you as a team work together more effectively?*

What are aspects of good teamwork? What skills are needed?

Have you taken time to brainstorm together?

How can you become aware of others' ideas to solve the problem?

How can all team members have the chance to present their ideas clearly?

Is everyone open to each others' ideas and interests?

Are you listening actively to each other?

Is everyone committed to solving the problem? How can you become committed?

How can you help others to become committed?

How can you share the needed leadership and tasks?

Does the team have a plan? Have you all agreed on a strategy?

Does everyone have a task to do? Is everyone contributing?

How does understanding others help a team (resolve conflicts, gain varied perspectives)*? Well yes, I think you are right. Patrice didn't want to take over, but she felt things had gotten desperate. Right, Michael would have liked to be more involved, but there was no room for him to step in! It's clear, Brian does have a different way of looking at this challenge situation.*

How do your ideas come together to work through challenges and make things happen?

Where do you see the habit of mind of Contributing Positively to the Group and Inspiring Teamwork in adults' work?

How does contributing positively to the group and inspiring teamwork help to make everyone's thinking and doing stronger?

4. Imagine Possibilities and Outcomes

Do you have a picture in your mind? What could happen? What could be?

What do you visualize?

What questions come up as you imagine possibilities and outcomes?

How do those questions develop the inquiry?

What will be the likely outcome if you try a different approach?

How does imagining what could happen help you with your work?

Where do you see the habit of mind of Imagining Outcomes and Possibilities in adults' work?

How can imagining outcomes and possibilities make your thinking and doing stronger?

5. Set Goals and Make Plans

What steps are you going to take to meet this goal? What is your strategy?

How does it help to take things one step at a time to meet a goal?

How does it help to take the time to make plans, employ strategy, and set goals?

How can taking the time to make plans and brainstorm strategy end up saving you time?

Where do you see the habit of mind of Setting Goals and Making Plans in adults' work?

How does setting goals and making plans help make your thinking and doing stronger?

6. Think Independently

Who has a new idea we haven't tried yet? I'm sure there is another way to look at this.

Take a chance and offer your thoughts! Take a risk!

How are you going to manage your work and see this task through?

How will you direct your own effort?

I think you are all set to work well. I'm going to leave for a while and see how you set about this task. Take it one step at a time. See how well you can manage the effort. You can do it! If you get stuck, first review what we have talked about and then try again.

Rose, how is your thinking or idea similar to Brian and Herbert's? How is it different?

What is a "stepping out" idea you have, Richard? It doesn't matter if it seems silly or weak at first, you can help the idea grow strong. Trust yourself.

What skills help you to think independently (mind mapping, outline ideas, plan strategy)*?*

Where do you see the habit of mind of Thinking Independently in adults' work?

How does thinking independently help your thinking and doing become stronger?

7. Use What You Know, Transfer Learning

Tell me what you understand and know about.

When have you used these skills or explored this idea before?

How are you using something you have already learned?

How are you transferring your skills and understandings to the task at hand?

Where else could you use these skills and understandings? In what other places or situations?

Who else builds and uses these sort of skills and understandings in the world (vocations, professions, life situations)*?*

How does using what you know and transferring your learning help your thinking and doing become stronger?

8. Step Back and Look at the Whole Picture

How are the different parts of this project, story, or task connected? What are the relationships? How are the parts dependent on each other?

Perhaps you need to expand your focus to make this project go better or become richer. Let's step back and take a look at the whole picture. How do the parts link to one another? Do you see connections? Can you build those links?

What skills help you to step back and look at the whole picture (drawing, graphing, outlining ideas, comparing and contrasting . . .)*?*

Where do you see the habit of mind of Stepping Back and Looking at the Whole Picture in adults' work?

How does stepping back and looking at the whole picture help your thinking and doing to be stronger?

9. Strive to Be Accurate and Precise

This project requires precision! There is little room here for errors. You have to be diligent and stick to it when it comes to being precise! In what ways do you think it is important to be precise as you work with this project?

Where else is there little room for error in things you do (solving a math problem, playing sports, playing music . . .)?

Where else do you need to be accurate and precise with your work?

Describe different ways you check work for accuracy, making sure it's right? What skills do you employ?

Where do you see the habit of mind to Be Accurate and Precise in adults' work?

How does striving to be accurate and precise help your thinking and doing become stronger?

10. Look Carefully

Why is it important to look carefully when working with this project? How does taking time to observe closely make a difference for this challenge?

Where else do you use the habit of mind to look carefully in school, at home, or in other things you do?

What are some adult jobs that require the skill of observing things closely? Yes, my dentist is also good with visual observation! Thank goodness for that!

How does looking carefully help your thinking and doing to be stronger?

11. Listen Actively

Why is listening actively helpful, if not essential, to this project?

What does it mean to listen actively?

What are other times when listening actively is helpful or essential?

Who felt they were really listening when Richard was speaking? What did the things he talked about make you think of? Who can restate what Tracy just said? Who can build on the idea that Philippe presented?

How well are you listening to each other today?

How can it be difficult to listen well? What are some things that can get in the way? Does listening well take patience? Focus?

How does it help with your work and thinking to be an active listener?

12. Support Ideas With Reasons Why

I see you feel strongly about your idea. Tell me why you are so sure. What ideas and reasons lead you to feel sure? What is your evidence?

What proof do you have to support your idea? What have you learned here with this project, and what experience do you have that provides proof for your ideas?

What could you research to uncover additional facts and reasons to better support your ideas and provide more proof? Compare your facts and reasons. Which of these facts or reasons hold the most weight? Which are the strongest to support the idea or concept?

What other skills besides research help you support your ideas?

Where do you see the habit of mind of Supporting Ideas With Reasons Why active in adults' work?

How does finding ways to support ideas with reasons why help your thinking and doing become stronger?

13. Persevere

You want to quit? Why? Let's look closer at why you want to leave this challenge. What is causing your frustration?

Your group has already worked well through some tough spots. Now you want to leave the project? I'm glad I found you just in time! Let's talk about it. What are things you can do when you are about to give up on a good, positive project or effort? What are things you could do to help you stick with this challenge? How can you manage your frustration and persevere?

How can you make this project more interesting for yourself? What effort and energy can you put into working here? How can you make this challenge your own? How does building a challenge and making it more your own help you persevere? How does it help you enjoy a challenge?

What helps you stick with a tough challenge? What are things that work for you (step back, look at the whole picture, look for ideas, take a quick break, laugh a little, draw out ideas)?

When should you ask for help? Right, a person can handle some frustration, but not a whole big armful! You need to know when to ask for help. So let's work together for a while.

Where do you see the habit of mind of Persevering in adults' work?

How does finding ways to persevere help your thinking and doing become stronger?

14. Communicate Clearly

You have a great idea there! You are on to something! Explain again what you just said. Take it slow, and take care to state your idea clearly. Think about how you are communicating your ideas so that we understand them more clearly.

When are others times you need to take this kind of care to present your ideas effectively (writing, drawing, speaking, performing music)?

Where do you see the habit of mind of Communicating Clearly active in adults' work?

How does finding ways to communicate clearly help your work and thinking?

15. Understand Others

What are the different contributions of your group, team, or class?

I'm curious. What are different ways you see each of your team partners thinking through ideas? Oh, Kyle likes to draw out her concepts on paper, which makes her ideas clear for all to see. Nicholas works quietly but then adds an important idea at just the right moment.

Oh, your partner isn't speaking to you right now? How come? You don't know? Have you tried asking why? Be brave! Oh, she does want to work with you! You thought she said something else! Good work clearing that up! Great risk taking!

Ursula, how is your thinking or idea similar to Renate and Berndt's? How is it different?

How is understanding other people's ideas and the way they think helpful and important?

Where do you see the habit of mind of Understanding Others active in adults' work?

How does understanding others help your work and thinking to be stronger?

Resources

Costa, A. L., & Kalick, B. (2000). *Discovery and Exploring Habits of Mind.* Alexandria, VA: Association for Supervision and Curriculum Development.

Tishman, S., Jay, E., & Perkins, D. (1992). *Teaching Thinking Dispositions: From Transmission to Enculturation.* Retrieved June 4, 2008, from http://learnweb.harvard.edu/ALPS/thinking/docs/article2.html.

Appendix E

Quick Link:
Target Inquiry Lab Skills

Fine Motor	Predicting, Hypothesizing
Number Sense	Brainstorming
Computation	Planning Strategy
Perceiving Symmetry	Perceiving Patterns
Estimation	Comparing and Contrasting
Measurement	Classifying Information
Data Analysis	Cause and Effect
Graphing	Sequencing Ideas and Information
Organizing	Observing and Recording a System
Problem Finding	Synthesizing Information
Problem Solving	Visualizing Outcomes
Abstract Reasoning	Designing
Spatial Reasoning	Analyzing
Construction	Evaluating
Mapping	Working with and Contributing to a Team
Using Vocabulary	Forming Relevant Questions
Interviewing	Researching
Oral Communication	Structuring One's Own Work Process
Discussion	Writing
Listening	Transferring Learning
Phonetic Pronunciation	***Add additional skills on back of page . . .***

Appendix F

Co-Educator Questionnaire

Open-Inquiry Instruction . . .

What most interests you about the inquiry learning format?

What aspects of the program do you feel will most help the children with whom you work?

Highlight or circle any of the following that are relevant to you:

Teaching for transfer

Cultivating flow

Working on developing multiple intelligences

Cooperative and group learning

Developing pre-writing experiences

Differentiation opportunities

Developing new teacher-student relationships in an altered "field trip–like" environment

Building habits of mind (see habit of mind listing), especially the following:

Building skills (see listing of inquiry lab target skill), especially the following:

Other Ideas, Questions, or Comments:

Appendix G

Lab Rubric: Inquiry in Action . . . Where Are You?

Lab Rubric: Inquiry in Action . . . Where Are You?

ACTION	HOT!	WARM . . .	CHILLY . . .
Identifying Inquiry and Getting Started	We have a picture in our minds of the inquiry or are well on our way exploring possibilities. We are open to what unfolds with the project. We are committed to try the inquiry.	We have some ideas for the inquiry but could explore more possibilities. The effort does not seem as vital as it could be. We don't yet feel totally committed to the inquiry.	It is very unclear what the possibilities are for this project. Energy for finding ideas and getting the inquiry off to a vital start has not yet grown. We have even thought, "Yikes! How do we get out of this project?!"
Helping the Inquiry to Grow and Finding Flow	Our ideas grow stronger as we brainstorm and think flexibly. We are fully focused. We ask many questions. Possibilities keep unfolding. We have "ah-ha!" moments while also hearing ourselves thinking, "What if . . ."	The effort is moving along but with little zest. We have a one-track plan with little room for other ideas to come in. New ideas, connections, and possibilities are not coming up as we work.	Not many ideas are surfacing. There is not much brainstorming in action. We feel stuck. Some of us are saying, "I'm bored." We have drifted away from the effort.
Working With Others and Making Contributions	We are exploring ideas together. We take time to listen. We find ways to combine our ideas and interests. We contribute our skills and understandings to the group effort.	We are working together at the same inquiry but seem to be missing a shared goal. We come up with new ideas but have trouble working out ways to use them.	Members of the group are working alone or are angry and not talking to each other. There is no common mission or goal. Any new ideas offered are getting lost.
Dealing With Frustration, Persevering	We find ways to work with our frustration. It is OK if we make mistakes—we learn and gain information from them. We ask for help if frustration gets too tough to handle. We will stick with this challenge!	The frustration is building, but we have not figured out how to deal with it. We make mistakes without thinking about and learning from them. We'll keep working, but for how long?	The frustration has grown beyond what we can handle. We are not seeking help. Mistakes are big trouble! Stay away from them! We want out of here!
Thinking About Thinking and Transfer of Learning	We take time along the way to reflect on our thinking and where it could go. We engage the habits of mind. We see many thinking skills and understandings in action. We are transferring our learning.	We are not taking time to review our thinking. We know that some habits of mind could be helpful but haven't thought of which ones. We are not highly focused to make connections.	This project has not become a vital thinking experience. We are not reviewing which habits of mind could be missing with our effort. The inquiry effort and energy feel flat.

An Eye on Open-Inquiry . . .

Student: _____ Class: _____

First Assessment, Date: _____ Second Assessment, Date: _____

Identifying Inquiries and Getting Started

_____

Helping Inquiries to Grow and Finding Flow

_____

Working With Others and Making Contributions

_____

Dealing With Frustration and Persevering

_____

Thinking About Thinking and Transfer of Learning

_____

Other:

_____

Other:

_____

From *Nine Thousand Straws: Teaching Thinking Through Open-Inquiry Learning* by Jean Sausele Knodt. Westport, CT: Teacher Ideas Press. Copyright © 2008.

Appendix I

Additional Inquiry Possibilities

The following projects add dimension to an inquiry learning lab. To aid in finding projects, names have been listed in quotation marks as suggestions for search terms to locate the project on the Internet or through various supply companies (see Appendix J, Potential Suppliers).

THINKING SCIENTIFICALLY:
Color Cube (Grades 3–6) *"Color Cube Puzzle"*

> **Inquiry Activity:** Work with and arrange various hues and values.

Color Box (Grades K–6) *"Montessori Color Tablets Third Box"*

> **Inquiry Activity:** Explore color properties.

Soap Film Geometry (Grades 3–6) *"Zoom Tool"*

> **Inquiry Activity:** Build geometric shapes and explore soap-film formations.
> **CAUTION:** Small parts.

Dinosaur Building (Grades 3–6) *"Medium T . Rex Puzzle"*

> **Inquiry Activity:** Students build, take apart, and rebuild the skeletal system of a large wood Tyrannosaurus Rex.

Shadow Puppets (Grades PK–6) *"Art Projector"*

> **Inquiry Activity:** Students create or follow visual instructions to make shadow puppets with light projected.

Color Mixing (Grades 2–6) *"Color Wheel"*

> **Inquiry Activity:** Students mix colors and spin them to observe mixing.

Point of Balance (Grades 2–6) *"Equilibrium Puzzle"*

> **Inquiry Activity:** Find the point of balance with metal arms and marbles.
> **CAUTION:** Small parts, marbles.

Shoe Box Capers Collection (Grades 1–6) *"TOPS Science"*

> **Inquiry Activity:** Various simple experiments—e.g., electricity, magnetism, pendulums. Box in shoeboxes with TOPS, including instructions with needed supplies.
> **CAUTION:** Possible small parts, including batteries, rubber bands, etc.

Open Box Exploration Collection (Grades PK–6)

> **Inquiry Activity:** Various—e.g., magnetism, fossils, simple machines. Assemble a large paper box with various items for open-ended exploration. Include various resources, magnifiers, or other supportive technologies.
> **CAUTION:** Possible small parts.

Name That Fish and What It Is Hiding Behind! (Grades K–6)

> **Inquiry Activity:** Put together a fish tank and have children identify different species of fish and aquatic plants.

Grow a Garden (Grades K–6)

> **Inquiry Activity:** Put together a greenhouse or work outside with children to grow various plants.

Where's Hubble? (Grades 2–6)

> **Inquiry Activity:** Locate the longitude and latitude on a lab map of the Hubble telescope satellite as it travels through the year, as well as other satellites at listed at Science@NASA: http//:science.nasa.gov/Realtime/jtrack/3d/JTrac3D.html.

THINKING VISUALLY, SPATIALLY, AND TECHNICALLY:

Scientists and Inventors (Grades K–3) *"Classroom Kit Number Four–Scientist and Inventors"* *(Learning Materials Workshop)*

> **Inquiry Activity:** Build a series of structures with simple machines.

Why Is the Keystone So Important? (Grades K–6) *"Roman Arch Puzzle"*

> **Inquiry Activity:** Build a wooden model of a Roman arch.

Masterpiece Memory (Grades 3–6) *"Art Memo Game"*

> **Inquiry Activity:** Find pairs and identify art masterpieces. Develop visual memory.

Memo It (Grades K–2) *"Haba Memo Game"*

> **Inquiry Activity:** Develop visual memory and find pairs.

Pipe Challenge (Grades K–6) *"Pipe Tree"*

> **Inquiry Activity:** Observe various diagrams and construct pipes into various formations. Design and draw your own new challenges with pipes.

Solid Wall (Grades K–2) *"H-Blocks"*

> **Inquiry Activity:** Among other structures, can you build a standing wall with no negative space between blocks?

Build and Construct (Grades 2–6) *"Erector, Capsella, Haba, Matchitecture, Fischertechnik ..."*

> **Inquiry Activity:** Build through instructions, or design and record (draw) one's own structures.
> **CAUTION:** Possible small parts, batteries.

Frame Builder (Grades 5–6) *"Wall Building Kit"*

> **Inquiry Activity:** Frame and build a model of a wall.

World Map Sleuths (Grades K–6) *"World-Sized Wall Map"*

> **Inquiry Activity:** Create a "Where in the world is . . ."–like project.

Buddha Board (Grades 1–6) *"Buddha Board"*

> **Inquiry Activity:** Brush water on board and black line drawing reveals, then slowly fades away. This is a great project to help children break through drawing inhibitions.

Pictionary Inquiry (Grades 3–6) *"Pictionary"*

> **Inquiry Activity:** Work on a dry erase board, easel board, or a chalkboard. Use just use the cards and not the board game.

Maze Collection (Grades K–2)

> **Inquiry Activity:** Work through various maze puzzlers—wood, magnetic, with tops, printed in book.

Claymation (Grades 3–6)

> **Inquiry Activity:** Find a "Claymation" program for the computer. Students build in clay and take digital camera shots to create animations.

Blue Value Dado Cubes (Grades K–6) *"Dado Cubes"*

> **Inquiry Activity:** Build constructions. Use drawing to understand various proportions and explore hue and value.

Wedgits (Grades K–6) *"Wedgits"*

> **Inquiry Activity:** Use spatial and abstract reasoning while building puzzle constructions.

V-Stick Structures (Grades 2–6)

> **Inquiry Activity:** Build structures with V-sticks (limbs or twigs) found in nature. Structures can be built large enough for children to use or small enough for troll dolls to inhabit. The roots of a tree form handy "caverns" to build a v-stick platform and roof structure for the trolls. **CAUTION:** Possible small parts.

THINKING MATHEMATICALLY:
Angle City (Grades K–6) *"Haba Ball Ramp"*

> **Inquiry Activity:** Spatial and abstract reasoning as building marble ramp constructions. How many different angles can you have in one marble run? Can you measure your angles? **CAUTION:** Small parts, marbles.

Green Blocks and Space (Grades K–6) *"Architek"*

> **Inquiry Activity:** Build structures using reference cards.

Architecto (Grades 1–6) (Similar to Architek) **"Architecto, Cliko, Equilibrio"**

> **Inquiry Activity:** Build structures from reference cards.

Tally Up! (Grades 1–3*) "Hens and Chicks"*

> **Inquiry Activity:** Collect pegs without causing the frame's spring to release. Tally mark each color collected, assign number value to each color, add up tally marks, add sums, multiply, and so on. **CAUTION:** Small parts.

From *Nine Thousand Straws: Teaching Thinking Through Open-Inquiry Learning* by Jean Sausele Knodt. Westport, CT: Teacher Ideas Press. Copyright © 2008.

Roll and Flip Numbers (Grades K–2) *"Wake Up the Giants" or "Shut the Box"*

> **Inquiry Activity:** Roll numbered dice, correlate with a numeral on the board, add or subtract, and flip up tiles.
> **CAUTION:** Small parts—dice (can replace with a large set of dice).

On the Wall Ball Ramp (Grades 2–6)

> **Inquiry Activity:** Create a wall marble ramp. Velcro fabric (available from fabric store) a bulletin board. Place Velcro receive strips on PVC pipes of various lengths.
> **CAUTION:** Small parts—marbles.

Accumulative Addition (Grades K–6) *"Shoot the Moon"*

> **Inquiry Activity:** Whatever planet you land on, put down its number, and add it to your sum. How high a score can you get in three minutes? Use an egg timer.

Weaving Patterns (Grades K–6)

> **Inquiry Activity:** Weave various color patterns on a tabletop or standing loom. Identify color properties as well as AB, ABC, ABCD . . . patterns.

Fractiles (Grades 2–6) *"Fractiles–7"*

> **Inquiry Activity:** Create an expanded tessellation-like pattern image with these magnets.
> **CAUTION:** Small Parts–magnets.

Frame Up Shapes (Grades 1–6) *"Haba Pattern Pieces and Rhombus Frames"*

> **Inquiry Activity:** Frame up pattern pieces inside frames.

Flags of the World (Grades 1–6) *"Montessori Flags of World"*

> **Inquiry Activity:** Identify and locate various flags on a world map.

Funky Chess (Grades 1–6)

> **Inquiry Activity:** With a provided collection of various found objects, identify your own chess pieces. List out your chosen pieces and the parts they play on a clipboard before you begin a game of chess (pawn: plastic goldfish; queen: salt shaker, etc.).

THINKING VERBALLY AND LINGUISTICALLY:

Tree Block Stories (Grades K–2) *"Tree Blocks" or "Tree House Blocks"*

> **Inquiry Activity:** Students build structures and arrange a home for a family. With writing prompts students create and record their stories.
> **CAUTION:** Some tree block products have a flax seed oil finish (allergies?). You can request unfinished blocks.

Dictionary Project (Grades 3–6)

> **Inquiry Activity:** Classic game of Dictionary. Students work in a group, taking turns as leader. The leader identifies a word from the dictionary and spells it out to the group. Everyone writes a made up definition for the word on an index card, except for the leader of the round, who writes out the true definition. The leader then reads all "definitions," and the group votes

on which is the real, "correct" one. How well one can write a believable definition is the quest. At the end of each game, the leader reveals the true definition.

Magnetic Poets (Grades 3–6) *"Magnetic Poetry"*

> **Inquiry Activity**: Students compose poetry and record poems in a "Magnetic Poets Society Journal."
> **CAUTION:** Small parts, magnets.

Write Your Name in Chain Stitch (Grades 2–6)

> **Inquiry Activity:** Students learn the chain stitch and add their names to the "Inquiry Lab's Heirloom Tablecloth."

Bilingual Food (Grades K–6)

> **Inquiry Activity:** "Bilingual photo cards" and plastic or wood food items are collected for group language explorations.

Lego Dacta Control Lab (Grades 1–6)

> **Inquiry Activity:** Learn computer "primitives" (the language of programming) and automate built Lego structures so that they move.

Story Line Ideas (Grades 1–6)

> **Inquiry Activity:** A series of photo cards are assembled for various age groups and interests. Students work in a circle and take turns revealing a card from the "deck" and add to a developing story line. The story can be recorded to so that students can listen to it again. Students can also then individually develop written pieces of their own that are based on the group's explorations. See how ideas develop further, and read the story back to the group.

THINKING MUSICALLY AND RHYTHMICALLY:
Music Harp (Grades PK–6) *"Melody Lab Harp"*

> **Inquiry Activity:** Students easily play music on a harp with song sheets that slip under strings. Note: Keeping the harp in tune requires expert help.

Sound Boxes (Grades K–2) *"Montessori Sound Boxes"*

> **Inquiry Activity:** Students sharpen sound and tone identification skills.

Keyboard (Grades 1–6)

> **Inquiry Activity:** Electronic keyboard with music for various levels of exploration (include headphones as needed). Note: It is best to find as simple a keyboard as possible with no "special" synthesizing effects or rhythms. The fewer buttons, the better.

Tone Wands (Grades 1–6) *"Tree Blocks Tone Wands"*

> **Inquiry Activity:** Students explore various tones and make music.

Wood Xylophone (Grades 1–6) *"Wood Xylophone"*

> **Inquiry Activity:** Students explore various tones and make music.

Percussion Tubes (Grades K–6) *"Diatonic Boomwackers"*

> **Inquiry Activity:** Students explore various tones and make music.

Tone Drum (Grades K–6) *"4- and 8-Note Tone Drums"*

> **Inquiry Activity:** Students explore musical and rhythmic possibilities with tone drums.

Calypso Steel Drum (Grades K–6) *"Child-Sized Calypso Steel Drums"*

> **Inquiry Activity:** Students explore musical and rhythmic possibilities with a steel drum.

Sound Studio (Grades K–6)

> **Inquiry Activity:** Listen to and identify various sound recordings or nature sounds, and gather ideas to compose compositions with a variety of simple instruments.

THINKING THROUGH STRATEGY GAMES AND PUZZLES:

Quoridor (Grades K–6) *(possible stretch PK–K)* *"Quoridor"*

> **Inquiry Activity:** Spatial logic strategy game.

Rush Hour (Grades K–6) *"Rush Hour"*

> **Inquiry Activity:** Spatial logic puzzler.

Katamino (Grades 1–6) *"Katamino"*

> **Inquiry Activity:** Spatial logic puzzler.

Namits (Grades 1–6) *"Namits and Namits Challenge"*

> **Inquiry Activity:** Verbal logic puzzlers.

Clothesline Brown Bag Team Builder Puzzlers! (Grades 3–6) **"Team Building Exercises, Experiential Learning, Hands-On Odyssey of the Mind Problems"** (see also Suggested Readings, Project Development and Support)

> **Inquiry Activity:** Find a variety of simple strategy team-building exercises, such as People and Pipes, found in Chapter Six, "Inquiry Project Sampler." Choose exercises for which the instructions and materials fit in a brown lunch or shopping bag. Suspend a clothesline across a corner of the room, and place bags on the line with clothespins or spring clips. Keep the challenge in each bag a mystery, or label as desired (see also Suggested Readings, Project Development and Support).
>
> The following are team-building strategy examples adapted from http://odyssey.mason.k12.oh.us/om5a.htm.
>
> ### Bridge the Gap!
> *Materials:* 75 toothpicks, 1 large ball of clay, 1 small basket with handle, 2 feet of string or twine, 1 box of large nails, 2 tables or chairs placed at a 1-foot distance from each other.
> *Challenge:* Build a bridge out of toothpicks and clay to span the gap between the two tables. Attach the basket to the bridge with string or twine. Test the strength of your bridge by placing nails in the basket one by one. How many nails can you put in the basket?

How Long Can You Go?

Materials: 1 piece of paper, 5 paper clips, 1 pencil, 5 adhesive labels, 1 straw, 1 pair of scissors, 1 yardstick.

Challenge: How long if a contraption can you make with the given materials? You will need the yard stick to measure.

Cheerio!

Materials: Container of Cheerios; nonfrosted, 18-inch piece of string or yarn; 2 pieces of 1-inch masking tape, sheet of typing paper, spoon.

Challenge: Assemble a garland of Cheerios by attaching the Cheerios to the string. Team members may not touch the Cheerios directly, but only handle them using any of the materials supplied. There can be no talking or written communication at any time during the challenge. Hand gestures or body language are allowed.

Appendix J

Potential Suppliers

ABC SCHOOL SUPPLY
http://www.abcschoolsupply.com

BACK TO BASICS
http://backtobasicstoys.com

BRAIN BUILDERS
http://www.brain-builders.com

CAROLINA SCIENCE
http://www.carolina.com

CONSTRUCTION SITE
http://www.constructiontoys.com

DELTA EDUCATION
http://www.delta-education.com

DISCOUNT SCHOOL SUPPLIES
http://www.discountschoolsupply

ETA CUISENAIRE
http://www.etacuisenaire.com

FAT BRAIN
http://www.fatbraintoys.com

FOX MIND
http://www.foxmind.com

HARRISVILLE WEAVING
http://www.harrisville.com

GUMMY LUMP
http://www.gummylump.com

HEARTHSONG
http://hearthsong.com

KAPLA
http://www.kaplatoys.com

KAPLAN
http://www.kaplanco.com

KID ADVANCE MONTESSORI
http://www.kidadvance.com

LAKESHORE
http://www.lakeshorelearning.com

LEARNING MATERIALS WORKSHOP
http://www.learningmaterialswork.com

LEGO EDUCATION
http://www.legoeducation.com/store

MAGNET KING
http://www.magnetking.com

MET MUSEUM
http://www.metmuseum.org/store

MINDWARE
http:www.mindwareonline.com

MODERN SCHOOL SUPPLY
http://www.modernss.com

PITSCO
http://www.pitsco.com

SAX ARTS
http://www.saxarts.com

SOUTHERN CONTAINERS
http://www.socontainers.com

S.S. WORLDWIDE
http://www.ssww.com

TREE BLOCKS
http://www.treeblocks.com

Appendix K

New Lab Challenge Idea!

New Lab Challenge Idea!

Appendix L

Student Lab Project Advice (for Clipboard or Notebook)

Offer some great advice to someone about an inquiry project you have worked on! *Make a drawing . . . diagram . . . write out ideas . . .*

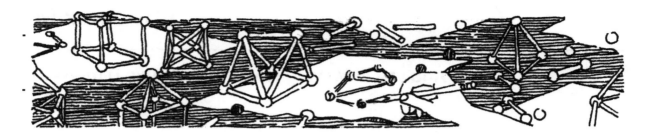

Analyze it! Moving from three to two dimensions.

Analyze It! What System Are You Using to Solve This Challenge?

Analyze it! What system are you using to solve this challenge?

Analyze It! How Does This Do That?

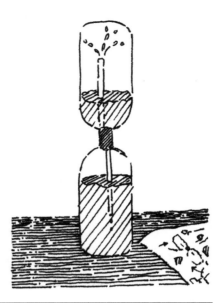

Analyze it! How does this do that?

Appendix N

Words for Thinking and Doing

Words for Thinking and Doing

abstract	concept	develop
accomplishment	conclusion	dialog
action	conditional	differentiate
algorithm	conduct	digest
aligned	conflict	discover
alternative	confluent	disposition
analogy	congruent	divergent
analyze	connection	dream
angle	consecutive	elaborate
anticipate	consider	element
apply	consistent	engage
assumption	constructive	estimate
bias	contrast	evaluate
brainstorm	convergent	evidence
bridge	counterbalance	expand
causal	creative	experiment
cause/effect	credible	explore
challenge	criteria	express
clarify	critical	fact
classify	critique	flexible
cognitive	curiosity	flow
collaborative	debate	focus
committed	deduce	formulate
communicate	deductive	frame
compare and contrast	defend	function
compatible	define	generalization
complex	deliberate	goal
concentrate	design	group

habit of mind	judge	possibility	study
hunch	link	predict	summarize
hypothesize	listen	principals	supportive
idea	merge	prioritize	synthesize
identify	metacognitive	problem finding	system
illustrate	metaphor	problem solving	test
imagination	method	procedure	theorize
imagine	mindfulness	process	theory
implication	navigate	productive	thinking
independent	negotiate	prove	tinker
industrious	observation	quest	transfer
infer	observe	question	understanding
initiative	opinion	questioning	value
innovation	order	reasoning	variable
inquire	outcome	recall	verify
inquiry	pattern	relate	verve
insight	perceive	relationship	visualize
inspiration	perception	representational	vital
inspired	perplexing	resolve	vivid
intelligences	persevere	sequence	vocalize
intuition	persistence	sequential	wonder
invent	perspective	series	wonderment
invention	point of view	speculate	zest
inventive	ponder	strategy	zinger!
investigate			

Adapted from: "A Language of Thinking Vocabulary" in Tishman, S., Jay, E., & Perkins, D.N. (1995). *The Thinking Classroom: Learning and Teaching in a Culture of Thinking*. Boston: Allyn and Bacon; and inservice handout presented at Kent Gardens Elementary, McLean, Virginia, by Gifted and Talented Itinerant Wendy Cohen.

Appendix O

Active Questions!

What possibilities do you see with this project?

What are your goals?

How do you keep working when things get tough? What helps you persevere?

What is something new you discovered?

What are you curious about?

Where have you used this kind of thinking before? What understandings or skills are you transferring as you work here?

What do you visualize? What pictures do you have in your mind as you explore possibilities with this inquiry?

What is your strategy?

What advice would you give someone who is about to work with this project?

What habits of mind do you have in action?

What habits of mind do you think you should consider putting into action?

Active Questions!

What intelligences do you have in action as you work on this inquiry project?

What questions do you find yourself asking as you work and explore?

How do adults employ the same thinking you are using here in their work?

What are the different parts of this inquiry challenge? Is one part more important? Which one? Why?

What makes your thinking great? What are your thinking strengths?

How is the team effort going with this project? What are the strengths of the team? What areas need help and development? How is each member of the team contributing?

What are some other ideas you could pursue with this inquiry?

What are new possible inquiry projects for our lab time?

Can you think of other questions?

From *Nine Thousand Straws: Teaching Thinking Through Open-Inquiry Learning* by Jean Sausele Knodt. Westport, CT: Teacher Ideas Press. Copyright © 2008.

Appendix P

Project Card Master Example

(List inventory number)

Strawberry Basket Number Sense!
(Title of project.)

Materials:
(List all needed supplies)

Ideas and Possibilities:
(Add general but open start-up guide questions)

Skills and Understandings:
(Add some of the skills and contents the the general inquiry generates)

Starting Up

Strawberry Basket Number Sense!
(Back of card; add title again)

(Add inquiry lab-time question ideas such as:)

Put together a starting list of questions for students, faculty, or parents to ask during the inquiry lab session.

What is a unit? Could one strawberry basket be seen as a unit of measure in your tower?

How do you need to employ the habit of mind of Being Accurate and Precise with this center?

What other habits of mind do you have in action today here?

What is your group plan to work with this center today? What are your team goals?

What is working well with your teamwork? What is not working well? How can you change the team dynamic and establish a better group working experience?

Review all the different ideas and contributions each of you is making. How are the various contributions and ideas similar, and how are they different?

What learning are you transferring as you work at this inquiry? What skills and understandings are you putting into action?

A strawberry basket tower has a beautiful green translucent quality. What does the word translucent mean? Let's look it up!

Questions!

Try an interview . . . .

Appendix Q

Beginning Middle End Graphic

Story in Action!

Beginning			Middle			End		

Store Sum Student Worksheet and Price List

Price List

_____

_____

_____

_____

_____

_____

_____

_____

_____

_____

_____

_____

_____

_____

_____

_____

_____

_____

Price List

_____

_____

_____

_____

_____

_____

_____

_____

_____

_____

_____

_____

_____

_____

_____

_____

_____

_____

Store Sums!

Appendix S

Magnet Mural Shape Possibilities

Magnet Mural Shape Possibilities

Select shapes. Enlarge in various percentages.
Shapes can be made up to two feet in length. Produce same shapes in various colors.

Appendix T

MI Student Interview Sheet

MI Interview of _____ **By**_____

Place Picture of Interviewee here.   Place Picture of You, the Interviewer, here.

How do you use all of your intelligences?

Interpersonal:

Body-Kinesthetic:

Naturalist:

Math-Logic:

Intrapersonal:

Verbal-Linguistic:

Musical-Rhythmic:

Visual-Spatial:

Mobile in Balance Building Instructions

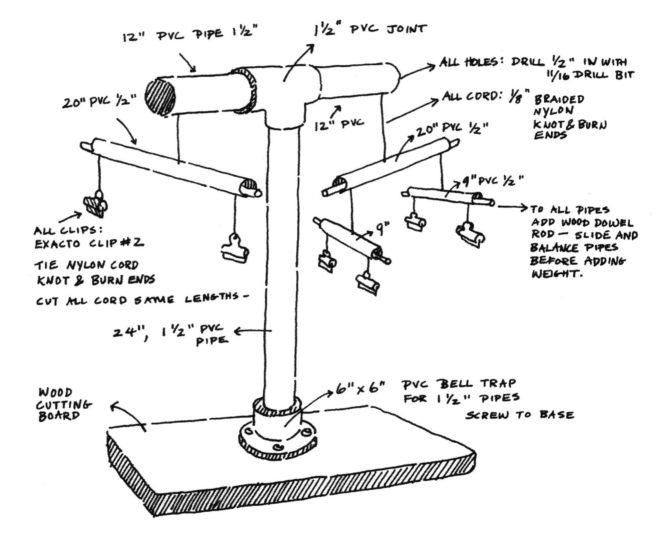

12" PVC PIPE 1½"

1½" PVC JOINT

ALL HOLES: DRILL ½" IN WITH 11/16 DRILL BIT

20" PVC ½"

ALL CORD: ⅛" BRAIDED NYLON KNOT & BURN ENDS

12" PVC

20" PVC ½"

9" PVC ½"

9"

9"

TO ALL PIPES ADD WOOD DOWEL ROD — SLIDE AND BALANCE PIPES BEFORE ADDING WEIGHT.

ALL CLIPS: EXACTO CLIP #2

TIE NYLON CORD KNOT & BURN ENDS

CUT ALL CORD SAME LENGTHS —

24", 1½" PVC PIPE

WOOD CUTTING BOARD

6" x 6" PVC BELL TRAP FOR 1½" PIPES

SCREW TO BASE

From *Nine Thousand Straws: Teaching Thinking Through Open-Inquiry Learning* by Jean Sausele Knodt. Westport, CT: Teacher Ideas Press. Copyright © 2008.

Build Habits of Mind!

1. **Be Adventurous and Open-Minded**

   Brainstorm many ideas. Be flexible with thinking and doing. Think out of the box!

2. **Wonder, Explore, and Ask Questions**

   Investigate and be curious. Seek new challenges or projects. Inquire.

3. **Contribute Positively to the Group and Inspire Teamwork**

   Offer your skills, understandings, and abilities to the team. Help the group to work well together.

4. **Imagine Possibilities and Outcomes**

   What could be? What will likely happen? Put a picture in your mind. Visualize.

5. **Set Goals and Make Plans**

   Establish workable goals. Design a strategy and steps to meet goals and objectives. Organize the effort.

6. **Think Independently**

   Think for yourself. Be bold in asking questions. Step out to offer a new idea. Build confidence for managing your own work. Review and think about your own thinking. Be metacognitive!

7. **Use What You Know—Transfer Learning**

   Use the skills and understandings you already have in new thinking situations.

8. **Step Back and Look at the Whole Picture**

   Get a full view of the project, event, or situation. Seek relationships. Understand how parts—things, ideas, beings, or purposes—connect and link to one another.

From *Nine Thousand Straws: Teaching Thinking Through Open-Inquiry Learning* by Jean Sausele Knodt. Westport, CT: Teacher Ideas Press. Copyright © 2008.

9. **Strive to Be Accurate and Precise**

   Be focused and organized when checking work for accuracy. Be tough in uncovering possible errors.

10. **Look Carefully**

    Observe critically and carefully to understand what you see. Gather visual information.

11. **Listen Actively**

    Listen and focus on understanding as you hear music, nature, or as others speak.

12. **Support Ideas With Reasons Why**

    Find evidence to prove your point. Weigh the importance of the facts and reasons found. Compare the importance of facts.

13. **Persevere**

    Find ways to deal with frustration and stick with difficult challenges. Ask for help if things get too tough!

14. **Communicate Clearly**

    Present ideas clearly and effectively as you write, draw, speak, or perform music.

15. **Understand Others**

    Be aware of others' thinking, abilities, interests, and feelings. Be perceptive and empathetic.

Resources

Costa, A. L., & Kalick, B. (2000). *Discovery and Exploring Habits of Mind.* Alexandria, VA: Association for Supervision and Curriculum Development.

Tishman, S., Jay, E., & Perkins, D. (1992). *Teaching Thinking Dispositions: From Transmission to Enculturation.* Retrieved June 6, 2008. http://learnweb.harvard.edu/ALPS/thinking/docs/article2.html.

Appendix W

Geodesic Dome Nonverbal Instructions

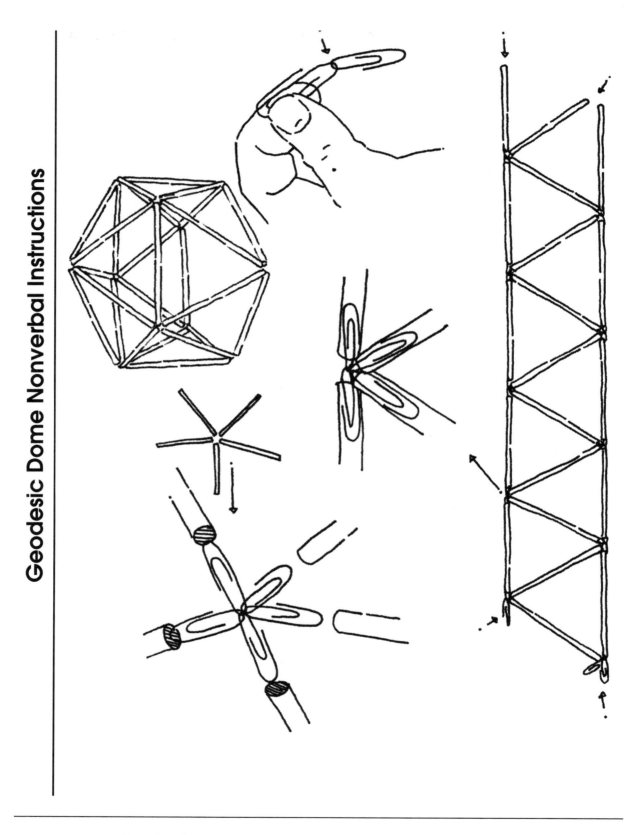

Appendix X

Strawberry Basket Clipboard Graphic

Strawberry Basket Number Sense!

Name	Number "Hunch"	Estimate	Exact Count

Appendix Y

Name That Bone!

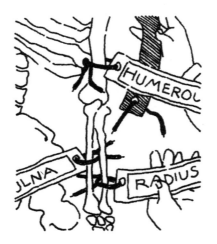

Name that bone! Draw a bone and identify it!

Theories and Methods

Barell, J. (2003). *Developing more curious minds.* Alexandria, VA: Association for Supervision and Curriculum Development.

Bellanca, J., & Fogarty, R. (1986). *Catch them thinking.* Palatine, IL: Skylight.

Bingham, A. A. (1995). *Exploring the multiage classroom.* York, ME: Stenhouse.

Blythe, T. (1998). *The teaching for understanding guide.* San Francisco: Jossey-Bass.

Bringuier, J. C. (1980). *Conversations with Jean Piaget.* Chicago: University of Chicago Press.

Brooks, G. J., & Brooks, M. (1993). *In search of understanding: The case for constructivist classrooms.* Alexandria, VA: Association for Supervision and Curriculum Development.

Bruner, J. (1960). *The process of education.* Cambridge, MA: Harvard University Press.

Bruner, J. (1971). *Toward a theory of instruction.* Cambridge, MA: Belknap Press/Harvard University Press.

Bruner, J. (Ed.). (1976). *Play: Its role in development and evolution.* New York: Basic Books.

Bruner, J. (1986). *Actual minds, possible worlds.* Cambridge, MA: Harvard University Press.

Cadwell, L. B. (2003). *Bringing learning to life: The Reggio approach to early childhood education.* New York: Teachers College Press.

Costa, A. (Ed.). (2001). *Developing minds: A resource book for teaching thinking.* Alexandria, VA: Association for Supervision and Curriculum Development.

Costa, A., & Kalick, B. (Eds.). (2000). *Discovering and exploring habits of mind.* Alexandria, VA: Association for Supervision and Curriculum Development.

Costa, A., & Lowery, L. (Eds.). (1989). *Techniques for teaching thinking.* Pacific Grove, CA: Midwest.

Crawford, G. B. (2007). *Brain-based teaching with adolescent learning in mind, second edition.* Thousand Oaks, CA: Corwin Press.

Csikszentmihalyi, M. (1990). *Flow: The psychology of optimal experience.* New York: Harper Perennial.

Csikszentmihalyi, M. (1996). *Creativity: Flow and the psychology of discovery and invention.* New York: HarperCollins.

de Bono, E. (1967). *New think: The use of lateral thinking in the generation of new ideas.* New York: Basic Books.

de Bono, E. (1992). *Teach your child how to think.* New York: Penguin Books.

Dewey, J. (1971). *The child and the curriculum and the school and society.* Chicago: The University of Chicago Press. Original works published 1902 and 1900.

Dewey, J. (1963). *Experience and education.* New York: Macmillan Publishing. Original work published 1938.

Dewey, J. *The school and society.* Chicago: University of Chicago Press. Original work published 1907.

Diamond, M., & Hopson, J. (1999). *Magic trees of the mind: How to nurture your child's intelligence, creativity, and healthy emotions from birth to adolescence.* New York: Penguin Group.

Fogarty, R. (1997). *Problem-based learning and other curriculum models for the Multiple Intelligences Classroom.* Arlington Heights, IL: IRA/SkyLight Training and Publishing.

Gardner, H. (1983). *Frames of mind: The theory of multiple intelligences.* New York: Basic Books.

Gardner, H. (1993). *Multiple Intelligences: The theory in practice.* New York: Basic Books.

Goleman, D. (1995). *Emotional intelligence.* New York: Bantam Books.

Jensen, E. (1998). *Teaching with the brain in mind.* Alexandria, VA: Association for Supervision and Curriculum Development.

Johnson-Farris, N. (1990). *Questioning makes the difference.* Marion, IL: Pieces of Learning.

Kao, J. (2007). *Innovation nation: How America is losing its innovation edge, why it matters, and what we can do to get it back.* New York: Free Press.

Knodt, J. S. (1997). A Think Tank cultivates kids. *Educational Leadership, 55,* 35–37.

Knodt, J.S. (1998). The Think Tank: A Discovery Room for Young Learners. *ALPS, Active Learning Practices for Schools.* Retrieved June 5, 2008, from http://learnweb.harvard.edu/alps/thinking/pop2.cfm.

Krechevsky, M. (1991, February). Project Spectrum: An Innovative Assessment Alternative. *Educational Leadership, 48,* 43–48.@BIB = The New City School. (1996). *Celebrating Multiple Intelligences: Teaching for success.* St. Louis, MO: The New City School.

The New City School. (1996). *Succeeding with Multiple Intelligences: Teaching through the personal intelligences.* St. Louis, MO: The New City School.

Paul, R., &Elder, L. (2000). *Critical thinking handbook: Basic theory and instructional structure.* Rohnert Park, CA: Foundation for Critical Thinking.

Perkins, D. N. (1992). *Smart schools: From training memories to educating minds.* New York: The Free Press.

Perkins, D. N. (1995). *Outsmarting IQ: The emerging science of learnable intelligence.* New York: The Free Press.

Perkins, D. N. (2003). *King Arthur's round table: How collaborative conversations create smart organizations.* Hoboken: John Wiley & Sons.

Perkins, D.N., Goodrich, H., Tishman, S., & Owen, J. M. (1994). *Thinking connections: Learning to think and thinking to learn.* Menlo Park, CA: Addison-Wesley.

Piaget, J. (1978). *Success and understanding.* Cambridge, MA: Harvard University Press.

Samples, B. (1987). *Open mind whole mind: Parenting and teaching tomorrow's children today.* Rolling Hills Estates, CA: Jalmar Press.

Sternberg, R. J. (1985). *Beyond IQ: A triarchic theory of human intelligence.* New York: Cambridge University Press.

Sylvester, R. (1995). *A celebration of neurons: An educators guide to the human brain.* Alexandria, VA: Association for Supervision and Curriculum Development.

Tishman, S., Jay, E., & Perkins, D. N. (1995). *The thinking classroom: Learning and teaching in a culture of thinking.* Boston: Allyn & Bacon.

Udall, A. J., & Daniels, J. E. (1991). *Creating the thoughtful classroom.* Tuscan, AZ: Zephyr Press.

Vygotsky, L. S. (1978). *Mind in society: The development of higher psychological process.* Cambridge, MA: Harvard University Press.

Wolfe, P. (2001). *Brain matters.* Alexandria, VA: Association for Supervision and Curriculum Development.

Theories and Methods Web Sites

Active Learning Practices for Schools, ALPS: http://learnweb.harvard.edu/alps/

Association for Experiential Education: www.aee.org

Association for Supervision and Curriculum Development: http://www.ascd.org

Duke University, Center for Inquiry-Based Learning, CIBL: http://www.biology.duke.edu/cibl

Exploratorium, Inquiry Connect: http://www.exploratorium.edu/ifi/resources/classroom/connect

Foundation for Critical Thinking: http://www.critcalthinking.org

Habits of Mind: http://www.habits-of-mind.net

IMSA Problem-Based Learning Network: http://www.imsa.edu/programs/pbln

Inquiry Learning Forum: http://ilf.crlt.indiana.edu

Inquiry Page: http://www.inquiry.uiuc.edu/index.php

Invention at Play, Lemelson Center: http://invention.smithsonian.org/centerpieces/iap/

IMBES International Mind, Brain and Education Society: http://www.imbes.org

Lemelson Center: http://invention.smithsonian.org/home/

Mind Matters: http://www.patwolfe.com/

The National Center for Teaching Thinking: http://www.nctt.net

North American Reggio Emilia Alliance: http://reggioalliance.org

Project Zero: http://www.pz.harvard.edu

Application and Project Support

Alvarado, A. E., & Herr, P. R. (2003). *Inquiry-based learning using everyday objects.* Thousand Oaks, CA: Corwin Press.

Arnone, M. P., & Coatney, S. (2006). *Mac, information detective, in the curious kids ... digging for answers: A storybook approach to introducing research skills.* Westport, CT: Libraries Unlimited.

Beachner, L., & Pickett, A. (2001). *Multiple Intelligences and positive life habits: 174 activities for applying them in your classroom.* Thousand Oaks, CA: Corwin Press.

Bowkett, S. (2007). *100+ ideas for teaching thinking skills.* New York: Continuum International.

Crabbee, A. B. (1986). *Creating more creative people.* Laurinburg, NC: The Future Problem Solving Program.

Crabbee, A. B., & Betts, G. (1988). *Creating more creative people: Book II.* Laurinburg, NC: The Future Problem Solving Program.

DeVries, R., Zan, B., Hildebrandt, C., Edmiaston, R., & Sales, C. (2002). *Developing constructivist early childhood curriculum: Practical principles and activities.* New York: Teachers College Press.

Eggen, P., & Main, J. (1990). *Developing critical thinking through science, book two.* Pacific Grove, CA: Critical Thinking Press & Software.

Eggen, P., & Main, J. (1991). *Developing critical thinking through science, book one.* Pacific Grove, CA: Critical Thinking Press & Software.

Emberley, E. (1994). *Ed Emberley's great thumbprint drawing book.* New York: Little, Brown and Company.

Emberley, E. (2001). *Ed Emberley's fingerprint drawing book.* New York: Little, Brown and Company.

Erickson, S., Seymour, T., & Suey, M. (2000). *Brick layers II: Creative engineering with Lego constructions.* Fresno, CA: The Aims Education Foundation.

Fleisher, P., & Ziegler, D. (2006). *Mind builders. Multidisciplinary challenges for cooperative team-building and competition.* Westport, CT: Libraries Unlimited/Teacher Ideas Press.

Goodrich, H., Hatch, T., Wiatrowski, G., & Unger, C. (1995). *Teaching through projects: Creating effective learning environments.* New York: Addison-Wesley.

Helm, J. H., & Beneke, S. (2003). *The power of projects: Meeting contemporary challenges in early childhood classrooms.* New York: Teachers College Press.

Ingraham, P. B. (1997). *Creating and managing learning centers: A thematic approach.* Peterborough, NH: Crystal Springs Books.

Lambros, A. (2002). *Problem-based learning in the K–8 classroom.* Thousand Oaks, CA: Corwin Press.

Llewellyn, D. (2002). *Inquire within: Implementing inquiry-based science standards.* Thousand Oaks, CA: Corwin Press.

Macaulay, D. (1973). *Cathedral: The story of its construction.* Boston: Houghton Mifflin.

Macaulay, D. (1975). *Pyramid.* Boston, MA: Houghton Mifflin.

Macaulay, D. (1998). *The new way things work.* Boston: Houghton Mifflin.

Marlowe, B., & Page, M. (2005). *Creating and sustaining the constructivist classroom, second edition.* Thousand Oaks, CA: Corwin Press.

Murphy, P., & Shimek, S. (Eds.). (1991). *The Exploratorium science snackbook: Teacher-created versions of Exploratorium exhibits.* San Francisco: Exploratorium Teacher Institute.

Petreshene, S. (1985). *Mind joggers: 5–15 minute activities that make kids think.* West Nyack, NY: The Center for Applied Research in Education.

Pollard, J. (1985). *Building toothpick bridges.* Boston: Dale Seymore.

Rohnke, K., & Butler, S. (1995). *Quicksilver: Adventure games, initiative problems, trust activities and a guide to effective leadership.* Dubuque, IA: Kendall/Hunt.

Ruef, K. (1992). *The private eye: (5x) looking/thinking by analogy.* Seattle, WA: The Private Eye Project.

Salvadori, M. (1990). *The art of construction: Projects and principles for beginning engineers and architects.* Chicago: Chicago Review Press.

Sikes, S. (1995). *Feeding the zircon gorilla and other team building activities.* Tulsa, OK: Learning Unlimited Corporation.

Stephens, L. S. (1983). *Developing thinking skills through real-life activities.* Newton, MA: Allyn & Bacon.

Tishman, S., & Andrade, A. (1997). *Critical squares.* Englewood, CO: Teacher Ideas Press.

Valentino, C. (1983). *Challenge boxes: 50 projects in creative thinking.* Palo Alto, CA: Dale Seymour.

Wurdinger, S. D. (2005). *Using experiential learning in the classroom: Practical ideas for all educators.* Lanham, MD: Rowman & Littlefield.

Young, D., & Pauls, M. (2001). *Puzzle play.* Fresno, CA: The Aims Education Foundation.

Zubrowski, B., & Fleishcher, S. (1981). *Messing around with drinking straw construction.* New York: Little, Brown and Company.

Application and Project Support Web Sites

Boston Children's Museum: http://www.bostonchildrensmuseum.org/index.html

Boston Museum of Science, Educators: http://www.mos.org/educators

Curriculum Activities for the Classroom: www.odysseyofthemind.com/curriculum.php

DK Images Encyclopedia: www.dkimages.com/discover/Home/index.html

Exploratorium Snacks (projects) Series: http://www.exploratorium.edu/snacks/index.html

Exploratorium Teacher Institute: http://www.exploratorium.edu/educate/index.html

Habits of Mind Book Lists: http://www.habits-of-mind.net/booklists.htm

Inquiry Page, Samples of Inquiry in Action: http://www.inquiry.uiuc.edu/action/action.php3

Investigative Learning at Ormondale: www1.pvsd.net/OrmWebsite/IL2/doing.htm

The Kennedy Center, Arts Edge: http://www.artsedge.kennedy-center.org

Lemelson Center: http://www.invention.smithsonian.org/resources/menu_edu_materials.aspx

NASA: http://www.nasa.gov

National Geographic, Education: http://www.nationalgeographic.com/education/

National Science Foundation: http://www.nsf.gov

The New York Times Learning Network: http://www.nytimes.com/learning/

Nye Labs: http://www.nyelabs.com

PBS Teachers: http://www.pbs.org/teachers

The Private Eye: http://www.the-private-eye.com

Salvadori Center: http://www.salvadori.org

Smithsonian Education: http://www.smithsonianeducation.org/educators/index.html

Tops Science Experiments: http://www.topscience.org

The Works: www.theworks.org

Zoom Activities: http://pbskids.org/zoom

Index

project development and, 116–17, 118, 119, 125, 216
transfer and, 34–36, 49, 50, 51
Tishman, Shari, 10, 24, 26, 34, 245, 253, 285, 307
Transfer of learning, 3, 10, 13, 18, 19, 25, 33–36
bridging, 34
Focus Themes and, 49–50, 51, 52, 53, 70–71
hugging, 34

project development, 117–19
surprises, 36
"station," 35

Writing, 2, 6, 18, 32, 41–42, 51
Focus Themes, 53, 55
prompts, 6, 10, 11, 48, 210
on display, 213, 215
student samples, 42, 225–33, 236–9
transition from open inquiry, 41, 221

About the Author

Jean Sausele Knodt, Artist, Educator

After graduating with a bachelor's degree in Studio Arts from Skidmore College, Jean completed her K–12 Art Education certification at Brandeis University. She earned her master's degree in Fine Arts from the University of Pennsylvania and attended the Skowhegan School of Painting and Sculpture. In addition, she focused on thinking-centered education by attending targeted conferences and educational programs, such as the Mind Institute of Project Zero at Harvard University. Throughout her development as an artist, Jean has taught and directed educational programs since the age of sixteen. She has also been active as a graphic designer, museum illustrator, professor of drawing and painting at various colleges and universities, and a college-level seminar leader on open-inquiry learning.

Jean became inspired about the possibilities of the open-inquiry learning format when she was asked to develop a critical and creative thinking lab at an elementary school. She found it a unique time and place to share the understandings and innovative spirit she gains through the process of developing her artwork. The lab emerged as an open environment that cultivates thinking and learning by helping children to continually visualize unfolding possibilities and establish constructive understandings by doing—much as an artist does.

Currently Jean consults, writes, and gives presentations about open-inquiry learning and continues with her artwork in painting and printmaking. Jean lives with her family in Northern Virginia.

Conference Call with the Author

Jean Knodt (pronounced "Connote") offers a no-charge forty-five-minute consultation to a collected group of educators, hospital or museum specialists, homeschool parents, or college classrooms interested in understanding more about putting an open-inquiry learning program together. Contact Jean by e-mail at the following address for further information and to schedule a group conference call: inspired.minds@rcn.com.